DIAMONDS AND
SCOUNDRELS

DIAMONDS AND SCOUNDRELS

MY LIFE IN
THE JEWELRY BUSINESS

ADRIENNE RUBIN

SHE WRITES PRESS

Published September 2019
Printed in the United States of America
Print ISBN: 978-1-63152-513-1
E-ISBN: 978-1-63152-514-8
Library of Congress Control Number: 2019940716

For information, address:
She Writes Press
1569 Solano Ave #546
Berkeley, CA 94707

Interior design by Tabitha Lahr

She Writes Press is a division of SparkPoint Studio, LLC.

Names and identifying characteristics have been changed to protect the privacy of certain individuals.

For my father, a man of integrity, who always had my back.
For Stan, my staunch supporter and the love of my life.
For Pam and Randall, my pride and joy.
For Galit and Loren, with great appreciation.
For Adam, Oren, and Ryan—my legacy.

CONTENTS

CHAPTER 1: From Whence Comes This Yearning? 1

CHAPTER 2: A Rough Beginning 13

CHAPTER 3: Learning from the Best 25

CHAPTER 4: Go for the Gold 32

CHAPTER 5: King Tut 36

CHAPTER 6: Juggling Time and Money 44

CHAPTER 7: From Gold to Diamonds 49

CHAPTER 8: When You Fall, the Only Place

    to Go is Up 60

CHAPTER 9: Staying the Course 72

CHAPTER 10 Buy, Buy, Buy 83

CHAPTER 11: Risky Business! 89

CHAPTER 12: A Full Time Job and Other Distractions 95

CHAPTER 13: Sergey, Dan, and a Special Offer 107

CHAPTER 14: A Penny Saved 116

CHAPTER 15: D & G Jewelry Manufacturing, Inc.,

    A Start-Up Company 120

CHAPTER 16: Flashback 128

CHAPTER 17: Every Man for Himself,

    and Every Woman 133

CHAPTER 18: Sudden Wealth 146

Chapter 19: ABCDEFG. 152

Chapter 20: Trust and Deception 161

Chapter 21: What's it All About, Alfie?. 172

Chapter 22: A Friend Gets in Trouble 177

Chapter 23: Shenanigans. 181

Chapter 24: The Last Straw. 189

Chapter 25: My Dad Slips Away. 196

Chapter 26: "You Can't Possibly Be That Smart". 200

Chapter 27: Diverting and Plundering the Profits 208

Chapter 28: Greedy Selfish Scoundrels 211

Chapter 29: Dan's Achilles Heel. 216

Chapter 30: Resilience 220

Chapter 31: Colored Gems, Inc.. 239

Chapter 32: Selling Diamonds Can be Tricky. 242

Chapter 33: Heedless Gall. 246

Chapter 34: Searching for Answers. 254

Chapter 35: Enough is Enough 258

Chapter 36: Assessing the Future 265

Book Club Discussion Questions 271

Case Study of The Diamonds and Gold
Jewelry Manufacturing Company, Inc. 273

IT COULDN'T BE DONE

By Edgar Albert Guest

Somebody said that it couldn't be done
    But he with a chuckle replied
That "maybe it couldn't," but he would be one
    Who wouldn't say so till he'd tried.
So he buckled right in with the trace of a grin
    On his face. If he worried he hit it.
He started to sing as he tackled the thing
    That couldn't be done, and he did it!

Somebody scoffed: "Oh, you'll never do that;
    At least no one ever has done it;"
But he took off his coat and he took off his hat
    And the first thing we knew he'd begun it.
With a lift of his chin and a bit of a grin,
    Without any doubting or quiddit,
He started to sing as he tackled the thing
    That couldn't be done, and he did it.

There are thousands to tell you it cannot be done,
    There are thousands to prophesy failure,
There are thousands to point out to you one by one,

    The dangers that wait to assail you.
But just buckle in with a bit of a grin,
    Just take off your coat and go to it;
Just start in to sing as you tackle the thing
    That "cannot be done," and you'll do it.

CHAPTER 1

FROM WHENCE COMES
THIS YEARNING?

Thirty-four years old, and what am I doing with my life?
Eight-year-old Pamela and five-year-old Randall were in
school most of the day, and we were living the privileged life
in a lovely home with a full-time, Spanish-speaking housekeeper. Stan made good money, allowing me the freedom to
play cards and tennis, study piano, learn to cook well, and have
lunch with friends, so what could possibly have been missing? I
needed more. More meaning, I suppose. (My carefree life was
becoming dull? How dare I say that?) I had too much energy.
What about my expensive college education? What use could
I make of that now? Did I have a purpose here on earth? How
could I make my mark in this world?

I was, quite frankly, just a lucky chief cook and bottle
washer, chauffeur, social planner, wife, and mother with a
loving husband who paid the bills for our happy family of four
in west LA. My diploma from UCLA had been filed away long
ago, along with my old teaching credential from the 1970s,
when women went to college to find a husband and become

a teacher or social worker or some such thing. A homemaker now, I was way too busy for a full-time job teaching or doing anything else. I did miss teaching though, having enjoyed it until our second child was born, so when Pam and Randy started school, I began substituting a couple days a week and actually looked forward to those morning phone calls when a French or English teacher was sick, and they needed me to replace her at a nearby high school.

Then one day everything was different.

I answered the phone at 7:00 a.m. and was told the science teacher was ill. It wasn't at one of the LA Unified City Schools, but at a private school for girls in the wealthy area of Holmby Hills.

"We know it's not your subject, but could you please substitute for the botany teacher today?"

Botany, not French?

Reluctantly, I agreed. The students were all teenagers, college bound and conscientious. I arrived that morning to learn the lesson at hand concerned the anatomy of flowers. The problem was I couldn't tell a pistil from a stamen, let alone what they were for, and the girls knew it. They were eager to learn from me, and I wasn't up to the job. "She doesn't know the answers," they said. Frustrated, I couldn't wait to get home at 3:00 p.m. Did I really miss teaching that much to continue like this? My husband Stan was a well-paid lawyer in a great law firm in Century City. As I was pulling in my driveway, I tried to justify my earnings: $46 in for the day, $6 out for the run in my stockings, $5 for lunch, something for gas, and taxes to pay. I could hear the country western music that wafted through the window from the radio of the young man painting our house inside. He earned $12 an hour, and *I* was the one with the college education. How did this make any sense?

Longing to make my days useful, I tried charity work.

My friend Joan had just lost her baby girl to cancer, so a group of us formed a new cancer fund for children. We became a strong organization, bringing in large donations every year at our charity ball. We also opened a children's store when a benefactor offered us free rent. We published cookbooks to raise additional funds, and as chair of the Cookbook Committee, I held a place on the board of directors. My committee and I tested recipes, created two cookbooks, and sold a lot of them. It felt good, very good in fact, until the day we lost the support of a major family foundation when Julie, our board treasurer, resigned. Her family was famous for their cosmetics, which were sold in every drug store throughout the world. They were big donors. I called Julie to ask what happened.

"Julie, you've been so dedicated, and your family is so important to us. What will we do without you? Why are you leaving us?"

"I got the Cancer Fund bank statement." Julie's voice was trembling with emotion. "And I was shocked to see that more than $50,000 had been withdrawn. No one told me. I thought it was a mistake. I was pretty upset and called Joan, since her husband and I are the only signers on the account. You can't just take that kind of money without a reason, and certainly not without a meeting and a vote from the board. It was a simple question. Joan started yelling at me because she thought I was accusing her husband of stealing it. We got into a huge fight. I'm treasurer. I'm responsible. I was concerned, not accusing. She took it the wrong way. It turns out her husband used the money for the Cancer Fund gift shop for fixtures or something."

"He took Cancer Fund money and spent it on the store?"

"Yes, but you can't do that. He can't do that. Not without board approval. I got so mad, and the more Joan said he was authorized to take money for the store, the angrier I got. I couldn't get through to her, so I resigned. I know the next board meeting is at your house next Tuesday, but I won't be there. I quit."

"But, Julie, we need you. Please don't do this."

"I'm sorry. I just can't stay on. Joan thinks she can do whatever she wants with our money, but I won't be a part of it. Not one bit."

The following Tuesday at my house, I spoke up and told everyone present about Julie's resignation and the significant loss of her family's future contributions. In front of the entire board, I made a plea directly to Joan. "Joan, you always tell us to think of the children. You should do the same. We can't lose Julie. Call her. Apologize. Get her back."

My inner voice was nagging: Adrienne, what are you doing? You think you can tell Joan what to do? You're not very politically savvy. This is her charity. You should keep your mouth shut and let her run things her way.

Joan couldn't believe her ears. I'd criticized her in front of everyone. No one dared tell her what to do. She wasn't changing her mind, not for the children, not for any of us. She called for a vote that would give her *carte blanche* to continue using the funds as she pleased, just as she had done in the past. I persisted. I asked for a discussion before we voted. Everyone on the board had raised substantial funds, through sales of crocheted blankets and other hand made products as well as a letter writing campaign, and I felt giving *carte blanche* over this money to any one person, even Joan, was simply wrong. Because of my argument, the vote was tabled and put off for a month. As I looked around the room, observing half the women knitting or working on needlepoint, and the other half afraid to speak up, I felt quite alone.

Days later, most of us on the board were going to a brunch at the Century Plaza Hotel to hear a famous author talk about her new best seller. As I was walking to my table, I saw Joan sitting with Bonnie, her best friend. I was anxious to talk to

Bonnie. A volunteer like the rest of us, she was in charge of the Cancer Fund store.

"Hi, Bonnie!" I exclaimed cordially. "Our second cookbook sold out and the printer asked for money for the next 5,000 copies. Would you send him a check from the Cancer Fund store?" Bonnie didn't answer. I tried to be upbeat and friendly. "By the way," I continued, "the third book is looking good. I heard your dinner party on Saturday was fabulous. We'd love to have the recipes to test them."

Bonnie was truly annoyed. "When I'm feeling a little *friendlier* towards the Cookbook Committee, then *maybe* you'll see the recipes."

"What do you mean, '*Maybe?*' Why are you mad at me?" I asked. "Think of the big picture. We're all just volunteers, and the cookbooks raise money. Everyone said your dinner was great, so let us test the recipes."

Bonnie gave me a look that could kill, raised her voice, and stood up, waving her arms at me, "I DON'T LIKE YOU. GO AWAY! GO AWAY!"

I instinctively stepped backwards. Startled by her threatening gestures, my brain reeling and my heart pounding in my ears, I quickly turned my back to her, unable to stop the tears from gushing, a reaction to the sting of her hideous words. How I wish I'd had the nerve to pick up the glass of water in front of her and throw it in her face. Instead, I proceeded to the front of the room toward my table near the stage, shaking from head to toe, too sick at heart to engage in trivial conversation or ingest anything but coffee. As the opening remarks began, a thousand thoughts distracted me. I wasn't looking for a fight. I'd been there from the very beginning. I was a founding member of the Cancer Fund, eager to do whatever it would take to eradicate cancer in children. Leaving the organization was unthinkable. But how could I stay? I had no choice but to resign from the board.

In my absence, the third cookbook would never be published. At home that afternoon, I sat down with pen and paper to write an eight-page history of my work with the Cancer Fund, detailing why I became involved and why I had to leave. My emotional distress became physical queasiness. This couldn't be the flu. It couldn't be, because we were leaving for Mexico City in two days. At the doctor's office, listening to me describe my symptoms, Dr. Paul assured me I was fine. He glanced at the letter in my lap I'd brought to reread in the waiting room and asked me what it was.

"Once you send that letter, all your symptoms will disappear," he said.

I left his office, went to Kinko's, and sent a copy of my letter to each and every board member. Dr. Paul was right. It was a catharsis and a cure.

So once again I found myself aching inside for something I could not define. Time on my hands was anathema to me. It was the age-old story of the over-educated housewife. I wanted so much to find fulfillment outside the realm of my husband and family and put my untapped talents to good use. But now I wanted to be paid for my efforts. A problem for me was that I believed I was not like most women. I was helpless when it came to interior design; teaching left me unfulfilled; fashion was not my *forte*; and volunteering for charity hadn't brought any satisfaction. On the other hand, I craved recognition. I needed to be needed, to be persuasive, and to have influence. On the phone with friends, I complained. "I'm too young to be wasting my time. I know I can be good at something," I repeated again and again. "I just have to be ready when the opportunity comes my way."

With my eyes open to all possibilities, I looked forward to our upcoming vacation in Mexico.

We'd been to Mexico once before in 1963, two months after our wedding. Back then Stan and I were just a happy pair of newlyweds combing the streets for silver tableware with wedding gift money to spend. The capital of Mexico was a city that sprawled in every direction, and for a first-time visitor it was overwhelming to navigate. There were dozens of historical sites to see, fabulous art in the museums and galleries, and diverse neighborhoods that covered large distances. The wide boulevards and grand parks were as beautiful as those in Europe, and the city was bustling. We found ourselves on Paseo de la Reforma, a wide boulevard with roundabouts and monuments, crowded with cars and pedicabs full of people everywhere. The pedicabs, mostly little Volkswagens, ran back and forth along the street, picking up people and dropping them along the way. Stan and I walked along the street, passing Sanborn's department store and many smaller shops. Block after block, just a young couple in love, we could see the sterling silver tableware for which the country is famous. Much of what we saw, however, was not well made. After an hour or two of roaming the street, we thought we'd be going home empty-handed, when suddenly we came upon a small shop, Joyeria Plateria San Francisco. The owners were there, a lovely couple, Francisco and Lotte Roth, Jewish immigrants from Hungary who had fled just before the Holocaust. Their store, like all the others, was filled with sterling silver pieces in all shapes and sizes, but unlike everyone else, they offered stunning Danish designs with high quality workmanship. We purchased several fine pieces and returned home with lovely wedding gifts.

Now fifteen years later, we were returning to Mexico City and thought we might find this special store once again. But the primary reason we chose Mexico for this vacation was to reconnect with a knowledgeable art consultant who had come to Los Angeles and encouraged us to visit him in Mexico, where he would introduce us to the fabulous world of Mexican art. Josh Kligerman was a tall man with wiry gray hair and an eye for the exceptional that made fine art so desirable. He picked us up at the airport, and over the next several days he brought us to the homes of the best artists Mexico had to offer: David Alfaro Siqueiros, Rufino Tamayo, Pablo O' Higgins, Augusto Escobedo, and Francisco Zuniga. Even though we didn't buy more than a couple of lithographs, a small watercolor, and an onyx sculpture, collecting fine art at reasonable prices would become our new passion.

We were staying in the Zona Rosa, a part of the city with fine shops, art galleries, and restaurants, and I was in the mood for shopping. Walking the streets close to Hotel El Presidente, we saw with delight Francisco and Lotte Roth's newly relocated silver store, a shop as elegant and as enticing as ever. As soon as we entered inside, even though more than a decade had passed, Mr. Roth recognized us immediately.

"I remember you!" he exclaimed. "I'm so glad to see you. You're a California lawyer, exactly what I need. Do you have a moment to talk?"

In addition to the beautiful tableware, a large section of the store was devoted to jewelry. While I was trying on various items, Mr. Roth and Stan sat on the sofa and discussed business. Half an hour later, when we walked out, my jewelry purchase in hand, I asked Stan what they had talked about.

"Mr. Roth has a sales agent in Los Angeles. She sells his silver jewelry but doesn't buy enough. She returns damaged goods for repair, and she hasn't paid her bill in months. He wants me to write a formal demand to pay him in full and terminate their relationship."

"Oh," I said immediately, thinking quickly of the fun I might have, "He needs a new agent. I'd love to sell his merchandise. It's beautiful and not expensive. As soon as we get to the hotel, I'm going to call him."

Stan sensed my restlessness. He was well aware of my need for validation as a person who could contribute, who could be successful and feel not only respect from others, but also self-respect, with an identity that encompassed more than that of wife and mother. He knew I was yearning for this. Every woman with brains and energy to spare needs to find a way to develop herself independently as a fulfilled, independent, and happy individual.

Stan had his law practice during the week and his golf on Saturdays, and he was also an active volunteer for the Arthritis Foundation—chairman of the board, in fact. When I asked him if I could work alongside him to raise money for arthritis, he gently explained that someone with more contacts and experience would be a better candidate. "I already have someone in mind who knows the president of Knudsen." Stan's response made perfect sense. After all, *I* didn't know anyone in the corporate world to sponsor the charity. I was just a capable young mother whose daily contacts were banal and unexciting. My life centered on our precious children and a one-syllable vocabulary that truly made me crave adult conversation.

"I get it," I said petulantly, with a touch of sarcasm. "I don't know anyone important who might be a big sponsor. *My* biggest contacts are the salesman at La Tijera Bootery and the box boy at the supermarket!"

During most of the twentieth century, the average woman was content to be a homemaker, and it seemed even the profession of choice for more than half of female college graduates was that of schoolteacher. Very few women back then dared to be lawyers or doctors. It was a man's world, one in which it was expected that the role of housewife, mother, and social planner would bring a woman all the fulfillment she could possibly need. Women who had to work did have jobs, but few women had a career. Ambition for a woman back then was a dirty word. I had two beautiful young children. Was there something wrong with me? Why was I aching to do more?

Here was my chance, an opportunity to spread my wings. I didn't know my search for excitement would eventually lead to buying and selling diamonds and gems, meeting scoundrels, getting scammed, or putting my life at risk.

I picked up the phone in our hotel room. "Mr. Roth, we just got back to the hotel. Stan says you're getting rid of your distributor. You need a new one, and I'M IT!"

"You're a nice lady," he said. "I like you very much, but you have a good husband. You don't need a job like this."

In retrospect, I realize how limited the concept of independent women was back then. Mr. Roth must have been referring to the fact that I didn't need the money, and I was going to have to insist.

"You don't know what I need," I said candidly, thinking of the large mortgage we'd just taken on our new home. "My children are in school now. I was volunteering for charity, but that wasn't enough for me. I love your silver jewelry. It's beautiful, and I know I can get people to buy it!"

Mr. Roth was not convinced. But I was earnest.

"I'd be so good at this. When I worked for The Cancer Fund, I was in charge of writing cookbooks, which sold all across the United States. The books sold out three times, more than 15,000 copies. In fact, we got them into Marshall Fields in Chicago, Neiman Marcus in Texas, and Henri Bendel in New York. If I can do that, I can sell your jewelry."

Fortunately, Mr. Roth believed me. His wife was a go-getter businesswoman, so he thought if I were anything like her, he might take a chance on me. The truth was, I knew how to cook and how to write, but I didn't actually get the cookbooks into any of those stores. It was someone else, a sales professional, who did that. I hadn't a clue how to do what I said I would. My entire knowledge of business involved selling Girl Scout cookies in the sixth grade.

Was this irrational thinking, a willingness to do anything, to grasp at any chance to fill the emptiness of my days? A life passing by without purpose or direction had fueled an illogical impetuosity.

The following morning, Mr. Roth sent a car and driver to take Stan and me to his factory, where together we selected the jewelry I was to sell. Mr. Roth showed us around. The upstairs showroom had wall-to-wall shelves displaying gorgeous silver candelabra, water pitchers, and other beautiful modern pieces. They looked as if they'd been made by George Jensen, the legendary silversmith from Denmark, whose modern, high-end designs were sold in the finest shops all over the world. Mr. Roth pointed out the most popular items. We sat at a large table with his son George, who worked in the factory daily while his parents tended the store, and together we made a list of the pieces I'd carry in my line. Mr. Roth began explaining how to get the business going. He told me to call the buyers at stores that might be interested, show the merchandise, and take their orders. And that was it! That was my introduction to the business world, my entire lesson, and the beginning of my career in jewelry. I named my company Avanti of California, which, in retrospect, sounds more like a clothing manufacturer than a jewelry importer. It was a terrible name, actually, but it identified my company with the factory, which was known throughout the world as *Avanti Internacional de Mexico. Avanti* is Italian for "advance" or "forward," which was appropriate for designs that were modern and trendy.

A novice with the nerve to tackle an intimidating responsibility, an experienced French teacher who was well versed in existential philosophy . . . this encompassed my comfort zone and my expertise. What did this have to do with business? Nothing. Still, I was industrious and wanted to learn. How hard could it be? Dismissing all negative thoughts, I was ready for action, with a bounce in my step. I'd soon become taller, bigger, stronger, more influential again, able to contribute and make some money in my spare time.

CHAPTER 2

A ROUGH BEGINNING

A beautiful line of jewelry was arriving, and I was counting the days. All I had to do was find the right buyers and take the orders. But wait! I needed jewelry displays. The Yellow Pages were as close as you'd get to Google in those days, and I used it wisely to locate where to buy the necessary displays. I also needed to clear the commercial shipments through customs, but I wasn't going to pay a broker a fee each time a shipment arrived from Mexico. How could I afford to hire a broker, who would charge a minimum of $200? To spend that much for a $2,500 shipment would increase the actual cost of each piece of jewelry by 8 percent. This would cut my 15 percent commission in half. I called customs directly. The chief customs officer for jewelry shipments to Los Angeles was a Mr. Arcos, and he was extremely kind. He said if I didn't wish to hire a customs broker, I could act as my own broker and import packages free of charge. All I had to do was drive three times to Mexicana Air Cargo at LAX and complete a substantial amount of paperwork each time a package was shipped. Mr. Arcos showed me how. Nowadays, with the heavy traffic in Southern California and price of gas, three trips to the airport wouldn't make sense to save $200, but everything was different then.

Before the first shipment arrived, Stan and I took a stroll along Rodeo Drive to see if any of the stores sold silver jewelry. Matthews was one of the more exclusive dress shops on the street. In the window were many of the same pieces of silver we had selected for my line. Naturally I planned to visit this store as soon as possible to tell the buyer I was the new agent for the product.

When the jewelry finally arrived from the factory, I laid it all out on the dining room table, changed the tags, and created a catalog. I changed the pesos to dollars and added exactly 15 percent, as Mr. Roth had suggested. The resulting prices ended in pennies and would make the buyers laugh. But finally, with everything nicely displayed on newly purchased velvet rolls in a small carry-on suitcase, I was ready to make appointments with buyers.

The first store I called upon, of course, was Matthews, since they already carried some of Mr. Roth's line. I was told to go into a large dressing room and spread out my wares on the carpeted floor. The buyer's name was Jeff. He couldn't have been older than twenty-five, and in such an elegant shop he appeared out of place wearing ordinary blue jeans and a long sleeve plaid shirt that wasn't even tucked in. When he entered the dressing room and saw the jewelry, he became angry.

"I'm already buying this stuff from someone else."

"Yes, I know," I replied, "but I'm the new distributor now. The lady you were buying from no longer represents the factory. I'm the new rep. You already know it's salable merchandise, and my prices are lower than hers."

"I don't care about the price. I get the price I want. And besides, I have an exclusive on the street."

Jeff didn't care about the price? My father had always taught me that what you pay for a product is important if you hope to sell it. So why didn't he care? My thoughts were scrambling in an attempt to understand.

"I'll give you the same exclusive, when you place your order. The rep you're buying from no longer has access to this collection."

I started sweating under my beautiful clothes.

"Nah, I don't think so," he said, waving his hands with a disgusted air, and with no further explanation, he added, "I think I'll be done with both of you." With that, he abruptly walked out of the dressing room, leaving me dumbstruck.

Who is he to tell me whether I can make a deal or not? Does my success depend upon him? He doesn't live in a gorgeous home like mine. He isn't married to a successful attorney. He doesn't have two beautiful children and a great life. Even if I'm not a success at this, I can still go home to happiness.

Admittedly, I *was* disappointed and even a little hurt, and I didn't like the feeling of having been dismissed so abruptly, especially by someone in his twenties, who, unlike me, didn't appear to have a college education. This young guy had the power to turn me down flat and bring on feelings of discouragement. He was supposed to buy from me! He didn't like me! My hopes were dashed in an instant. I gave myself a mini pep talk and thought, *It might take a bunch of "no"s before I get a "yes," and the faster I can get through those "no"s, the faster I'll get that big sale.*

What do you do when you hurt? You try to brush it off, and then you find a friend.

I put all the jewelry back into the carry-on bag, picked myself up off the floor of Matthews' dressing room, and walked across the street to Van Cleef & Arpels, where I could bare my soul. Daniel Ryan was the manager of this wonderful exclusive jewelry store on Rodeo Drive. I sat in his office a while and listened to his good advice.

"Reach the resident buyers downtown and exhibit at the appropriate trade shows," he said. Then he asked Carole, his secretary, to look at my line, and he called upstairs so the Van Cleef & Arpels jewelers who worked in the building would come have a look as well. They were impressed with the workmanship and ordered a few small things for their families.

"We can't wear silver at work," Carole told me, "because Van Cleef sells only 18 karat gold, but I really like these bracelets and I'll just have them gold plated."

I was glad to have this first order, albeit a small one, and immediately felt better. Leaving Van Cleef, I walked back across the street to the store right next door to Matthews, where they had beautiful Danish silver jewelry displayed in the window. A well-dressed woman greeted me. Her name was Gunn Trigère. Gunn smiled at me with my small suitcase.

"I have a line of beautiful silver jewelry. Would you like to see it?"

"Of course!" she replied enthusiastically. "If it looks like what you're wearing, I'd love to see it. Can you come tomorrow morning at 10:00?"

That was my first big sale. Her purchase order, mostly necklaces and bracelets, filled the entire page of my order form. What's more, Matthews no longer had an exclusive on the street.

If I've made it sound easy, it certainly wasn't. Realizing I had to drum up my own business, in the months that followed I kicked myself into gear. First, I contacted the resident buyers in downtown Los Angeles and participated in a four-day show at the LA Apparel Mart. The resident buyers consisted of a few specialists who consulted with buyers from out of town and helped them find what they were looking for. They knew where to find all types of merchandise, so naturally I wanted them to become familiar with my line. I rented a tiny room in the building with a desk and a few chairs. This proved to be a total bust. Not knowing whom to call, I hadn't contacted anyone to let people know I would be there. The buyers who came all had appointments with others, and no one stopped to see me.

Well, that was a wasted effort. There must be another way to reach buyers.

I contacted the California Gift Show, which was a bi-annual event where retailers came to buy for their stores. I was told to talk to a man who wanted to share his booth. So I called him, and we agreed that instead of paying for half the booth, I would help him sell his clothing line. I exhibited along side him, sold his clothing and my jewelry, and decided to take my own booth space the next time and every six months after that.

What I didn't know was that a huge adventure was unfolding, and it would continue for thirty-five years. A small hobby can grow and mushroom into a real business, even if part time. Every day while my children were in school, I would get in my car and drive all over town, searching for upscale stores to carry my line. I began boldly making cold calls. I went into Saks Fifth Avenue and asked to speak to the buyer. The national jewelry buyer for Saks was Maryanne Mooney, but she worked in the New York office. The jewelry manager at the Beverly Hills store loved what I was wearing and arranged for an appointment with Miss Mooney, who would be coming to town shortly. Within two months of starting my little import business, I landed one of the most sought-after clients. Saks put me on the map, so to speak, with an order for eight stores all over the country. In fact, I had to dig into savings to pay Mr. Roth for the order, and then wait for Saks to pay me in thirty days. What I hadn't expected was that Saks didn't pay on time, and after three months had passed with no response to my billing statements, I had to resort to sending Saks a Western Union telegram. That seemed to do the trick, but then they took a discount, which had never been discussed or agreed to. Stan had to write a legal letter to get payment in full.

It was a feather in my cap when Mr. Roth came to New York on a pleasure trip with Lotte, his wife, some time later. They were unaware I had sold to Saks Fifth Avenue and couldn't believe their eyes when they saw their jewelry in the cases there.

It was about this time that I realized a fifteen percent commission was too low for everything I was doing. I was not just representing *Avanti Internacional de Mexico*. I was operating my own business as Avanti of California. None of the stores wanted to receive shipments directly from the factory and deal with customs. So not only did I have to find the accounts, but I also had to bring the shipments through customs, separate the orders and ship them myself to each store, bill the accounts, and wait for payment. I needed a larger margin to make my efforts worthwhile and eventually hire an employee. Stan was supportive. He could see I was trying very hard. He also trusted that I was smart enough to know what I was doing. He didn't meddle or offer advice and never complained that I was running the business out of our home.

I'd had the line for six months when I tried to sell to a wholesaler of fine jewelry on Hill Street in downtown Los Angeles. He sold gold jewelry primarily and told me he didn't want any silver. "I'd much rather make a profit of 10 percent on gold than three times that much on silver." Silver was cheaper than gold, but clearly, it was much harder to sell, mainly because gold was the metal of choice for jewelers, and at thirty-five dollars an ounce, gold was truly inexpensive at the time.

I muddled through a lot of attempts to sell to jewelers who weren't interested. I couldn't understand why they didn't want my product, since I thought it was so fabulous. I decided to try Bullocks Wilshire, a fine department store catering to the affluent residents of Hancock Park. The buyer at Bullocks loved the Avanti tableware—beautiful salt, pepper, and sugar holders, which were sterling, clad with enamel in beautiful colors. She definitely wanted these, but she didn't buy the jewelry, nor did she reorder the tableware after everything had sold out.

I sold to Gumps in San Francisco. Stan had an Arthritis Foundation meeting in this beautiful city, and I tagged along with my samples. At five feet two inches, 115 pounds, in a suit and high heels, I dragged my suitcase along the streets from Union Square to Post Street; and then, an hour later, leaving Gumps with a nice order for enameled salt and pepper dishes, I was ready for my next appointment around the corner, less than a block away.

My feet were killing me. I couldn't lug my suitcase another step and hailed the taxi driver, who was waiting curbside.

"Sorry, lady, I'm not driving you there. It's around the corner. You can walk."

"Please take me. I can't drag my suitcase any farther. Will you do it for a $10.00 tip?"

"Oh, all right. Get in the cab."

With shipments coming in, I hired a UCLA student to help me with my orders. This did not turn out well. I suspected something amiss when the young woman showed up for work one day wearing a smock with gigantic deep pockets. It was the perfect smock for a thief to wear. Wary now, I searched the storage closet that housed all the silver. Then I asked her, "Where are the enameled salt dishes? I see we still have all the mushroom pepper shakers, but no salt dishes?" Of course, I did know the answer. If she'd realized the mushrooms were for pepper, she probably would have stolen those as well. The day she wore that smock was her last day on the job.

Stan and I traveled frequently together when he was chairman of the Arthritis Foundation. I always brought the collection. He would conduct meetings all day, while I would search through the hotel phone book to find stores to carry the line.

Selling on the road is exciting, because you never know how the day will turn out. There were many times when I drove around town and sold nothing at all, or days when I sold very little. There were also the rare days when a casual appointment turned into something fun, such as the time I went to Geary's, one of the finer stores in Beverly Hills. They wanted one hundred of the pretty silver puffed hearts to be delivered in time for Valentine's Day.

I kept myself open to surprises. In later years, after I'd given up selling silver and started selling gold and diamonds, I went to see a cousin in Atlanta. Cousin Sara loved jewelry, and she knew all the jewelers in her hometown. She drove me around Atlanta to see every jeweler she knew, although I made very few sales. One small store there ordered a single pair of gold and diamond huggie earrings for $75.00. At the time, this small item was hardly worth shipping, but by the time I retired, this same store had ordered thousands of pairs of these from me. Over a ten-year period the huggie earrings brought in hundreds of thousands of dollars, and they are still selling to this day. This is what makes business compelling. The unpredictability of finding new customers rather than having a pre-determined set salary made every day exciting.

Although I had graduated from UCLA, I had never taken a single course in business. My education now came from attending the school of the streets, where you fend for yourself and learn by doing and paying attention. The buyers at I. Magnin & Co. department stores taught me how to get paid on time. They paid their discounted orders first, preferring terms such as 3/10/ EOM, which meant a 3 percent discount would be taken, and the shipment must arrive ten days before the end of the month prior to the actual due date, giving them at least forty days to sell the merchandise before having to pay for it. If I wanted Avanti to be in their catalog, or at least get an insert to advertise my pieces in their monthly statements to customers, I would have to pay a substantial fee for photography. I gladly agreed to the fee, stipulating that it could not be higher than 5 percent of the total order. Who knew that it was the manufacturers and importers who paid for all the ads in those department store catalogs?

The order for I. Magnin was complicated. The buyers wanted three bangle bracelets, to be sold as a tri-color set, the three bangles worn together, one plain silver, one rose gold vermeil, and one yellow gold vermeil. They also wanted one hundred necklaces with three-dimensional fruit charms—a small pear in plain silver, a small banana in yellow gold vermeil, and a small apple in rose gold vermeil. These would hang from a black silk rope with a sterling silver clasp. Very excited to get this order, I contracted to make these custom pieces, even though I didn't know who could make the vermeil. The factory in Mexico certainly didn't do it. Vermeil is a special type of gold plating over silver, and even though I thought it would be easy to find a local company to do it, I was overly optimistic. Many vendors could do yellow gold vermeil over silver, but no one seemed to have experience with rose gold. It took weeks to locate The 1928 Jewelry Company, the only supplier in the country that used rose gold vermeil. They made gold-plated replicas of jewelry in rose gold in the vintage style from that era. I went to see them and showed them the samples, and they agreed to do the job at a reasonable price. I did not get this in writing, which turned out to be a big mistake.

When the six hundred fruit charms and bracelets arrived from Mexico, I separated them for the yellow and rose gold vermeil and dropped them off in person to have them gold plated. The next morning, I got a phone call with bad news. The 1928 Jewelry Company had changed its mind and refused to do the work. They considered me to be a serious competitor. It was a low blow. Stan was at home when I got the bad news. I was sitting on the bed with the phone in my ear and a look of dismay on my face.

"What are you going to do?" he asked. I had six hundred pieces I had to pay for with no resources to finish the order. What *was* I going to do?

In the 1970s, we didn't have personal computers. Individual effort was what counted most to achieve what you wanted. Some would say it was luck that I found another gold-plating company willing to create a formula for rose gold vermeil. But I would say, on the contrary, it was effort and persistence and the refusal to take no for an answer that led me to the solution. With the help of the silversmith who was making the clasps for the one hundred black silk rope necklaces, I met the right man. Lenny Goldberg was a gold plater who had never made rose gold vermeil, but he promised he would figure out how to do it. He was up for the challenge. Through trial and error, he figured out how much copper to add to the gold. The result was perfect, and the pieces for I. Magnin & Co. were delivered on time. They sold out. I was paid on schedule, and Lenny got a nice gift basket for rescuing me.

So it was that, in my first year of business, there were some bumps in the road. When my "sure" sale at Matthews fizzled, I succeeded with the luxurious Trigère shop. When an employee became a thief, I was forced to work alone. When The 1928 Jewelry Company refused to gold plate my order, I suffered great anguish, yet persevered to find a solution. No matter what, I had to keep going.

One Saturday evening our insurance agent and good friend Lloyd took us out to dinner. "Why does your husband let you work?" he asked me. My hair stood on end.

"*Let* me work? My 'work' is part of who I am. It's a strong part of my identity."

"How much money can you possibly make?" he asked.

Stan answered his questions with this retort: "It's not how much money she makes that's important. Adrienne is so busy, she has no time to spend money shopping." After we laughed at the joke, he added, "Besides, it satisfies her soul."

My self-respect and the respect of others that barely existed when I'd been a teacher were growing. I had to feel productive, even though I didn't fully understand why. I did ask myself, why wasn't my life, defined as wife and mother, enough for me? Stan was doing well, and I certainly didn't need to work to support my family. What I craved was a clearer sense of my role here on earth and my place in society. Who was I, this person with untapped, wasted talent and energy? Venturing out into the world, suffering there, struggling there, and most assuredly, not failing there, would validate my existence in a different way. And of course, I loved the thrill of making my own money without a boss or regular hours. That was the fun part. Even if I worked part time, the person I could become would depend on the choices I would make and the actions I would take. The world was full of adventure, prizes, and promises. Through sheer will I would go after it all, capture the "brass ring," and become someone different in the process. I knew instinctively I had to make important choices for myself, because if I didn't, life would make them for me.

Those lofty words belie the hard part I would discover later. Most successful wholesalers in business have to have new, beautiful designs every year. They need to go after the big buyers who are constantly searching for product. They need to work hard, not part time. They get financial help from the banks (because after all, business is capital-intensive), they have courage, and they take serious, calculated risks whenever the opportunities present themselves.

All this, of course, was completely off my radar. It was simply too soon to know this now. And it was way too soon to know how exciting it would be to join the world of jewels and gems, competing for profits in a world where few women ventured, a world dominated by men. I certainly couldn't have imagined I'd end up in a legal battle with my Russian partners or that my daughter would fear for my life because she truly believed they might have me killed.

CHAPTER 3

LEARNING FROM THE BEST

One night for dinner we invited Daniel Ryan, the manager of Van Cleef & Arpels who had helped me on my first day on the road. Daniel brought Catherine as his date, a cute, energetic French girl in her twenties. She had been living in France with her father and was importing silver jewelry from Mexico to sell there. The two of them went to Taxco, Mexico, where they gathered a collection to distribute to French boutiques throughout their country. Like me, Catherine had started a business herself, as an importer of silver to sell in her country.

When Catherine was still a teen, she lost her mother to cancer. My own mother had passed away when I was four. Nevertheless, we were both blessed. I grew up believing that with my mother up in heaven watching over me, no matter what, I'd be fine. Aunt Estelle had told me so. Catherine was an only child, while I was the eldest with three younger brothers, but both of us were instinctively fiercely independent and bossy, running the show at home and figuring out how to get whatever we wanted.

Like Catherine, without a mother's kinship, I had learned to be self-reliant at a very young age. Somehow I knew that it was totally up to me to go after what I wanted in life. I developed the strength, fortitude, and determination to forge ahead unaided, on my own. I would be a risk taker. Like Catherine, I would welcome challenges with courage, sometimes even heedlessly in search of the Golden Goose of reward.

As Catherine began her story, I focused on her every word as she told us that night at dinner how she started her business.

In her charming French accent, she described her very first months' long stay in Taxco, where she met Mexican silversmiths whose families had worked with silver for generations. I was truly interested in her story, since I wanted to expand my collection, and I asked her all sorts of questions. I had heard that the entire town of Taxco was made up of silversmiths who made jewelry by hand at home, but I had no idea how to locate these people. Catherine told me to go to a hotel at the top of the hill where there was a square in the center of town, near a large church. It was the best hotel in the tiny town of Taxco. Once there, Catherine said, I should turn left and look for a cantina on the right. If I walked in and asked for Pedro, he would take me to the homes and workshops of the best silversmiths in all of Mexico.

I couldn't wait to take Catherine's advice. I was eager, excited, and bright-eyed, my insides fluttering as I imagined with delight the tantalizing goodies I might find for my buyers. Stan and I planned our next vacation, another trip to Mexico. But it seemed Mr. Roth had retired, and his son George had taken leadership of the factory. George was not exactly thrilled with the news that we wanted to go to Taxco, since he was concerned about the competition. He really didn't want me to carry lines other than his.

"Why do you want to go to Taxco?" he asked.

"Oh, I must go. I need rings and earrings and small items you don't offer."

Realizing I could not be dissuaded, George insisted on driving us there. Then when we got there, he pretended not to know where the silversmiths could be found.

"Let's go to the cantina to see if Pedro is there," I proffered.

It was easy. Pedro was standing in the doorway of the cantina, exactly where Catherine had said he would be. He was only too eager to take us from house to house and from workshop to workshop, where I found so many new designs. This was truly a cottage industry of silversmiths working at home. I only found out later that George had asked Pedro not to take us around, but Pedro received a commission on every piece I purchased, so he took us everywhere. Unable to prevent me from buying, George left and went on to Acapulco, while Stan and I stayed in Taxco a few nights on our own. At first, Stan thought it was fun to look at rings. However, as can happen with handmade merchandise, quality control became a problem. We examined rings all day long, three days in a row, and rejected a great many when the workmanship wasn't satisfactory. After poring over rings all day and looking for imperfections, each night when we closed our eyes we slept with visions of rings dancing in our dreams. When I think of it now, I realize how much Stan loved me and did for me. Otherwise, why would he spend days looking at $2.00 rings, when back home as a lawyer he could earn so much more?

We discovered silver peddlers in underground rooms by the church, where women sat at benches with their parcels for sale. However, on the third day of buying, Stan suddenly got a horrible toothache. He couldn't help but complain. We were visiting a tiny silver workshop that belonged to Ernesto Purdy, an Australian businessman who had moved to Taxco years before. Ernesto had stunning earrings, Danish and Italian in style. Not having painkillers, Ernesto gave Stan some Tequila to numb the excruciating pain of his toothache. Of course, that was fairly useless. We quickly made our way back to Mexico City on a bus, with Stan grimacing at every bump in the road. At least in Mexico City they do have good dentists. George's wife Sara had a dentist she recommended highly, and he treated Stan's abscess immediately, relieving him of the pain.

On the flight home, Stan said, "All you spent in Taxco was $2,000." With earrings costing $4.00 a pair and rings costing $2.00 apiece, I had over 500 items to ticket, catalog, and get customers to buy. Considering the low potential profit and the amount of effort entailed, I had to agree that those five days in Mexico had been an extremely poor use of Stan's precious vacation time. Even so, Stan was my staunch supporter.

Darling Stan—a rare find, lucky for me. There has never been a better husband—kind, smart, generous, considerate, and loving, a man who wanted more than anything for his wife to find inner happiness and fulfillment. He encouraged me in every endeavor, without a hint of negativity or skepticism, no matter what crazy choices I made. Once I started to develop my own identity separate from wife and mother, he would say, "Life with Adrienne is anything but boring." Surely without Stan there to support me, I could never have done half the things I did.

Back home I couldn't wait to tell Catherine all about our trip. She had been to France in the meantime to visit her father and check on her silver business, which was doing well. Her father was in charge of sales, and Catherine wanted him to take over the entire business so she could move to the States. She searched for something made in France to sell here. While visiting one of her customers in St. Tropez, she noticed a new trend: funky, colorful, inexpensive plastic pins were being sold in almost every clothing store. She bought them and showed them to me. Personally, I couldn't believe anyone would wear such things. If you had good jewelry, shouldn't you wear that, not cheap, colorful plastic? Yet according to Catherine these pins were the rage, especially in Paris and Saint Tropez. Thinking they would sell in the States, and hoping to make Los Angeles her home, Catherine—ever the entrepreneur—purchased a few dozen samples from a French clothing store to show to buyers in California. She had the right idea to buy one of each design at the retail price, because that way she could develop a complete sample line without having to make a big outlay of cash. The factory that manufactured the pins in Paris required a minimum purchase of each design. Not knowing which would be the most popular, she didn't want to buy in quantities until she had orders to fill.

With a large selection of designs, Catherine attached the pins to velvet boards, tagged them and produced a full-color catalog. These pins were from one to two inches in size, colorful plastic shapes of animals, ice cream cones, ladies' hats, umbrellas, baby buggies, and so forth. Weird, I thought. Why would anyone want to wear a pink and white plastic ice cream cone pin on a sweater? Catherine asked me who I thought might buy these. I couldn't answer. They were so odd. She had paid around $3 a pin. The factory would have charged her half the price for quantities, but a substantial minimum order would be required. Even though she paid full retail for her samples at shops in Paris and San Tropez, the investment was small. She could show the samples, take orders at $3.00 a pin, and double her money later, when she placed her order direct from the factory at a cost of $1.50. She decided to call her new company *La Vie Parisienne*.

When Catherine flew back to Los Angeles with her sample pins, I invited her to stay as our houseguest. Undaunted by my lack of enthusiasm for her product, Catherine took her wares to the shops in Westwood near UCLA, to West Hollywood from Sunset to Melrose, and to every boutique she could find. In her appealing French accent, she explained to the shopkeepers that she was taking orders during the month of August, when the French factory was closed, and delivery would be toward the end of October. She worked the streets, making cold calls, just as I was doing, but within six weeks she had amassed orders totaling $15,000—meaning she had sold 5,000 pins! I was flabbergasted. When she ordered in quantity from the factory in Paris, her profit for six weeks of selling those funky pieces of plastic would be $7,500. Unlike me, she could double her money on her product.

Needless to say, within a year Catherine became well established in Los Angeles. At the same time, my own business was floundering. Silver was becoming increasingly difficult to move. I was stymied and becoming discouraged and decided to call Catherine.

"Why don't you take my pins and try to sell them?" she suggested. So I did, and I sold them to every store I visited. I also set up her line in my booth at the gift show and opened accounts for her there.

Catherine and I were alike in many ways, but very different in others. Stan always thought she was a bit "kooky." In her younger days, she'd had many men in her life who adored her, but she never committed herself to any of them. Eventually, once her business was well established, she went to Russia to adopt a young boy and raise him as her own in Los Angeles without a father. The two of us went our separate ways and lost track of one another over time. I do know this: Her company, *La Vie Parisienne*, is still thriving, and she spends most of her time now in France.

Catherine never waited for opportunity to knock on her door. She created it by knocking on doors herself. She even bought a building in Santa Monica with a partner, leased it out but kept a place for her office overlooking the Pacific Ocean. Years later, she would design her own collection of vintage jewelry with crystals made in her own factory in a small town in France. As an entrepreneur, she was a great influence in my own life. Because of Catherine, I knew you could start a business with baby steps, grow it, and start another. I began to see the business world in a bigger, broader way.

Catherine had known that sales in silver were slowing down. That's why she sought a new product. As it happened, I would have to do the same.

CHAPTER 4

GO FOR THE GOLD

It is widely known that precious metals are precious because they last forever. Platinum, gold, and silver can be melted, re-worked and repaired an infinite number of times. That's what makes them precious. I had now been selling silver for one year, and sales were slow—very slow. My buyers were not selling what they had bought, and some were stuck with inventory for a long time. I wasn't happy about this. My goal was to help people, not hurt them. Instead of silver, they were selling inexpensive gold chains. One day while taking in some silver for repair, I overheard the jewelers in the repair shop talking about gold. I learned valuable information from them. Gold was in great demand at the moment and easy to buy, especially gold chains from Italy. You just put the chain on the scale and weighed it, and you knew how much it cost. The price was fixed by London's spot market twice daily. Machine-made chains didn't cost much to manufacture. You would take the price of gold, add a little for labor and customs, and you'd know exactly how much to pay for it. It occurred to me that if produce or meat is sold by weight, I could do the same with gold. It was a no-brainer.

A no-brainer? Really? Don't you know buying gold can take serious money? Aren't you doing this for fun, part time?

Actually those thoughts never entered my head. Without hesitation, the decision was made. I would sell gold chains and buy them by weight. It was easy to find importers of gold chains from Italy here in Los Angeles. Furthermore, I could sell by the piece. Almost all the jewelry buyers would pay a little extra for the convenience of having my personal service and a 30-day open account for payment. I decided to invest, even though I didn't know anything about gold chains. They baffled me in their similarity. With no experience, it took me an hour to select a tiny sampling, just a handful for $3,000. I remember how my heart was pounding and my hand was trembling as I wrote the check, wondering if I was guessing right. The chains were so thin. Who would want them? There were so many similar styles and lengths—box, Figaro, curb, herringbone, marine link—all of them necessary to have a broad selection.

Although I began buying the chains from a wholesaler, it wasn't long before I found a direct supplier in the guise of Agosto and Pedro, two Italians with an office in downtown LA. These two men were factory reps who sold to every gold dealer and wholesaler on Hill Street, where the jewelry mart was located. Buying from them put me on a level playing field with all the other downtown dealers.

During the day, when the children were in school, I would wrack my brain to find the best jewelers as clients. I was driving anywhere and everywhere, from the valley to the marina or from home to Pasadena, to show both gold chains and silver jewelry to jewelers, gift shops, and clothing boutiques. Los Angeles, a series of suburbs and towns that lead endlessly from one to another, held a myriad of possible prospects in need of product to sell. Gold chains were wildly popular, they were inexpensive, and they made fabulous gifts, so every small boutique was buying them. But in silver only the small charms were selling. The beautiful, Danish-style modern cuffs and long silver necklaces were dead. The buyers, most of whom owned small shops, would tell me what they needed, and they all wanted gold. They usually told me to bring them specific styles, lengths, and price points. Being a start-up one-woman operation, I was the one who found the clients, took the orders, purchased the product, shipped the packages, billed the clients and collected the payments. It was a process that required diligence more than brains, but I liked it better than teaching in the LA city schools where my valuable talents had been so unappreciated.

Not all days were good ones. I have memories of driving back from San Diego alone late at night, hungry and tired, having missed dinner with my family. My energy was sapped from every inch of my body after a long day of calling on jewelers with poor results. Utterly fatigued and anxious to get home, I gave myself a pep talk. "You must keep going. No regrets for having tried. Today was a setback, but you are not a loser and must never give up without giving your all."

I never thought of quitting.

Always searching for new buyers, I decided to check out the stores at the Bonaventure Hotel. Winbell, a Japanese gift shop didn't carry gold jewelry, but right then and there the owner made the decision to do so. Within an hour, I walked out with an amazing $4,000 order for gold chains. I called my husband right away at work, so excited to tell him that my surprise of the day had just tendered a $400 profit. It was an adrenaline rush, and Stan laughed at my joy.

I tried not to let my work impact on my family, but there's no question it did. I shudder to think of the time our son was left stranded after religious school. Class was over at 5:00 p.m., but 6:00 p.m. had come and gone, and where was I? Overtired and overworked (self-induced to be sure), I'd simply forgotten to pick him up. Poor kid, eleven years old, standing outside as the streetlights illuminated, the school principal at his side. And poor me, I still shudder with shame to this day.

Wife and mother or career girl: pick one or the other and do it well. Relinquish the role of wife and mother to have a strong career? Unthinkable! Struggling with internal conflict, I found myself apologizing. To compromise here or there was not a solution, and yet that was what I was doing. On occasion the family would suffer, and if not the family, the business. My mother had never worked as far as I knew, and after she died and my father remarried, my stepmother never worked either. Wives weren't expected to have a career, and most men back then felt diminished somehow when they did. It was a bad idea for a woman to make more money than her husband. My stepmother told me so, and she was very wise. "Dear Abby" in her *Los Angeles Times* column insisted that when the man of the house is the primary breadwinner, the marriage has a better chance of surviving. Stan disagreed completely and said he'd be delighted if my income surpassed his. Still, we all thought that Stan was an unusual guy, because it seemed that nothing could destroy his self-confidence. Even so, my mom's words were stuck in my head. If it meant I could make millions, I could never sacrifice my family for personal success.

This was a conflict that never went away. I cannot say I have regrets, but I wonder sometimes if my meaningful career could have been placed on hold until it no longer affected those nearest and dearest to my heart.

CHAPTER 5

KING TUT

In 1978, King Tut was the rage. LACMA (our Los Angeles County Museum of Art) hosted a major exhibit full of fabulous Egyptian artifacts and jewelry from ancient times. It was a groundbreaking exhibit from the Cairo Museum, an enormous installation of fabulous pieces. As the exhibit toured several cities in the States, all things related to Egypt became popular. In jewelry, it was scarabs and images of Nefertiti. If you visited the UNESCO gift shop on Westwood Blvd., you would find wonderful exotic replicas, unusual gift items and extraordinary, inexpensive fashion pieces. The buyer for UNESCO was Esther Morgenstern, a lovely European lady in her late fifties, and she had great taste. She especially loved my things from Taxco and became a wonderful client. When the Treasures of Tutankhamen were on exhibit, she showed me the scarab rings and Nefertiti pendants she had purchased from an Egyptian vendor whose name was Mohsin. I thought I'd like to sell these things also and asked her to have Mohsin contact me the next time he was in Los Angeles.

Mohsin lived in New York, was married to a former flight attendant, and had three children. One day, during the Tutankhamen exhibit, after taking an order from the museum shop at LACMA, Mohsin came to my house to show me his collection. His rings were unlike any I'd seen in Mexico, with large stones and intricate details. We struck a deal. I was going to rep his line and share his booth at the San Francisco Gift Show, where I had not exhibited before.

It costs thousands to take a booth at a show, a 10' by 10' piece of draped carpeting one could call one's own for five days. It was one thing to exhibit in Los Angeles, where the booth was the only cost, where a hotel and restaurants were unnecessary and where the buyers were close to home, close enough to visit all year long while the children were in school. It was another thing entirely to exhibit out of town, where the costs were triple. But San Francisco was not that far, and if Mohsin was paying for the booth, and if I stayed with my dear friend Irene, my only expenditure would be the nominal airfare for the one-hour flight each way. Seize the day. Stan wouldn't mind. Without hesitation I relinquished my responsibilities to our housekeeper at home, and with great anticipation I made the arrangements to go. This was a chance to meet buyers whose stores were distant from home, and when they would see my beautiful modern collection of silver so seductively priced, like everyone else, they'd be tempted beyond their control.

The bi-annual gift show in San Francisco is open to retailers only, not the public. Joining Mohsin in his booth would be a chance to see which of his items were the most popular. It would also give me the opportunity to see Mohsin at work and to learn how he sold his collection. After the show, he would give me his line on consignment, and I would take it from there, showing it to my retailers, sending him orders that he would ship to them.

At the show, my blind desire for success did not serve me well. I was impatient and impulsive. Day one I was full of hope, but by day two, full of despair. Anxious for sales, I would unwittingly cause harm to my neighbors.

Our booth was in a large room, nothing more than an empty space divided with poles on stanchions from which flimsy curtains hung. There were three exhibitors in our row. Mohsin's booth was on the corner. Next to us was a company selling lovely reproductions of famous paintings, such as the *Mona Lisa*, and they were mounted in authentic, expensive carved wood frames. On the far corner was a booth where the vendors sold clothing.

Mohsin's booth was exactly 10' by 10', with two six-foot jewelry showcases he had rented and placed in an "L" to form the corner aisle. I asked Exhibitor Services to put a tall showcase against the back curtain so I could display my tableware and various styles of Italian gold chains. According to the agreement between Mohsin and me, I was not to sell my silver jewelry at the show, because I wasn't paying for the booth, and offering my silver jewelry would compete directly with him. So instead of silver jewelry, I brought the sterling silver tableware, a pair of large sterling silver candelabra, a sterling silver tea service, water pitchers, and other dining accessories.

Each day of the show, we would arrive early with our wares and put them on display, and each night we would pack them up and take them to a security lock-up room. My pieces were large and cumbersome, as well as valuable. Mohsin's pieces were small. He could fit them easily into a small carry-on bag, but my suitcase was enormous and heavy. Pulling it to and from the security vault in my business suit and high heels wasn't easy, but to make matters worse, one of the wheels was slightly bent, causing it to fall on its side again and again when I tried to roll it down the aisle.

Mohsin's booth shared a common wall of curtains with our neighbors who were selling the art. On their side of the curtains, all around the perimeter of their double-sized twenty-foot-long booth, they'd hung heavy, framed paintings from wires attached to the poles, against the flimsy temporary drapes as a backdrop. The paintings were perfectly lit with individual lights attached to the poles above, creating an authentic gallery experience. Mohsin and I set up our booth in less than an hour, but our neighbors spent the entire day just to hang their paintings and light them with special fixtures they'd brought for this purpose. It was a painstaking process, well worth the effort because by the end of the day their large booth looked like a room in a museum. It was quite an accomplishment for them.

The third booth in our row, with clothing for sale, was 10' by 10', not difficult to set up. Those exhibitors had just a table, two chairs, and racks of clothes. They didn't even use extra lighting.

When the first day of the show began, we were all eager and optimistic. But by the end of the day, the only person who had sold a lot was Mohsin. I certainly didn't sell anything, and our neighbors didn't either. I told Mohsin no one was looking at my things at the back of the booth, and I wanted to move the tall showcase from the back curtain to the side curtain in order to create some interest. We decided to wait until morning to move it. The showcase was tall and heavy, and we were tired.

The next morning, after a late night with very little sleep, I arrived at 7:00 a.m. at the show, anxious to get started. Bleary eyed, I dragged my very large, heavy suitcase filled with the bulky sterling silver candelabra, tea service, water pitchers, and gold chains from the security room to the booth. The bent wheel was my nemesis, as the lopsided suitcase toppled over again and again on my way down the aisle. As dressed up as ever in my high heels and suit, I struggled with it for several minutes. Seeing a young lady in distress, a young Chinese man came to help me bring my wares to the booth. Finally, with my suitcase parked safely inside the booth, I stared at the six-foot tall trophy case, trying to figure out the best way to move it. Alone now, an hour and a half before the show was to open, I began to tug at it to move it across the carpet to the other side. I should have waited for Mohsin but thought I could do it myself.

What happened next exactly, I can't say. I was tugging as hard as I could on the showcase, and I accidentally pushed it into one of the poles holding the curtains up. Suddenly, all the poles and curtains began to sway back and forth. I watched them, stunned and helpless, as one section after the other toppled to the floor. One by one, the poles hit the carpet, bringing the curtains, paintings, and lighting down with them in a heap. From left to right, the entire row of booths collapsed, like a stack of dominoes standing on end, or a house of cards flattened in the wind.

Trembling and sweating, I wanted to jump out of my skin. I just couldn't believe my eyes. The beautiful art gallery next door was gone. Mark and Harry's paintings were scattered all over the rug. Their lights, so painstakingly placed, were helter-skelter everywhere. Our booths were flattened. What now? Could I possibly disappear? I was to blame for this, and there was nowhere to hide. Pacing back and forth, I alone could hear my silent scream, "Oh, no, no, no!"

Ours was the first row, right by the entrance. Someone notified Exhibitor Services that an entire row of booths was down. Mohsin walked in at 8:30 and began yelling, "Why didn't you wait for me?" Exhibitor Services had started putting everything back together, repositioning the toppled poles and curtains to recreate the row of booths, but they weren't about to hang or light our neighbors' paintings free of charge. Upset and nervous as to what Mark and Henry would say when they would walk in and see their booth in a shambles, I waited for the worst. Just before 9:00 a.m., Mark arrived. Taking his first step into the doorway, he saw his paintings on the floor and his curtains in a heap, his lighting destroyed. His hand flew to his forehead in disbelief. He shook his head, blinked his eyes, spun around, walked out, and then walked in again, not quite understanding, as if in the midst of a bad dream.

"Mark, I'm so sorry! I can't believe what I did! This is all my fault. I'm so sorry!" I was squirming and wringing my hands. "I came early and tried to move my showcase myself, against the side curtain so people could see my things better. But I couldn't move it. It was too heavy. It was stupid not to wait for help. The whole row collapsed before I could do anything. God, I'm so sorry!"

"What? What did you do?" he asked, not understanding my words, incredulous that his booth was a total disaster.

"I tried to move the showcase. It hit a pole. Then everything went down. It just happened so fast. God, I'm sorry. I hope nothing is damaged. Exhibitor Services can put the paintings back. I'll pay them to hang them and relight them just like before."

Of course, I had to make the offer, no matter that they'd charge union prices and I might have to pay two men for an entire day's work.

It took Mark a while to comprehend the reality, as he collapsed in a chair to watch the men from Exhibitor Services plant the poles and rehang the curtains. Finally, he said, "Adrienne, we don't need to hang the paintings. We'll just line them up on the floor, unlit. It's hard to hang them and not worth the effort. Yesterday, as great as they looked, we didn't sell a single one."

I guess Mark knew that this was not the show where he belonged.

Maybe because I was young and attractive, or because we were exhibitors bound by the same negative sales situation, Mark and I became friends after that. He even moved my heavy tall showcase into *his* much larger booth against our common curtain, where my wares could be better seen. I was forgiven. I may have hurt him, but he tried to help me anyway, and I felt huge gratitude for his generosity.

It was here at this show where I met a wonderful lady, or at least I thought so at the time. Her name was Margo. She was there to buy jewelry for her own business and turned out to be a fantastic saleswoman who loved to travel, loved jewelry, and loved the art of selling even more. She offered to join me to help me sell at future shows, wherever they might be. I also met Elsa, another fantastic salesgirl. She lived in San Francisco and wanted to work at the shows. Eventually I would hire them both, and we would become a staff of three.

During the entire show, with the exception of Mohsin, all of us in our row had negligible sales. Yet my presence there had taught me something important: People wanted jewelry. Mohsin had sold a lot of it, so if I rented my own booth and displayed my own jewelry in San Francisco, I could be successful also. It didn't hurt that at the end, Mohsin gave me his line to distribute without charging me a penny.

I did fairly well with Mohsin's King Tut jewelry, opening accounts under his company name and sending him the orders, which he shipped from his office directly. Shopkeepers were delighted to buy such timely pieces. For my efforts, I was to receive a fifteen percent commission, but Mohsin didn't pay me anything at all. I called him repeatedly, listened to his excuses, pleading with him, yelling at him, and waiting impatiently. Was this to be the first of many letdowns?

I believed in people, took them at their word. I was like Little Red Riding Hood, unafraid of the wolves in the forest and ignorant of the dangers that lay ahead, unable to imagine the troubles I might encounter in my path. This was just the beginning. Was I unsophisticated, gullible and exploitable? Perhaps. But an easy mark for those who chose to take their advantage, never!

After about six months, when it became obvious Mohsin simply wasn't going to pay me, I took matters into my own hands. I had a jewelry party and invited my friends. They purchased Mohsin's rings right out of the line at wholesale prices and paid me for what they took. I sent Mohsin his due but deducted what he owed me. Then I returned what remained of his line and moved on to the real thing: jewelry with gemstones.

I would not be the helpless damsel, not then, not to this day.

CHAPTER 6

Juggling Time and Money

I came across a wonderful best-selling book, *Dress for Success*, by John T. Malloy. When you are in sales, the first impression you make says a lot about who you are. This was especially important in the 1970s, when women in the workplace were rarely taken seriously. To create the perception that you as a woman were as capable as a man and just as serious about the business at hand, you had to dress the part. A revealing décolleté or tight fitting short skirt would send the wrong message. To be treated as an equal, I dressed the part I wanted to create. Proper business attire meant conservative colors, a suit with a skirt and a nice blouse, or a great looking blazer. Even so, my attire didn't always convey my no-nonsense businesslike passion. I shall never forget the arrogant Israeli wholesaler on Hill Street, who'd been successfully selling gold chains for years. Alon patted me on the head as if I were a child. *Pat me on the head?* Even though he didn't mean to humiliate me, the act itself was demeaning. I wanted respect, not a pat on the head. It felt as if I could never be an equal in his eyes. I wanted to ask him, "Would you pat me on the head if I were a man like you?" I bit my tongue instead and swallowed my pride.

A typical work day for me was spent driving to see buyers in the morning, and afternoons driving the children to gymnastics, T-ball, ballet, little league, tennis, swimming lessons, basketball, and flag football practice. I had always known that the emotional stability of our children depended on our being there for them. And we were. My dad, retired for many years, would help me with errands, sometimes shipping packages, sometimes driving carpool. The first three years of my business, Stan and I traveled often to Mexico. In 1979 our children, Pam and Randall, came to Mexico with us for a month. We made many friends there, met many people in the art world, and at one point even considered owning an art gallery. But since the busiest days for art dealers are weekends when I wanted to be with my family, owning an art gallery was out of the question. The years when our children were small were some of the happiest years of my life, even though I was really too tired to appreciate that then.

Other activities, besides my constant dieting and exercising, included swimming hundreds of laps in our pool and jogging six times around the park almost every morning. I enjoyed cooking and entertaining at fancy dinner parties, reading for our monthly book club discussions, researching diets and vitamins relating to health and longevity, teaching French to the gifted a few hours a week at Warner Avenue Elementary School, attending football games with Stan at the coliseum on Sundays when the Rams were playing, and almost always having the whole family to dinner on Friday nights. For a while, I held French classes for children in our dining room. It was only when the children were at school during the day that I'd network constantly to look for new product and buyers. As the business began to encroach on my family time, I cut it back and resolved even more to be a better wife and mom. Back then my little business was, after all, just a part time job.

Despite my busy schedule, I persisted. In my quest for new products to sell, I found two factories in Thailand and Hong Kong in need of distribution in California. They had reasonably priced, high quality ruby and sapphire rings. Gradually I built the inventory, so that when I exhibited at trade shows, I could offer a full line of lovely, inexpensive pieces of jewelry.

The trade shows were hard work. Most of them were out of town, requiring airplane tickets, hotels, twelve-hour days, standing on your feet indoors on carpet-covered concrete at convention centers under hot lights while professionally dressed, and skipping lunch if business was brisk. Exhibiting at the shows meant weekends away from Stan and the children as well as a lot of missed social events. To save money, I always set up the booth myself, which required hanging the lights and preparing the showcases. At first, I didn't have anyone to help me set up and tear down. It was a herculean job for one person, arriving each morning at 7:00 a.m., two hours before the show opened, to put the jewelry out, and leaving an hour after closing each night to take it all to the security room. In Los Angeles, my dad would come to help. He was constantly worried that someone would rip me off. But in San Francisco I was alone all day every day, and I couldn't leave the booth unattended to grab a bite of lunch or even visit the lav.

You are stupidly frugal to do this alone. Spend the money and hire Margo and Elsa next time.

The San Francisco shows were twice a year, five days in the winter and again in summer. I'd wait until the night before my flight to pack my bags, but Margo was ready days in advance, with her hair done and makeup in place. She was a great schmoozer and instinctively knew how to get customers to buy. Everyone loved her, including me. She was energetic, upbeat, charismatic—a real people person. When Elsa came on board a year later, the three of us were an unstoppable team. Each day would begin with breakfast at 6:00 a.m.—shower, dress, hair, makeup—and a taxi to arrive by 7:00. We'd pick up our merchandise from the security lock-up each morning and spend the next two hours filling the glass-enclosed, lockable showcases. We'd stand on our feet selling from 9:00 a.m. to 6:00 p.m., with barely a moment for a quick sandwich, and at closing time, take another hour or so to pack the jewelry and bring it to the security lock-up for the night. It was grueling but profitable most of the time.

No one said I had to do this, but I did it because I knew no other way to be successful. I just couldn't allow myself to fail. I'd even lie awake in bed trying to think of more appealing displays or better ways to advertise. Through most of my career, we did six of these shows a year. Occasionally they would be back-to-back, one week after the other, three in the winter, and three in the summer, in Los Angeles, San Francisco, and Seattle, truly sapping my energy for days afterwards.

I was asked many times if I felt like giving up or if I thought my family was suffering because I was so driven. As hard as it was, I loved the challenge. I was excited to be in the thick of the business world. I justified it all by telling myself that the most strenuous part was doing the shows, and that was just six weeks a year.

During the first years, I always traveled with the jewelry in small carry-on suitcases. It was easy when I was selling silver. I didn't worry about thieves and tricksters. As my merchandise grew in value, I became more prudent. The airports to and from the shows were a constant challenge, especially the x-ray security screening. Not knowing any better, an agent looking at the screen scanner might ask, in a voice that could be heard from one side of the airport to the other, "What'cha got in here, jewelry?" And I'd answer just as loudly, "No, ma'am. There's no jewelry in there." Then I'd hand the agent my business card. Since they always wanted to open the bags, I'd ask for a private room in which to go through my belongings.

I developed nerves of steel and eyes in the back of my head. I never used the word jewelry when in a public place or taxicab. My three bags were known as Hewey, Dewey, and Louie, in case anyone was listening, and if anyone needed to know what they contained, my answer was, "Gifts." After all, I *was* going to the Gift Show. When carrying the goods to and from airports, the confidence and calm I portrayed to others belied a vigilant observation of my surroundings and the fear I felt inside. Wary of thieves, I appeared unafraid, although I was constantly cautious and silently on guard, with eyes wide open and my bags one hundred percent in sight at all times, until feigning bravery was no longer necessary and unshakable courage eventually became second nature.

CHAPTER 7

FROM GOLD TO DIAMONDS

At the end of three years, I actually had amassed a decent collection of inventory. In 1979 Ronald Reagan had just been elected president. During Carter's administration, the cost of living had increased dramatically, all across the board. Oil, groceries, and real estate had all succumbed to terrible inflation. With the anticipation of Reagan as president, and the Iran-Iraq war continuing, the price of gold and diamonds began to skyrocket. There was talk that the price of gold would go from $400 an ounce to $1,000 an ounce, and silver from $5.00 an ounce to $40 an ounce.

The prices went up so fast that if I didn't replace my inventory on the same day I sold it, I wouldn't be able to do so the following day without adding money from my own pocket. As a result, I had to remove all the price tags and resort to selling by weight according to the gold market spot price each day. Every piece went on the scale, like a commodity, as the price kept going up. The good thing was that I got rid of all my heavy silver. With its new high cost, I could sell all my old inventory for a profit at the same old price that suddenly seemed so low.

There is no question that those who had a lot of gold and silver inventory made money during this period. At the shows, some of my customers were buying for resale, but many were individuals seeking wholesale prices for personal purchases. As the price increased, it became easier to sell jewelry than ever before, even at higher prices. People were investing, not just buying. But selling to individuals at the gift shows was not my main business. I truly needed and sought out more retailers to sell to. In my haste to get good clients, I made a few mistakes—and the one I made at the Bonaventure Hotel in downtown Los Angeles was really a doozy.

During this period, the Japanese tourists were flooding our shores with money to spend. Busloads of tourists were buying everything in sight, mostly high-end brands, such as Gucci, Chanel, and Louis Vuitton. My Japanese clients at the Bonaventure Hotel, one of the finest places to stay in downtown Los Angeles, were doing well with their gold chains, and I went to visit them often to update their stock. I tried showing them my gemstone collection, but they simply weren't interested. They wanted gold and nothing else. So I decided to look for another prospect nearby. Wandering through the hotel promenade, I noticed a truly outstanding jewelry store. It had plush sage color carpeting and green suede fabric on the walls, expensive Plexiglas acrylic cases throughout the store, a shiny copper ceiling, and beautiful displays with all kinds of rings, Cartier handbags, Dunhill lighters, and fabulous jewelry. I met with the owner, a Mrs. Yu, who was charming and very much interested in looking at my collection.

I didn't understand why Mrs. Yu was so adamant about showing me how wealthy she was when she asked for an open account. She was Korean, but her husband, who was off in Japan, was supposedly a well-known Japanese shipping magnate. I was so impressed with her store that I merely glanced at the business documents and didn't bother to check her credit. I should not have been so easily fooled by her beautiful premises. What really mattered was whether or not she paid her bills. It would have taken just a few phone calls to know that she didn't, and that giving her goods was an enormous credit risk. Mrs. Yu wanted five thousand dollars' worth of gemstone rings and pendants. I gave her many nice things right on the spot with a 30-day open account. Then, a few days later, she called me to request diamonds for special clients—two carats and up—and I was only too eager to oblige. She was a real go-getter, and I liked that. I had no reason to believe she would ever cheat me.

I must digress to say that my Japanese clients a few doors away were among the most honest people I have ever known in all my life. Months before, my father and I accidentally shipped them a package that included not only their order, but someone else's order as well. They'd found it perplexing and called to alert me. Had they kept the package that belonged to someone else, I never would have known and would have lost several thousand dollars to my carelessness. It was beyond their realm of thought to take something that didn't belong to them. However, my experience with Mrs. Yu was a different story.

My knowledge of larger diamonds at that time was extremely limited, since all my diamond purchases were small melee, meaning stones that weighed less than a tenth of a carat. I was far from proficient at using a diamond loupe to see the flaws or inclusions inside the stones, and I doubt I could have detected a good cubic zirconia from a real diamond, or as they say in the industry, a simulated stone from a natural one. However, I did know a diamond dealer I trusted, and I went to see him.

"Maurice," I explained, "I have a client with a beautiful store at the Bonaventure Hotel. She asked me to bring her a few nice stones, at least two carats each."

"How well do you know this woman?" Maurice asked.

"I just met her. She has an impressive store, full of expensive jewelry and accessories that are all name brands."

"Listen," Maurice said, "I don't know her, but I know you. I trust *you*, you understand."

Maurice really liked me and wanted to help, but he added most emphatically, "I'm dealing with *you* and not with her. This is your customer."

"I'm not worried. Her husband is a big shipping magnate in Japan."

Maurice gave me five stones on my signature, a total value of $96,000, and he told me to add a 4 percent commission for myself. He did not want to know my customer. He was dealing only with me, and I would be responsible for the bill, with the understanding that Mrs. Yu could return the stones if there were no sales. The five stones were loosely stored in little folded papers. Maurice advised me to keep them safely in my bra while I was walking around downtown. That was so strange. I remember telling myself, "No one knows you are walking around with diamonds in your bra, Adrienne. You are fine."

I walked to my car with the diamonds in my bra, drove to see Mrs. Yu, and gave her the five diamonds in exchange for her signature on a memo that said the stones were mine. I gave her permission to offer them to her customers, with the clear understanding that by my consigning them to her, she held no right of ownership. I didn't own them either and had signed a similar memorandum for Maurice. Title would not transfer to her until she paid me. She was to let me know in a few days. If she sold them and handed me a check, only then would the consignment become a sale to be invoiced. If not, the diamonds would be returned.

That afternoon at our son's little league baseball game I thought, "Wow, if she keeps all the diamonds, I'll make an easy $4,000!" But there would be nothing easy about this transaction.

A few days later, I called Mrs. Yu and was told two of the stones were "sold." Mrs. Yu's customer was a real estate broker who would take them as soon as escrow would close at the end of the month on a house she sold. A third stone was under consideration as well. I picked up the other two diamonds and returned them to Maurice. "Remember," he said, while deleting two stones from the paper I'd signed, "I'm dealing with *you*, and not with her."

Then my troubles began to unfold, as I attempted to collect either the remaining three diamonds or the money for them. Over the following few weeks, Mrs. Yu gave me one crazy excuse after another. "The diamonds are in Japan." "The escrow was extended." "I'll have money for you soon." I would go to her store, and she wouldn't be there. A few more weeks passed.

I'd been in situations like this before with deadbeat customers. I'd figure it out once again, wouldn't I?

Summer was approaching. We had plans to go to Europe on a month-long vacation with Stan, Pam, and Randall, but I didn't want to leave without first resolving the situation with Mrs. Yu. Finally, utterly frustrated and not knowing any better (as Stan never tried to teach me California law), I persuaded Mrs. Yu to write postdated checks to me for the three stones she had kept. I later learned that this was a big mistake, because in spite of the memo she had signed which said the title to the diamonds was mine, accepting the checks from her automatically transferred the diamonds from my ownership to hers. Once I attempted to cash the checks, which all bounced, legally the stones belonged to Mrs. Yu. I held on to the checks, believing they'd be good in the not too distant future.

Stupid independent girl. Your husband is so smart, and you didn't ask him?

Brash, foolhardy, overconfident, reckless—and yet, adventurous, bold, and daring . . .

Maurice was concerned. He came to our house the night before we were leaving for Europe. The value of the unreturned diamonds totaled $60,000. We sat at a card table in the family room, and I showed him the three checks, which were stamped "NSF," meaning non-sufficient funds.

Maurice put his hand on top of mine on the table and asked, "If she doesn't pay you, are you going to pay me?"

I answered, "Maurice, you know I could probably get out of paying you if I wanted to. But I have to sleep at night, and I'm obligated to pay you, and I will. But I can't pay you now. I'll figure this out when I get back from Europe. Please be patient and give me time."

In spite of the fact that I knew in my heart I would pay him, he left the house that night worried that I might not, that he might have to sue me, and that the litigation might be difficult if he were to fight me with Stan on my side.

We left for Europe the next day, and after three weeks abroad, I called my dad from Greece to see if he had been to see Mrs. Yu. He wasn't truthful when he merely said she hadn't been in on the day he stopped by. He didn't say that he had been to see her every single day, that she was never there, and that many of the better pieces in her store were no longer there, either. What he also didn't tell me was that he had started smoking again from frustration and stress, that he had gone to see Maurice and had offered him $45,000 on the spot instead of the $60,000 I had signed for, or that Maurice had turned him down. I knew none of this from our phone conversation. Dad wanted to spare me, but he also knew I'd object if he interfered. Did I need rescuing? Absolutely not! I'd gotten myself into this mess, and I'd find my own way out. I would never allow myself to be so beholden to my father.

Our month-long vacation had been a whirlwind. But it wasn't all vacation. In Israel I purchased small diamonds for my mountings, in Egypt I searched for pendants with hieroglyphs, and in Greece I found a manufacturer of gold jewelry sold by weight. I had often admired the stiff open bangle bracelets with rams' heads at the tips, so typical of Greek and Roman times, and so hard to find elsewhere. Stan was my rock, even on vacation. He rationalized that my buying while traveling would allow part of our trip to be tax-deductible. It was important for my business to include new things, and my collection needed constant updating to keep my customers happy.

After four weeks abroad—having enjoyed Paris, Israel, Egypt, and Greece—our family of four flew back home. Even before unpacking our bags, Stan and I drove to the Bonaventure Hotel to see Mrs. Yu.

Surprise! The store was padlocked shut, and all was dark inside.

Stan and I immediately went to see the hotel manager. "What happened to *Le Diamant*, your jewelry store on the fourth floor?" we wanted to know. "Is the store temporarily closed?"

"We had to shut them down. The rent is six months past due."

Another tale of woe, another calamity. How is it possible Stan didn't criticize me? If he felt angst, worry, or distress, he didn't let me see it. I, on the other hand, was outraged and ready to fight. I had to get those diamonds back, or the money for them!

The next day, I went to the police and the district attorney to show them the bad checks. I learned that the police had found seventy-seven pawn tickets from a pawnshop in Las Vegas, for the jewelry and diamonds Mrs. Yu had pawned there. Mrs. Yu, once a wealthy woman, was addicted to gambling. She owed her favorite Las Vegas hotel a substantial sum for her gambling losses, and she had quite a long list of creditors. Now that her store was closed, she had to file for bankruptcy protection, both Chapter 11 and Chapter 7. Chapter 11 would allow the company to reorganize and keep creditors away during the process. Chapter 7 would allow company assets to be sold to pay company debts. However, it turned out that Mrs. Yu's personal debts were far greater than her assets, particularly because a well-known jewelry business in town, Terrell and Zimmelman, had a second mortgage against the Yu family home.

After four years of part time work, the small business owner I thought I was had become the number one major creditor in a bankruptcy case.

Just put your head down and keep moving forward. What else can you do? Sooner or later you'll figure it out.

I put aside my thoughts of woe and called George at *Avanti Internacional*. I needed his permission to bring back the unsalable silver and take something else in exchange. I was in a pickle playing with the big boys now, and the sooner I could get rid of the leftover silver, the better.

Whenever we went to Mexico, we would buy things for ourselves: silver, leather goods, and art. But this time, with such a broad line of jewelry selling well in the States, I decided to take gold jewelry to Mexico to sell to our friends there. We were going for the weekend, purely a business trip, and I was well prepared. I brought some hoop earrings made in New York to sell in Mexico, along with gold charms as well. As it happened, on that trip I sold very little of the gold I brought. George exchanged my unsold silver for new pieces, simply dollar for dollar, not bothering with an invoice or the usual paperwork for customs, and our favorite artist Zuniga had nothing we could buy. The one thing I did accomplish was to exchange my larger pieces of silver jewelry for smaller ones that were easier to sell.

Flying back Sunday afternoon, we realized we hadn't

actually bought anything in Mexico this time. But when we filled out the customs declaration form and checked "Nothing to Declare," the customs agent at LAX didn't see it that way.

"Madam," he asked, "what is all this gold jewelry you have here with price tags?"

"This is jewelry made here in the States, in New York. I took it to Mexico to sell, but I couldn't sell it and brought it all back. I didn't buy it there."

"Do you have any proof of purchase? Any invoices from New York?"

"Not with me. But I do have them. They're in my office."

"You'll have to bring them to me. In the meantime, we'll keep these things here."

Wha . . . ?

He set the gold jewelry aside. He then asked, "Do you have anything else to declare?"

"No!" I said with conviction. "I told you, I didn't buy anything."

He searched the luggage and saw the bag of silver jewelry—new pieces that had been exchanged for old.

"What is this?" the agent asked.

"I didn't buy that," I said. "I had this unsalable silver and brought it back to the factory in Mexico, and they gave me this in exchange. They didn't give me an invoice. I didn't pay anything. It was a simple trade."

"Well, you need an invoice and a Certificate of Origin from Mexico, or you have to pay duty." He set the entire bag of silver next to the gold. "Bring the documents, and you can get it all back."

What a hassle. I didn't do anything wrong, technically. They want the paperwork, that's all.

Stan was visibly annoyed but said nothing. He was tired and anxious to get home. I watched as he moved as far away as possible to the edge of the luggage table and sat down, his back to me, holding his head in his hands with his elbows on his knees, pretending he didn't know who I was. By this time everyone on our flight had left the terminal, and it seemed we were now under investigation.

The agent asked one more time, "Are you sure you have nothing more to declare?"

"I have nothing to declare. I didn't purchase *anything* in Mexico so there is *nothing* to declare."

The remaining customs officers in the building came over to see what was going on. We were there for almost forty-five minutes, while they looked through my checkbook and handbag.

Sure enough, the agent found something else.

"What is this?" he asked, removing a pillbox-sized container from inside the zippered compartment of my purse, the same one I used for travel all over the world.

"Oh, that!" I exclaimed. "I completely forgot about that! Those are the tiny diamonds I purchased two weeks ago in Israel. I forgot I even had them with me." After the trip home from Israel, I thought only of Mrs. Yu. I had so much on my mind.

He took the diamonds into custody, as well.

I grabbed my handbag, turned it upside down and shook it. A silver heart pendant fell out. "Here!" I said, handing it to him.

We were lucky they allowed us to go home.

The next day I called Mr. Arcos. It was he who had taught me how to be my own customs broker just a few years before. As overseer of all jewelry that cleared customs in Los Angeles, he was familiar with every jewelry factory that shipped their goods into the city, whether by air or sea. He knew all the exporters by name, he had seen their invoices, he knew their prices, and he was familiar with their merchandise. He also knew exactly what had transpired the day before and was expecting my call. In fact, my confiscated gold, silver, and diamonds were in his office, sealed and locked in a safe. Mr. Arcos couldn't have been kinder. He told me what I had to do. In the end, arriving with invoices for everything, including the unsold silver I'd exchanged, I retrieved all my confiscated merchandise for $65.00. It was a tiny price to pay, all considered.

Even with that reprieve, Mrs. Yu's bankruptcy weighed heavily on my mind.

CHAPTER 8

WHEN YOU FALL,
THE ONLY PLACE TO GO IS UP

A young woman lawyer had been working at Loeb & Loeb a short time when I hired her. She had little or no experience in bankruptcy court, but she was smart, and Stan had confidence in her. Everyone thought the case of Rubin vs. Mrs. Yu would be good experience for her. She would represent me against all the other creditors. The Trustee, who represented all of the creditors including me, took charge of Mrs. Yu's debts and assets. He was a very nice man I would meet a few months later.

Summer went by quickly. It was time for me to pay Maurice. I really didn't know where I would find the $60,000 to pay him. We set up a meeting, and it was then that Maurice informed me that my father had offered him $45,000 as payment in full more than two months earlier. I was so glad Maurice had refused my dad's offer. I certainly didn't want my father to pay. As generous a man as he was, I was far too independent and never wanted to accept money from him. But this time, Dad really wanted to help, and I reluctantly accepted a loan. He gave me a check for $25,000 to give to Maurice as a down payment, and he said quite clearly, "I won't need this back until January." Maurice agreed to take the balance in monthly installments of $5,000 until the entire $60,000 was paid in full. He refused to take less than the total price. However, to help me, he gave me $15,000 in gold chains. They cost him less than that, but for me, it was a sizeable and generous discount. I was fortunate, and I knew it.

After this, for the next several months my part-time job became a full-time job. I needed to earn $10,000 a month to pay Maurice and my dad on time. I hired a UCLA student to do my grocery shopping and be with Pam and Randall after school, and for the next several months I saw my family only during dinnertime.

My children suffered. They must have, because I wasn't there. I was stuck now. I'd screwed up. I had to make the money back. I couldn't let my dad take the fall. If I worked hard, I could pay it all back by January.

In the meantime, my lawyer was working on the bankruptcy case. Everything in Mrs. Yu's store was to be put up for auction. The proceeds from the auction were to be divided among the creditors, only after the Bonaventure Hotel received the unpaid rent and the Trustee received his fee. I was the creditor who was owed the largest amount, so naturally I took great interest in the value of the assets remaining in the store. The Trustee appointed by the bankruptcy court was in charge of organizing the auction. He eventually retrieved two of my diamonds from a pawnshop in Las Vegas, as well as the third one, which had been found in a Kleenex box adjacent to the safe in the back of Mrs. Yu's store. He would hold a second auction and sell the three stones at a later date.

The first auction was to take place in November in the Trustee's office. Obviously I wanted the auction to bring as much money as possible, and I had many questions for the Trustee, including how he was advertising the sale, whether or not the merchandise had been appraised, and so forth. He was experienced and had been in charge of such sales many times, but he had probably never dealt with as meddling a creditor as I. When I learned he didn't advertise the sale, other than to notify his personal list of prospects, and that there had been no appraisal of the merchandise, I was upset. I insisted he should advertise in the *Los Angeles Times*. I told him I would prevent him from holding the auction by claiming he had not done what was necessary to obtain the most money for his creditors.

"I'll tell my lawyer to block the sale," I told him. "You have to advertise it."

Apparently, that wasn't normally done. He simply was not going to advertise the auction. To placate me, he told me to bid. If the bids were low, I could get a bargain. I had no interest in bidding, however. I was already short of cash, doing my best to pay Maurice.

"What if you don't get a good price?" I asked. "What if there aren't enough bidders?"

"I won't sell the contents of the store unless I get a good price."

"And what price is that?" I wanted to know.

"I can't tell you, because you might be a buyer."

"I can't be a buyer," I insisted. "Where would I get the money? I have to pay for the diamonds. I'm not a buyer. I promise you, I can't buy anything right now."

"Okay, I'll tell you. But if I tell you, you can't bid. We'll hold the auction in my office and you can attend, but I can't tell you my minimum if you're planning to bid."

"I'm not a bidder. If you won't tell me your minimum, I won't let you sell without an appraisal and an ad in the *Times*."

He took a breath. "I'm not going to accept anything less than $50,000."

I supposed that would have been okay.

There was a five-day period when interested parties looking to buy could go into the store and examine the contents before the sale. Since I wasn't a buyer, I didn't go.

The day of the auction my lawyer, my father, and I went to the office of the Trustee. We were quite surprised to see only one bidder, a woman with a $20,000 cashier's check for the whole store. The Trustee could not hold an auction with only one bidder, so he took the offer under consideration and dismissed us. He decided to hold another auction a month later, when perhaps more buyers might attend.

A month later, we showed up for the auction once again, only this time the same woman buyer came with a cashier's check for just $18,000. There were no other offers. Not knowing what else to do, still bound by his promise to me that he would not sell the assets for less than $50,000, the Trustee told us we were all invited to join him in court, where he would present the offer to the judge and objections could be heard. Of course, I was completely unprepared for this turn of events. Less than half an hour later we were in court, and I found myself standing in front of the judge pleading that it would be a terrible injustice to the creditors to accept $18,000 for the entire contents of Mrs. Yu's store.

"Your Honor," I begged, "you cannot accept so little money. The value is at least $150,000. Eighteen thousand is way too little."

"What do you suggest, madam? What choice do I have?"

"If you let me take this merchandise in my car to sell to stores, I'll bring you more than double that amount."

The judge seemed very old and grumpy to me. He stated quite emphatically, banging his fist on his podium, "Not one piece of merchandise is leaving that store until bought and paid for!"

I held up the multi-page inventory list. "Your Honor," I pleaded again, "this isn't right! These pieces are valuable, and to accept only $18,000 is a terrible mistake."

"Madam, if you think it's worth so much, why don't you buy it?"

"I can't buy it," I said. "I promised the Trustee—" I couldn't finish my sentence because the Trustee jumped to his feet, waived his arms to get the judge's attention, and interrupted, "If Mrs. Rubin wants to buy it, she should do so, Your Honor." He sat down and waited for the judge to reply.

The judge then said to me, "Mrs. Rubin, what is your offer? I shall be obligated to accept this offer of $18,000, unless you offer more."

I knew right then that I had to buy it.

I had to think fast. I asked the judge, "Will you allow them to open the store for me, so that I can examine the merchandise, as other interested parties had the opportunity to do? That way you will get my best offer."

"Absolutely not." The judge emphasized each and every word. "No one is going to open the store for you to have a look around. You must present an offer now."

"I want to make an acceptable offer, but I didn't know this was going to happen. I didn't expect to be here, and I don't have a cashier's check with me."

The Trustee jumped to his feet, interrupting a second time, "Your Honor, I know Mrs. Rubin's husband. I can wait until tomorrow for a cashier's check."

We were granted a five-minute recess. A colleague had come to the sale just to observe. He was interested in buying the showcases and the safe, to be sold on a later date. He whispered to me, "That woman with the $18,000 offer, I know her husband. If she's paying $18,000, the merchandise is worth $40,000. If you need money, I'm glad to lend it to you."

I stood once again in front of the judge, stammering, "I—I'm not sure. I really don't know what to offer. I haven't examined the items, and I don't even know where to begin." I felt like a child standing there in front of His Eminence.

"You must offer at least $20,000."

"I will certainly offer you $20,000," I answered timidly, "but that's not my highest price."

The Trustee wanted to wrap things up. He stood up quickly and said quite simply, "I recommend that we sell the contents of the store to Mrs. Rubin for $20,000."

As the judge proclaimed, "So be it," his gavel hit the podium with a bang.

What just happened?

As I was leaving the courtroom, rather dizzy from this event, I spotted a pay phone and called Stan. "What happened at the auction?" he asked.

"Are you sitting down?" I asked him right back. "I bought the entire contents of the store for $20,000!"

After I described the entire episode, Stan asked me, "Where are you going to get $20,000?"

I answered rather gingerly, "You know the money in your Keogh plan . . . ?"

The following day, early in December, I delivered a cashier's check to the Trustee for the contents of Mrs. Yu's store, and he, in turn, instructed the manager of the Bonaventure Hotel to remove the padlock for me. My father came along. I was filled with anticipation, never having actually examined what was in the store before. My plan was to check everything off the list of inventory before packing up and going home. Like a kid in a toy store, I was thrilled beyond belief that it was all mine. And for only twelve cents on the dollar! There were opal, jade, sapphire and pearl rings, necklaces, pendants, dozens of loose stones, lots of fire opals, Dunhill lighters, Cartier and Chanel handbags, Etro vests, jade trees, unusual desk lamps, and designer scarves. I was dazzled.

We weren't in the store an hour when the hotel manager came in. "Mrs. Rubin," he asked, "would you be willing to sell anything today before you go? I'd like to buy something for my wife for Christmas."

"Of course," I replied. "Please look around. Everything has a price tag, and your cost is 40 percent of the marked price, a 60 percent discount off retail."

He bought a few pieces and sent his office assistants and secretaries to buy things also. I was so busy showing and selling that I had very little time to go through the inventory list. The next day was the same. Guests of the hotel came in to look around and buy. By the fourth day the sales totaled $10,000. I certainly wasn't ready to leave. However, the other jewelers in the hotel promenade complained because it was close to Christmas and they weren't making any sales, so the manager came to tell me that I really had to pack up and go home before the week was over. I did as he asked.

That Saturday night, December 13, 1980, Stan and I went to a Christmas party at the home of our close friends, Lynn and Jim. Among the fifty people there was a man who manufactured gold jewelry in his factory in downtown Los Angeles. He was most interested to hear my story. Apparently Mrs. Yu had approached him at some point, wishing to buy from him with a thirty-day open account, but he had checked around and heard she was no good. We were huddled with our cocktails, and I was at the end of my story when Stan noticed the two of us talking and came over.

"Now," Stan said, "all she needs is a place to sell it."

"I've got a place on Los Angeles Street," the man replied.

"You can use my front room, have a big sale, and advertise in the *Los Angeles Times*. I won't charge you anything. You'll rent some showcases, and I'll put some of my jewelry out also."

"Wow, that sounds great," I said. The two of us immediately sat down on the living room sofa away from the other guests at the party and created a newspaper ad on a sheet of scratch paper we found:

LE DIAMANT

Major Downtown Hotel Jeweler

BANKRUPT!!!

Up to 70 percent off!

Four days only

**December 22 - 25
10:00 a.m.—4:00 p.m.**

Los Angeles Street at 20th Avenue

OPEN CHRISTMAS DAY

**Fabulous jewels, opals, pearls, Italian gold,
Dunhill lighters, Cartier, Chanel, jade trees
and more!**

On Monday morning, I placed the ad in the *Times*, rented two showcases, and hired a security guard. The factory was located on South Los Angeles Street, a part of the city that didn't appear to be very safe. The building was one story, right up against the sidewalk, and there wasn't a lot of traffic, pedestrian *or* automobile. The sale would be held only during daylight hours, from ten o'clock in the morning until four in the afternoon. At the start of each day the jewelry would be put on display, and before closing we would put it back in the safe. It was all well insured.

The ad in the *Times* worked wonders, and were we busy! My dad drove with me each morning, and helped me sell all day long. We were on our feet the whole time and couldn't even stop for lunch. The fourth day was Christmas, a Thursday. We changed the ad and made it twice the size, emphasizing the last day of the sale. I wasn't sure anyone would come on Christmas Day. Might we get customers with Christmas bonuses in their wallets or those who needed a last-minute gift on their way to Christmas dinner?

At 10:00 a.m. Christmas morning the showroom was full of people, three deep in front of the cases, waiting to be helped. The line of customers waiting to come inside went around the block. The security guard held anxious customers at the door, letting them in one by one as other customers exited. People came from all over the city, even the wife of one of Stan's partners, who must have been as surprised to see me selling as I was to see her shopping. As soon as I could get to the phone (In those days we had to authorize credit cards over the phone.), I called my house.

Pamela answered, "Oh, hi, Mom! How's it going?"

"Where's Daddy?" I asked.

"In the Jacuzzi outside," she replied. Stan often used the Jacuzzi to ease the pain of his osteoarthritis, which plagued him constantly.

"Tell Dad I need him down here right away! Can you

think of anyone else who might come down here and help with our sale? I can't believe so many people came on Christmas Day! It's a madhouse."

In fact, I needed numbers for the customers to pull from a machine, like they use at delis and bakeries.

Stan arrived within the hour. Unable to stand because of his arthritis, he sat on a stool behind the showcase opposite me and helped many customers with their selections. His arthritis was painful, however, and he wasn't in the mood for negotiating, as often as not giving pieces out at large discounts just to move on to the next customer.

At the end of four days, my gold inventory was decimated. Several nice pieces from Mrs. Yu's store were sold, and I had collected over $65,000. I needed to replace the gold immediately. But the best part of all was that I had plenty of beautiful items left over, and enough cash on hand to reimburse my father and Maurice.

On the tenth of January, I handed my father a check for $25,000 to repay September's loan.

"Is this check good?" he asked.

"Of course, it's good," I said.

Dad was truly surprised, as he never actually expected to get his money back. I went up in his estimation a thousand fold. Maurice was paid in full as well.

It was a relief, but more than that, it was an accomplishment. I'd gotten myself into the mess, and through sheer resolve, I got myself out. I had to. Pure grit, gumption, and staying power. I knew I could do it. I'd never give up.

If I learned anything from this, it was not to be so trusting. My faith in others turned to caution, as I looked forward, debt free, to the days ahead.

Now it was on to the shows with great hopes of selling the rest of Mrs. Yu's beautiful merchandise.

The shows were not open to the public, only to the trade, so every buyer had to show proof of a business or retail store, usually in the form of a resale license, in order to obtain a badge. My booth was in the jewelry section, where exhibitors were allowed to sell on a cash-and-carry basis and deliver on the spot. The gift section, about ten times larger than the jewelry section, was for order-taking only. Owners of gift shops and buyers from department stores around the country would come to buy for the upcoming season, and usually after buying and replenishing their inventory in the gift section, they would browse the jewelry section to buy something for themselves at wholesale prices. We always did well with smaller pieces of jewelry, but it was quite an eye opener when Mrs. Yu's fancy pieces sold even more quickly. All this time I'd thought the shows were for stores to place orders for new merchandise, not for individuals who wanted expensive jewels sold one piece at a time. Suddenly I realized I'd be even more successful if I could upgrade my collection and offer truly high-end pieces.

In the spring of 1981, the Trustee in Mrs. Yu's bankruptcy case was ready to sell the three diamonds I claimed belonged to me. They would hold an auction in a small room in downtown LA. I told two friends about it, and they both came. Both were diamond dealers. It didn't occur to me that they might know each other, but even if they did, I thought they'd compete with each other at the auction. The problem was that no one else came to buy. The two men started to bid for the stones. The first and second stones went for a decent price. Then suddenly, in the middle of the third sale, one of the two men got up and left, claiming he needed to talk to his office and would return shortly. When he came back, he pretended he was no longer interested. What none of us knew at the time was that he had left to call the other man's office secretly and make a deal that they would be partners. They'd own the stone together and chill the bidding. This stone went for a fraction of what it should have.

I knew both of these men well, and since I had brought them to the auction, which they otherwise would not have known about, I felt betrayed. Once upon a time we had eaten together at the same table. Now they were laughing on their way to the bank at my expense. I was still a babe in the woods of commerce; I still had a lot to learn. In the end, my lawyer and I settled my claim for the diamonds, and the Trustee gave me $35,000 for them, less than half of what I hoped for. The actual wholesale price should have been much more. Nowadays, with the Internet, they would have sold for their true value.

One would think this double cross, by two men I knew personally, would have affected my faith in the men in this business. But I understood well that when it came to making money, any legal means of doing so was considered acceptable. I was the naïve one who let it happen. Blaming myself for not understanding how the game was played, I'd be wiser and more astute in the future.

CHAPTER 9

STAYING THE COURSE

"S tan, why does your wife work so hard?" friends would ask. "She certainly doesn't have to."

Indeed, why did I work at such a difficult vocation, when money was not an issue? I was a wide-eyed innocent in a crafty, often deceitful world, an inexperienced woman playing the game of buying and selling mainly for fun to see how high I could climb. It certainly wasn't ambition that turned me on. I'd started a business not knowing where it would lead. I couldn't suffer the thought that I'd been wasting my time.

Yet even so, I often wondered what was so commendable about this business. How was it even laudable to buy from one place and sell to another, the same product with a marked up price? Most of the time I was merely finding items to sell, purchasing here and offering them there. I had "an eye" for putting together a new collection every year and figuring out future trends to make a profit. I was good at it. But how could this be my purpose in life? I thought a lot about doctors who save the lives of their patients, lawyers who help their clients find justice, and teachers who inspire and motivate their students. And when it came to the product of jewelry itself, I was baffled by its perceived value. As a gift, it was a symbol of love. As a possession, it had intrinsic value. But I couldn't imagine why a diamond could cost so much, when other things were so much more useful.

I traveled constantly. One day on 47th Street in New York City, a dealer offered to buy my entire collection.

"I can take it all off your hands," he said. "I know I can sell most of it right away. But I won't leave you with the dogs. I'll take it all."

His offer was ridiculously low. I couldn't even counter.

"No thanks," I answered politely. "You're not even in the ballpark."

No way would I sell it all for a song. I knew I offered pretty things and had a knowledge of what they should cost. Wasn't that worth something? Give it all up for so little compensation? Banish the thought!

Our cousin Aleeza, who also sold fine jewelry, invited me to join her on a Sunday morning at the Pasadena flea market, an outdoor football field where the Rose Bowl is held. This was not in an indoor convention center, but simply on the dirt track outside. I wondered if it wasn't risky, taking expensive merchandise to sell in such a public outdoor place. But, always ready for anything, I got up at 3:00 a.m., the appointed time to be ready when Aleeza picked me up to drive there. It was pitch black outside, the damp chill seeping into our bones. We set up the space in the dark, laying a rug under our feet. I wasn't properly dressed, too cold to describe, and with so little sleep could barely stand up straight. By three o'clock that afternoon, having missed a good night's sleep and a Sunday with my family, I was on my way home, having sold less than

$100 worth of merchandise. We all make mistakes in life, and this was the dumbest but certainly not the worst of the many I've made. Still, Aleeza had said she made money there, and if you don't try something once, you'll never know.

My philosophy was to try all possibilities. Some people seem to be born lucky, but I tried lots of projects to make my own luck. I knew that to be lucky, I needed to be open to new experiences and not over analyze them. Serendipity, "fortunate happenstance," comes to those who keep trying.

There were occasional losses. As a wife, mother, and want-to-be businesswoman, I was constantly overtired, but that didn't prevent me from visiting clients after hours. At times like that, haste and fatigue could lead to mishaps. Harry from Goldline in Beverly Hills called me from his factory one evening after dinner and said he needed gold chains. As I pulled up to his office on South Beverly Drive, there were a couple of swarthy looking men getting out of a Rolls Royce in the parking space behind mine. One was wearing an open shirt, and his entire chest was covered in a vulgar display of heavy shiny gold chains. Apparently all three of us were going to see Harry. As we stood there and rang the doorbell together, my heart was beating faster than a drum. It was dark outside. Inside, Harry's phone was ringing nonstop, even at eight o'clock at night, and I noticed he was not his usual self. He seemed agitated. His nose was running, and he kept sniffling. I showed the chains, and he bought a few, but I couldn't wait to get out of there. "Those guys are dealing drugs," I surmised.

The following morning, I realized I had left a velvet roll full of gold chains at Harry's place. "Harry," I said on the phone, "I left one of my chain rolls in your office. Can you please check?" He told me it wasn't there. *Deceitful scumbag.* I insisted he had it and went to see him, to no avail. After that, I was done with him for good.

As risky as it was to take gold in my car to sell late at night, even in Beverly Hills where the police were always nearby, it was absolutely abhorrent to deal with liars, junkies, or dope heads.

It was twenty-five years later when Harry came to the LA gift show and spotted me in my booth. By then he had been in and out of jail. It's interesting that he was glad to see me. He was off drugs then, and when I asked him about the chain roll, he admitted I had left it there. He did not apologize to me, and I dismissed him as another simple casualty in the course of doing business.

Always searching for retailers, I made a lot of cold calls. If you knock on enough doors, someone will buy. I stopped on Pico at a jewelry store in Beverlywood. Although I didn't know it at the time, the owner was an old acquaintance from high school days. He didn't buy much, but it was there that I met Rachel, another young woman entrepreneur. When she saw I had come there with goods to sell, she asked for my card and contacted me the next day. She had a full time desk job, but sold pieces at discounted prices to fellow employees during lunch hour. The jeweler in Beverlywood gave her items on consignment at prices just above his cost, and I did so as well. She was successful, since she worked at a large company with women who loved her candor and enthusiasm. Over the years she became one of my good clients, albeit after-hours at my house, taking up my precious time on weekends or after dinner on weekdays. I tried to accommodate her, even though I realize now that my time would have been better spent tucking my children in bed and spending time with Stan.

This is simple proof that any would-be entrepreneur with a little imagination can make extra money at her day job.

Another young woman I met, who had two children the same ages as Pam and Randall, was a phenomenal salesperson.

At the time, her husband was having difficulty getting his real estate business off the ground, although he is quite successful today. They had just moved to Los Angeles from South Africa, and with four children in the family, this energetic gal did what she could to put food on the table. Having come from Johannesburg, she knew people in downtown LA in the diamond business. One diamond manufacturer trusted her enough to give her jewelry to sell, no payment up front, so she could show friends, neighbors, and any possible interested parties. Every day before lunch she would drive to the high-rise office buildings in Century City, and in one office after the next, she would announce herself, "The jewelry lady is here!" Everyone loved her, and she certainly did very well.

She was an amazing salesgirl. She could make everyone believe she was offering the most beautiful gem in the world for a fraction of its true value. Working at the gift show alongside me, she sold a little ring that I'd had in stock a long time. As soon as the customer left with her purchase and was out of earshot, she said proudly, "Well, I certainly pulled that money out of her purse!"

I was in awe of this woman. Yet at the same time, that was not the way I did things. For her, every opportunity to make a sale was a challenge. For me, it was more about helping others acquire what they needed and having them come back for more. I must say, though, when it came to making a sale, she was truly gifted.

In the beginning, at the Los Angeles show, I carried the goods (which eventually included diamonds) to and from the show in the trunk of my car. Two or three of us would travel to the convention center together. As inconspicuous as we tried to be, troublesome things did happen. My rear tires were slashed more than once. This was a ruse would-be thieves would use to get the driver to open the trunk to access the spare tire. I never did open the trunk, but simply drove to a gas station on a bad tire. Damaging a wheel on your car can't compare to the risk of losing thousands of dollars in jewelry, or putting your very life at risk.

At one of the shows, I did fall prey to a band of Columbian con artists in front of the Los Angeles convention center. I had been warned about professional thieves and their tricks, especially the Colombians, who were among the most notable drug lords trafficking in cocaine in the 1980s. The first day of the show, I pulled up to park in front of the convention center with four bags of jewelry in the trunk. One of my sales staff was with me, but neither of us noticed the big guy who was waiting some distance away on the sidewalk next to the entrance. He was tall, well dressed, and looked like he belonged there. We didn't pay him any mind at first. But suddenly he came upon us, just as Rachel and I were putting two bags on the luggage cart. We were working quickly and ignored him until he threw a large bunch of one-dollar bills on the sidewalk and yelled, "You dropped your money." I glanced at the money at my feet and held fast to my bags. But at that exact moment a car pulled up next to mine, and before I realized what was happening, another guy jumped out of his car and grabbed the other two bags from the open trunk of my car. He was so quick, only taking a split second to make his move. I held fast to my other two bags, ignoring the money on the sidewalk, and, completely dumbfounded, watched the thieves drive off, burning rubber as they sped away with two of my bags in their car before I could even turn around.

Just like that, all my rings were gone. In a split second . . .

Bad guys are everywhere. Don't you know, Adrienne, everyone wants what you have? Get used to it. It's part of your everyday life now.

Luckily there were two corroborating witnesses to the crime, and I was insured. Keeping meticulous inventory records paid off, as I had proof of purchase of every single item. Full reimbursement by my insurance company took only thirty days. Then it was business as usual again, except after that I was wiser and even more careful than ever before.

Okay, I admit it. I was gutsy, but also occasionally not in my right mind. According to my insurance policy, as long as the goods were in my possession, they were covered. But I couldn't leave them in the car while running a quick errand, not even to use a restroom for five minutes, or they wouldn't be insured, and I certainly couldn't ship them on the plane as luggage to an out of town show. I'd had as many as four bags, and they had to be with me at all times.

My father worried about me constantly. I couldn't tell him about the risky situations I'd found myself in. He didn't know about my slashed tires or the times when I was clearly being followed. It was a given that Columbian thieves were in LA, looking for easy prey, using tricks to catch jewelers off guard. When leaving the parking lot at the LA show, I saw my tire had been slashed. I told everyone in the car to roll up the windows and lock the doors; we weren't stopping until we would find a gas station, and then we would all surround the trunk to protect the merchandise while the attendant removed the spare tire. On another occasion, I was sitting in a small jewelry store in the Westfield Century City mall, with rolls of gold chains open on the counter while the owner was making his selection. As I was showing my wares I noticed a tall, skinny man peering at my open bag through the store's front window. Then, as I was walking toward the escalator to go to my car, dragging my bags behind me on my luggage cart, I saw the same man sitting on a bench. As I turned the corner in front of him, he stood up and started following me. With my heart pounding in my chest, I quickly ducked into Macy's department store. I was definitely not going to risk being accosted in an underground parking lot!

A salesgirl stood behind the cosmetics counter right by Macy's entrance. I didn't hesitate.

"Can you help me?" I asked. "There's a guy outside following me around, and I'm afraid to go to my car. I parked two levels down. I don't dare go down there by myself."

She could see I was nervous. "We have security. I'll call one of our guys to walk you to your car."

The guard came right away. As the two of us left Macy's, I looked around. The man I feared had disappeared. I was ever so grateful that day to reach my car in safety.

My father didn't comprehend my desire to achieve success in business. He would have much preferred to give me money than to see me work. No one but Stan could ever grasp my need to establish a separate identity, a strong and stable sense of who I was or who I could be. I was a wife and a mother, first and foremost, steeped in the traditional values of creating hearth and home for my family. That took priority. Everyone told me that should have been enough. Everyone thought I was crazy to do what I did. No one understood that I was aching deep inside with a yearning to experience more, achieve recognition, and explore opportunities to accomplish something. I would thrive on the pursuit of success, no matter how elusive, and relish the opportunity even as the challenge increased. I had so much energy and a high sense of self-esteem, and having decided that my most important goals in life had already been achieved, I enjoyed the chance to play the role of a merchant and a peddler. It was fun to make my own money, and even more fun because the people I bought from and sold to had no knowledge of the truly rich life I enjoyed at home. Because of Stan, I could experiment with confidence. Because of my strong commitment to forge ahead in the face of adversity, my sense of self evolved. It didn't seem to matter that, with all my expenses, I wasn't earning enough to support my family. I didn't need to do that. And that's why, through it all, my father never stopped asking me to quit the business. "You don't need to work," he'd say. "Why do you do it? I'll buy your business, and you can be free."

Dad didn't understand my need to work, just as he couldn't possibly fathom man's need to climb Mt. Everest. He came of age during the Great Depression, when food was scarce and there were very few jobs, and almost everyone struggled to survive. I, on the other hand, knew naught of poverty. Grateful for this, I simply couldn't quench my unbroken desire to accomplish something. To master a task with your head held high, to be independent and inventive, wouldn't this bring a sense of purpose to my days? I wanted to be influential. I yearned for some indescribable thing, for a life that meant something. Would such an achievement remain forever beyond my grasp?

Even though I was selling far more gold than silver, Stan and I still traveled to Mexico from time to time. We had many friends there. It was always wonderful to see everyone. We'd visit Mexican artists, go to fabulous dinner parties, and dine at the best restaurants and in the finest homes. At *Avanti Internacional*, George was also selling more gold than silver. Even though he manufactured chains in his factory, he often ran short of supply. He sometimes needed from one to two kilos, as many as five hundred to one thousand chains of one particular style. Before each trip I would go downtown to my Italian friends, Agosto and Pedro, who supplied all the gold dealers in town. I wasn't just buying silver in Mexico but delivering gold there as well.

On this occasion, George wanted me to bring him a few hundred pieces of a thick yellow gold rope chain with a white gold box chain intertwined, a very particular style that the Italians made better than anyone. Agosto and Pedro had on hand only half of the quantity George had asked for. I bought every piece they had, their entire stock, but it wasn't enough.

"Is this all you have left?" I asked them. "You must have sold a lot of it to dealers on the street here. I need more. Who has it?"

I went up and down Hill Street to look for more. I knew a large chain dealer at the California Jewelry Mart and began there.

"Do you have the rope chain with the white gold box?" I inquired.

"Yes, we have a few," the salesman said, offering me a dozen pieces or so.

"Is that all? I really need more; any length is fine."

"If you have a moment, I'll check in the back."

The dealer went to a room in the back. He returned a few minutes later. "Sorry," he said, "This is all I can give you this week. Come back in a week or so, and I'll have more."

And so it went the rest of the day, as I made my way in and out of elevators, picking up whatever the dealers in upstairs showrooms had on hand. The funny thing that happened at the end of the day was, after collecting as much of this design as I could find, I bumped into Agosto on the street. He said with a sudden realization, "Oh, it's you, isn't it? You're the one!"

"What do you mean?" I asked. "What did I do?"

"Everyone's been calling me all day for the rope with the white gold box chain you got from me this morning. You're the one they want it for."

There was no question that gold chains were popular. All the women were wearing them, from the trendsetters in Beverly Hills to the checkout girls at the supermarket.

One day Stan and I were traveling to Hawaii for an annual meeting of the Arthritis Foundation. Our dear friends, Lynn and Jim, were also going to the meeting. On the plane, Lynn began talking to a man sitting nearby. When she found out he had a store in Maui that sold leather goods and jewelry, she became all excited. "You have to meet my friend, Adrienne," she told him. With that, she got up and came over to tell me she had someone to introduce me to. His name was Jeff Thompson, and he quickly became a customer. His opening order was for a few dozen gold chains worth about $10,000, and over the next six months he reordered and paid on time. Then he called to announce the opening of a second store and asked if I would send him gold chains on consignment for his grand opening. He wanted to make a big splash with lots of gold chains for a week or two. Of course I would help him out! I used my credit line to send him over $40,000 worth of fine Italian chains, but this time, he didn't pay, and he didn't return any of the goods. He said business was slow. He needed more time. It was September. By December, he still hadn't paid, nor had he made any attempt to send even a partial payment to me.

In January, Stan and I went to Maui again for another special meeting of the Arthritis Foundation's board. We both were looking forward to this trip. We'd have beautiful weather on a lovely beach, and I could use the opportunity to see my deadbeat customer. Actually, Jeff's new store turned out to be quite attractive, and a lot of gold chains were on display. Jeff met with me for lunch and gave me postdated checks, each a month apart. However, just before it was time to cash the first check, I received a phone call asking me to wait a little longer. So I did, but the check bounced anyway. Jeff was truly a deadbeat. I was concerned, since $40,000 was a significant sum. Then I got the idea to cash all the checks at once at the end of the month, just before payday, when he'd be paying his employees. The checks went through, and I was paid in full. Had I not taken such a bold step, who knows how my own credit standing would have been affected? *I had to keep an eye on the money*, always balancing that fine line between maintaining good relationships with my customers and taking care of my business at the same time.

CHAPTER 10

BUY, BUY, BUY

One evening Stan and I were out with our friend Daniel, who was still the manager at Van Cleef & Arpels. Daniel complimented my necklace and ordered one for the boutique on Rodeo Drive. He also mentioned a jeweler in Milan that he thought I should meet. The jeweler, Piero Milano, was a very well known, highly respected collector and wholesaler of the finest jewelry in the world. Stan and I planned a trip to Italy, to tour the country, but especially to see Mr. Milano.

I shall never forget this trip. It was 1982, and our first stop was in Milan at the fancy hotel, the Principe Savoy. I had made an appointment in advance with Piero Milano for 9:00 a.m. on the morning after our arrival. However, that Monday morning I awoke terribly ill. I called to say I wasn't coming and would be there in a day or two. I had such a bad cold, a sore throat with swollen glands, bright red tonsils, and a fever. The hotel concierge sent a doctor to our room. He was a most distinguished looking gentleman, with gray hair, a gorgeous silk suit and tie, as impeccably attired as any best dressed Italian. He took my wrist to check my pulse and noticed my beautiful newly acquired 18 karat gold Piaget Polo watch. Stan thought he would charge more for his services after seeing my watch, but I didn't care. I seldom took it off. I was surprised when the doctor prescribed a suppository.

"The pain is in my throat and head," I said, "not in my rear end."

Nevertheless, the medicine worked wonders, and I recovered in just two days. I did tell Stan that if you have to be sick, the Principe Savoy is the place to be. It was a full-service hotel, both elegant and comfortable, with wonderful wholesome chicken soup delivered at any hour of the day or night.

The Piero Milano showroom, on the second floor of an old building in the center of the jewelry district not far from the famous Duomo Cathedral, was an extraordinary place to visit. Stan and I took a taxi there, walked up the stairs, rang the buzzer, and were cordially greeted. After several introductions, we were invited to sit at a counter that was about twenty-five feet long, facing the staff on the other side where most of the jewels were kept. The main showroom where we sat was flanked with offices on both sides. On the walls were poster-sized photos of the factory in Valenza, depicting rows of jewelers at their benches, making pieces by hand. On the left side of the showroom stood full-sized flags of various countries, an homage to clients who came from all over the world. Facing us on the other side of the counter were carts piled up with suede jewelry rolls, each one filled with the finest inventory. An enormous safe was directly opposite our seats. From time to time, the staff would retrieve more jewelry from drawers under the counter. The quantity and quality of jewels and gold were staggering to see. We were about to peruse what I thought to be the most extensive and beautiful jewelry collection in the world. I must say I had no real appreciation for fine jewelry until I saw the Piero Milano collection.

Mr. Milano came out of his office to greet us and asked Shira, his salesgirl who knew English well, to show us whatever we wanted to see. I started looking at necklaces and matching bracelets without stones. Everything was put on the scale and priced according to gold weight and labor. The gold price was calculated on the value of the dollar, which in 1982 was quite favorable. After three hours of gazing at shiny gold, I was told it was lunchtime. Mr. Milano, quite the gentleman, invited Stan and me to have lunch at a long table with his staff at a fine restaurant. The food was delicious. Afterwards, we went back to the showroom, where I continued to pick and choose from the enormous selection offered. The day went by quickly. By 6:00 p.m., I was still eager for more, but the showroom was closing, and we had to leave, only to return the next day and the day after that. The pieces I would bring back with me would upgrade the look of my entire inventory.

Leaving the showroom at 6:00 p.m. allowed us an hour and a half to shop for clothes, as the shops all stayed open until 7:30. The US dollar was stronger than ever, so in European currency everything from the most famous designers was affordable. I went home with a pile of new clothes, and Stan bought a few things as well. Our last day in Milan, we went to a leather factory. The prices were so low that we bought a huge amount of leather goods—several handbags to keep or give as gifts, jackets, and a suede skirt with fringe—so many items that we needed an extra suitcase to put them in, and we bought that as well.

Stan was such a sweetheart. He came to support me, helping with difficult choices, but for the most part, he would sit while I worked, reading the *Herald Tribune* and working on the crossword puzzle of the day, looking forward to fabulous lunches and dinners, and shopping from 6:00 p.m. to 7:30 p.m. for great Italian clothes. Mr. Milano, whose English was minimal, made jokes with me in French, about how Stan was able to sit and relax in the showroom while I did all the work. Mr. Milano was well schooled in French, and since I was a former French teacher, we got along quite well. He explained to me how important it was for him to continue to work himself, since so many jewelers and their families—over 350 people in Valenza—depended on him for their salaries.

Imagine that I needed three full days to see the Piero Milano collection! And I'm sure I didn't see it all. He had a completely separate walk-in vault for sets of major jewels, part of which I saw on my last day. And there was an entire section of jewelry that Shira said I didn't need to see, since it wasn't appropriate for the American market—mostly 18 karat beads and extremely large heavy gold ornaments. Mr. Milano didn't work with 14 karat gold, only 18 karat and above. Much of his merchandise was hand-made, labor intensive, and, in my opinion, definitely worth his wholesale prices.

On the second day, when I was looking at jewels with stones, Stan became quite interested. He saw two pieces he wanted to buy for me, an unusual emerald and diamond ring, and a Cartier style diamond bangle bracelet. I was thrilled beyond belief. I would take orders from these two items, but they would be mine! Mr. Milano explained that a buyer from a world famous jewelry company had ordered the same bangle bracelet I was getting. The only difference was that mine would not bear the famous company signature. We were told how that buyer had asked Mr. Milano to raise the price on the invoice so he could receive a kickback. Somehow this didn't surprise me at all. I didn't know how to offer kickbacks discreetly to department store buyers, but I imagined it was done all the time. I didn't own a vacation home to offer my buyers, the way Mrs. Roth did, and I didn't think of raising the price to offer a baker's dozen, or throw in an extra piece with the order that store buyers could keep for themselves. If someone had told me this was how things were done, I'd have joined in the fray and chalked it up to the cost of doing business. But I was Miss Naïve Goody-Two-Shoes, far from worldly-wise. I had a lot to learn.

That night Stan and I went to the La Scala Opera House. Listening to the concert, I was on top of the world. I thought only of gems and jewels, and the two beautiful pieces Stan bought for me. Dazzled all day long from staring at shiny diamonds and gemstones, my eyes hurt terribly, yet I was happy, feeling so loved by my husband. I thought about my stepmother and her appreciation for fine jewelry. Finally, I understood why she had loved it so much. She was up in heaven now, pulling celestial puppet strings, and I was doing her bidding.

During my third day at the Piero Milano showroom, two native African women swaggered in. Apparently they came often to buy gold to bring back to Africa, and they always had a lot of cash. These were large women, buxom and broad, very loud, and extremely self-confident. Wearing bandanas on their heads, beach thongs on their feet, and bright, colorful clothing, red and yellow from head to toe, with only their toes peeking out of their billowy skirts, they spoke fluent French but with an accent. Their taste in jewelry seemed outlandish to me, and they always tried to get a better price on their purchases. Italians don't negotiate on their prices, and Mr. Milano never backed down when dealing with the Africans. They would scream and yell at him in French, and he would scream and yell right back at them. I watched these attempts at negotiation in amusement. No one knew who sent these women, or where they got their money, but they came to the showroom regularly and were good customers. My mind wandered when I witnessed their interactions. Were they African princesses from Gambia? Congo? Maybe they were sisters who had wealthy husbands that sent them on spending sprees to keep them happy. Later Mr. Milano told us a story about how they would smuggle money out of Africa. They would roll it up tight, seal it in plastic, and put it in their vaginas. According to Mr. Milano, one of them "went pee-pee on the train," and the money fell out the hole in the toilet onto the train track, and she lost it all. As I pictured this happening, I was not just amused but extremely grateful, at least, that I didn't have to smuggle cash to make my purchases.

This was my first buying trip to Italy, to be followed by many more. I would meet many other dealers, factory owners, and wholesalers, and my business would steadily grow, as I would soon become known for having the finest 18 karat gold collection from Italy.

But it wasn't just my jewelry line that was special; my new Italian handbags were exceptional, too, as I would discover after attending a crowded flea market a month later in Mexico.

CHAPTER 11

RISKY BUSINESS!

I was enjoying my new Italian handbags, especially one particular large black shoulder bag that I wore almost every day. It had two zippered compartments and was extremely useful for transporting goods to and from suppliers in downtown Los Angeles. I'd had this purse less than a month when George asked me to bring another package to Mexico with thousands of dollars worth of gold chains. This would be a short trip to Mexico City, from Saturday through Monday. Stan and I would stay with our friends Sylvia and Manuel. Even though they had a beautiful home in a gated community, I felt safer keeping the heavy gold package in my new shoulder bag, on my shoulder, rather than leaving it in their guest room. My bag with $40,000 of gold would stay with me all weekend.

On Sunday the four of us decided to visit the flea market, always colorful and unusual. It was more crowded than usual, with people elbowing and bumping up against us right and left. I held tight to my bag and after a few hours returned to the house without incident, or so I thought. On Monday, I delivered the heavy package of gold safely to George and spent the afternoon with his family. Then we went to pack our luggage quickly for the flight home.

Stan was helping me put my things in the suitcase, so I gave him my new black shoulder bag.

"Please wrap it carefully in tissue paper," I advised. "It's my new Italian bag and should be protected."

"This is your new bag?" Stan asked. "Look at this!" The bag had been slashed with a knife all along its side.

I suppose this is a testimonial for the craftsmanship of fine Italian handbags, since nothing had fallen out. I couldn't imagine losing $40,000 of gold chains! A few months later when we went back to Italy on a buying trip, the factory repaired the bag quickly, simply by replacing the side panel.

Good fortune followed me faithfully, as somehow, I escaped disaster once again.

Winter in Los Angeles, dark outside by 5:00 p.m., found me at Nubar's factory, picking up an order of gold charms. Nubar wasn't there. Broadway was not a well-lit street at night, and I had promised my father I would not walk around downtown in the dark. My father would ask me over and over, "Please, Adrienne, leave downtown before the sun goes down. I worry about you."

"Dad," I told him, "don't worry. I will never walk to my car alone downtown when it's dark out."

Since it was winter and the sun had set, I asked the factory foreman if someone could walk with me to my car, a couple of short blocks away. A young factory worker appeared, and we walked together to my car. We barely spoke, since his English was limited. I don't think he was much older than twenty-five. When we got to my car, I politely offered to give him a ride back to Broadway. The two of us got in my car.

Sometimes even those you think you can trust will behave badly.

I was about to start the motor, when suddenly this young man grabbed me and started kissing me! I threw him off with a scream, in no uncertain terms! It wasn't difficult, as fortunately he backed off at once. But then without a word or any warning, he unzipped his pants and started to masturbate. I watched in shock but unafraid, as neither of us uttered a sound. When he was done, I gave him some Kleenex, started the car, and drove him back to Nubar's factory in silence. Some may find this funny, but at the time, for me it was anything but. I was happy to escape unscathed. I couldn't tell a soul, mainly because doing so would elicit advice I didn't want to hear.

Audacious or intrepid, unsuspecting or dauntless, unafraid or just lucky—I was still not able to talk about this for many years.

The next two years, life went on as usual and my business continued to expand. Then in 1983 at the gift and jewelry show in Los Angeles, a man with the last name of Joshahari came to the booth wanting to start his own jewelry business. Just like Rachel, he also had the idea of making extra money by selling jewelry to fellow factory workers during his lunch hour. At first he ordered a few things at the show and again on the phone from time to time. Later I came to trust him, and before long he was coming to the house to pick up his orders and see the newly arrived items. After six months, it was time for the gift show again. Joshahari called to ask what time the show started and when it closed. He said he definitely was coming to see the new collection and would probably be there the first day of the show.

Joshahari didn't come to the show. He didn't come the first day or any day, for that matter. However, he called my cell phone repeatedly to inquire as to our opening and closing times. These calls worried me. On the last day of the show, when we were closing at noon, he called again, this time asking if we needed help to pack up and close the exhibit space before going home. I was so annoyed. I certainly didn't want his help or anyone else's after the show was over. Packing up and going home was risky, and only the most loyal, devoted individuals were to be there. This time my father wasn't with me. He was in Acapulco. Before leaving town, Dad asked Stan to pick up the merchandise from the show and bring it safely home.

Here's the truth: It's my merchandise. I bought and paid for it with, at that point, six years of hard work. I knew how to travel with it, more than anyone else could possibly know. Those bags were like my babies. However, because of my father's request, Stan left his office in Century City and drove downtown to pick up the four bags and bring them home from the Convention Center. I am not sure if Stan had ever been followed before or was even concerned about being followed, the way I always was. He had never traveled alone with the bags, nor had his tires ever been slashed. He had never been followed in a mall on the way to the parking lot. He was not the one with nerves of steel and eyes in the back of his head. Why hadn't my father trusted *me* to bring my bags home safely?

While we were packing up our lights and show para-phernalia, Stan picked up the four bags at 1:00 p.m. and drove home with them, into our garage, arriving around 1:30. He was rushing because he had an appointment in his office at 2:00 and didn't want to be late. He had a lot on his mind. The housekeeper was there, but Stan didn't honk for her to come outside. He opened the trunk, took two bags in the house and went to open the safe, leaving the other two bags in the unlocked trunk with the garage door open. When he came back to the car, the other two bags were gone!

Stan stood at his open trunk, his now *empty* trunk. Was he going crazy? Where did the bags go? Weren't there two more? Had the housekeeper brought them in? No, she was still vacuuming upstairs. So where were the bags?

It wasn't like him to be hasty, inattentive, or imprudent, even for just a moment. He simply wasn't experienced in carrying jewelry. Vigilance and constant watchful concern were learned traits that I'd developed. This wasn't expected of him.

Had he even wondered a tiny bit that someone might have followed him home, or had he thought to look in his rearview mirror just to check? And then he'd left the trunk unlocked and certainly made it easy for whoever might have tailed him. With that disturbing thought, Stan rushed to the office, where his client was already waiting for him.

Did I think it was Joshahari who had robbed me? No one else had called to verify again and again exactly what time the show was closing. No one else knew where I lived. However, we didn't witness him taking the bags out of the trunk. In fact, he never called to ask for merchandise again, not then, not ever. I was very angry, and it took several months to get over it.

I wasn't angry with Stan. He had a lot on his mind and wasn't thinking of the danger. What upset me most was not having been trusted to take care of everything myself. Why was I perceived as less capable, when in fact, I was more competent, more experienced, and more adept than anyone at watching over my valuable collection? Had I not been a woman, my father would not have asked Stan to bring the bags safely home, and everything would have been different. The irony here is that most of the time, a woman loves to have a man as her protector, myself included. My father and my husband were doing what they thought was best for me. So how could I be angry with them?

It took time to process my feelings. I was exasperated, dismayed, vexed beyond words, resenting their intrusion but glad for their concern.

At least the insurance covered my losses. But I had a nightmare that would change the course of the future. I dreamt that two robbers rang the doorbell of our house. Our housekeeper opened the door, and they shot her before forcing me to open the safe, a gun at my back. After a terrifying dream like that one, I had to move the business out of the house.

During my fiasco with Mrs. Yu, Stan never criticized me. He never once said I had been careless or negligent. When I asked him why he had never uttered a single word of criticism, he said he had known I already felt awful, and criticism wouldn't help. So I didn't criticize him for leaving the two bags in an unlocked trunk, or for not waiting for the housekeeper to come outside. But I did let everyone know emphatically once and for all that more than anyone else I could be trusted to handle the jewelry myself.

We entertained often at home. At one of our many garden parties, we invited one of Stan's clients, an older gentleman and a long-time friend of my father. He owned a four-story building in downtown Beverly Hills, with retail stores on the street and offices above. At the party I told him I was looking for an office for my business, and he offered me space in his building at a most interesting rental rate. I grabbed it and took a five-year lease with a five-year option to renew. I ordered the showcases, telephones, and new stationary, and purchased a tall safe, filing cabinets, desks, chairs, printer, fax machine, and more. A complete security system was installed, including an electrically locked door and buzzer. Four months later I moved in. This would be my home away from home for the next fifteen years, and I would no longer have to schlep bags of jewelry to stores on a daily basis. Most important of all, the merchandise would be out of the house. The business was no longer a part-time hobby. It had become a profound part of my life.

CHAPTER 12

A FULL TIME JOB AND
OTHER DISTRACTIONS

The downside of moving the business out of the house was that I was expected to be at work every day during business hours. I now had a place of business open from 10:00 a.m. to 6:00 p.m., and needed a full-time employee, one who was well screened and would not steal.

When I had first started the business in 1976, my dad told me not to rely on business from friends, and I never did. Some customers support their friends who open a business and make an effort to buy from them before shopping elsewhere, with the idea that all merchants need to make a profit, so why not give the business to a friend. But I wanted to help my friends acquire pretty things and felt compelled to offer them lower prices. Ultimately, as more and more clients became friends, this was not good for the bottom line, especially now that I had more expenses to pay. But that wasn't so terribly important, since Stan was always the primary provider for the family. I had the feeling that I was "playing store," as we had done as children.

Because we were located inside a building and not at the sidewalk, there was no street traffic. I was now saddled to the showroom and no longer running around to see my customers with the jewelry in the trunk of my car. At this point almost all my business was done at shows or over the phone. I also sold at Arthritis Foundation events to benefit the charity. I'd close the showroom, bring the collection to the annual meetings, set up showcases and donate the profits. It was great fun.

After five years at the Bedford Drive location, it was time to renew the lease. I asked for more space. The owner of the building had passed away, but the management hadn't changed. The building manager gave me five hundred additional square feet at the same rental rate. He measured each and every square inch, including the thickness of the interior walls.

Wait. He's not just measuring the rooms? He's measuring the thickness of the interior walls? I have to pay rent on the space the walls take up?

Suddenly a light bulb went off in my head. I'd much rather be a landlord than sell jewelry. A landlord collects rent every day, including Saturdays, Sundays, and holidays, with increases every year. Jewelers get paid only when inventory is sold, and the longer the inventory sits unsold, the more the investment diminishes in value. I had perhaps $250,000 invested at cost in old inventory. This was dead money, which could have been used as a down payment on a small piece of real estate where I could be charging someone rent. The dead money was a quarter of a million dollars I could never get my hands on, because during the time it took to sell old inventory, the rest of the inventory continued to age.

This idea of owning real estate remained front and center in my mind. As I drove around town looking at all the buildings, I wondered who were the landlords and how much they earned. As a jeweler I was merely buying myself a job with a hefty investment in inventory and a return of $70,000 to $80,000 a year. I imagined what it would be like to receive monthly checks and yearly increases without having to work from 9:00 to 5:00. I started to fantasize how many landlords there were in the small city of Beverly Hills. How many were retired, like my dad, playing cards or golf at the country club every day?

Am I in the wrong business? I'm working my tail off to sell the old stuff in order to buy new things and can never get my hands on the money.

It was a perpetual challenge.

While the addition to the showroom was under construction, I took the opportunity to go to the Basel jewelry show in Switzerland to see new vendors. Basel is perhaps the largest and most important jewelry show on the planet with three large venues: one building dedicated for watches, one for jewelry manufacturing machinery, and one for fine jewelry and gemstones.

Flying to Switzerland on a buying trip sounds far more exotic and fun than it was. I was alone. I had to make decisions, and not all of them would be sound. It was really hard. And yes, there was a chance to hook up with a handsome man after dinner, but I simply wasn't interested.

What's it like to walk the aisles of a trade show, by yourself, in a city far from home? No matter where you are, it's hard work. Finding suppliers with enough of the right product at the right price takes patience and concentration. At this particular show, with vendors from all over the world, I met Roberto Casarin and his rep, Timothy King. They had fabulous rings, and they promised to visit me in the States in the near future.

One month later, Timothy King came to my showroom with Roberto's exports for me to buy. And not long after that, he introduced me to a client of his who wanted to sell her things to me. Temi B. was a young woman like me who purchased mountings and filled them with stones to sell at the shows. She was having trouble selling her expensive diamond necklaces, and Timothy told her I could probably sell them for her. Her father, who accompanied her to my showroom, was a diamond dealer who wanted to show me his diamonds as well. Their prices were enticing, and their merchandise truly beautiful.

"I have a charity ball this weekend," I said. "Would you like me to wear one of these necklaces and find a buyer for you?"

Temi gave me a necklace to wear to the event, on a memo with my signature. That Saturday night I put the necklace on and looked in the mirror. It took my breath away. It was stunning!

I put a scarf around my neck to cover the necklace and went to the ball, not wanting to attract attention when getting out of the car. Then once inside, I put the scarf in my coat pocket. While walking around and perusing the items in the silent auction, I was greeted by one of the dinner guests, Arthur B. He came over with his wife Norma to say hello, and it was then that we discovered we would be sitting at the same table. Art and Norma couldn't help but notice my beautiful necklace. Unbeknownst to me, they had been looking for one. A bit later at the table, Norma sat down without her husband, as he was still in the auction room. Our mutual friend Lynn, who was sitting between Norma and me, said, "Adrienne, you've got enough jewelry on. Norma needs a diamond necklace. Let her wear it a while."

Arthur soon sat down to dinner across from me. "Adrienne," he asked, quizzically looking at my neck, "where is your gorgeous diamond necklace?"

Without saying a word, we all turned our heads to gaze at Norma. When Art followed our gaze and looked at his wife, he asked in front of everyone, "How much is this going to set me back?"

"About the price of a small Mercedes."

Art asked me to dance to get the exact price, so others wouldn't hear.

A few days later, Art and Norma came to my showroom to purchase the necklace and a pair of earrings to go with it. That same week, I sold a five-carat diamond that belonged to Temi's father. Timothy King's little introduction resulted in more than $100,000 changing hands. From that day on, Temi and I continued to sell each other's pieces.

Through the 1980s, I traveled to Italy often. With my knowledge of French and Spanish, I could understand the Italian language fairly well, but when I tried to make myself understood, I had great difficulty. After a harrowing experience at a Milan post office, where trying to communicate almost brought me to tears, I decided to take beginning Italian classes at UCLA in the summer. Being able to speak a little bit would help me enormously. For six weeks straight, I could be found on campus Monday through Friday from nine in the morning until noon. At the time I had a full-time employee in the showroom, so I was afforded this luxury.

By the end of summer Timothy quit his job as a rep for Roberto Casarin and asked me if he could work for me. I couldn't pass up this exciting offer. After all, he had opened accounts all over the United States when he was with Roberto. Plus, he spoke Italian perfectly and would be a great asset on buying trips. We decided to form a new company, Adriana K Collection Jewels, featuring high-end, 18 karat gold Italian imports. Adriana is the Italian spelling of my first name, and K is the first initial of Timothy's last name. I thought the name sounded Italian and had a nice ring to it, but I probably would have decided on a different name had I realized that the letter "K" doesn't exist in the Italian alphabet. It was only after our business cards, order forms, Fictitious Name Statement, and bank account were in place that I heard the Italians refer to us as "Adriana Kappa," using the word "Kappa" from the Greek alphabet.

To enhance the collection and make it more enticing for Timothy's accounts, the two of us planned a three-week buying trip to visit the small Italian factories in Valenza Po, an area known for manufacturing the finest jewelry in the world. Stan didn't want to go, as he knew it would be tedious work for me, and he would be bored to tears in the tiny town of Valenza.

Valenza, often referred to as "The City of Goldsmiths," had 1,100 jewelry firms and 18,000 inhabitants. It was a boring place to visit—gray, industrial buildings on both sides of the streets, and little or no signage. A newcomer wouldn't know where the jewelers lived or worked, completely understandable given the wealth of gold and jewels behind their closed doors. Figuring out how to find them was daunting even with Timothy's perfect Italian. The town was large enough to support one restaurant but no hotels, so Timothy and I had to book our rooms at a hotel out of town, in Alessandria, a half hour's drive away.

Many if not most of the jewelers in Valenza did their work at home, learning the craft as it was passed from father to son and from generation to generation. Unlike the larger Italian jewelry manufacturers in Rome or Vicenza, where jewelry is made in quantity for the masses, the jewelers in Valenza made higher end, individual, labor-intensive pieces. It was a cottage industry; there was no real distribution center and no place other than the one retail store near the marketplace to find the beautiful jewels for which the town was so famous. We certainly weren't going there to buy retail. Locating the finest jewelry manufacturers would be no easy task, since the jewelers of Valenza didn't travel to the States. They didn't go to international shows or even have a website. Since most of them worked from home, they would be impossible to find even with Timothy's perfect Italian. We went to the Chamber of Commerce and were given the address of a small exhibition hall where many of the jewelers of Valenza advertised their designs. It was actually a small building with one large room, with glass display cases on the walls. Each showcase held, at most, a dozen jewelry items along with the manufacturer's business card. We spent a full day walking around the hall and looking at the displays. Finally we had a list of our favorite jewelers to visit. Timothy made appointments with them for the next two weeks.

The result of this research was our purchase of an amazing, absolutely sensational collection from the finest jewelers in Italy. We ordered one piece each of many beautiful designs. Timothy would take the line on the road visiting upscale jewelry stores to take orders, and I would stay home to run the business from the showroom in Beverly Hills. Some of our new collection looked like the exquisite pieces from Buccelati or Bulgari, just as beautifully made and similar in style. We ordered many of our imports as mountings, so we also had to purchase diamonds back home in Los Angeles and hire diamond setters to set them there. It made no sense to have our pieces finished in Italy, where diamonds were more expensive. I hired Nina, a young, energetic gemologist to help buy the stones. She was a recent graduate from the GIA, the Gemological Institute of America, where she had learned how to grade stones. A great asset, she loved working with clients as well. Her first day on the job business was slow, so I asked her to put the jewelry boxes in order. She did as asked but not without snickering, "That's why I became a graduate gemologist, because what I really wanted to do was organize the shelves."

Timothy went on the road every day and opened several new accounts. At first he traveled from New York to Florida to visit the jewelers he had met when he'd worked for Roberto.

However, his expenses were very high. His draw was $1,000 a week. And there was his airfare, rental car, hotel, and meals, plus the costly insurance for a traveling salesman. Insurance is necessary, though, evidenced by the fact that the very first week, Timothy lost part of his line on the streets of New York while talking on a pay phone.

Timothy's story sounded a bit fishy, but how could I know for certain if he was lying or telling the truth? Wouldn't he notice a thief's hand as it cleverly reached into his case, even if he'd been on the telephone? The thought did occur to me that he could have easily sold part of the collection and kept the money. I swallowed the $5,000 insurance deductible and reordered a new line of samples, setting us back several weeks while we waited. I still wonder to this day if Timothy was just another scoundrel who scammed me too. In fact, our business partnership would last only a year.

Our main marketing strategy was to exhibit at the jewelry trade shows in New York and Miami, where upscale retailers looking for high-end, 18 karat gold imports could find us. We would meet prospective buyers at the shows, and Timothy would visit them throughout the year to boost business. The stores that carried our line catered to a wealthier clientele. To find these accounts required research and a great deal of travel. Timothy did what he could, but high-end jewelers were few and far between, perhaps only one or two per city. Turning a profit was extremely difficult. By the end of the first year, in spite of fairly good sales, Adriana K had lost over $40,000.

So, by mutual agreement, Timothy left, and Nina left as well. I kept the company name and continued traveling to Italy alone and doing the shows, enlisting good friends to help sell. Suzanne and Lynn were fabulous at sales. Between Avanti of California and Adriana K, I exhibited at eleven shows a year.

I felt as if I were on a steep slope, climbing ever so slowly.

I had two companies, one that concentrated on high-end jewelry, while the other concentrated on lower-priced gift items. I needed to focus on one or the other but just couldn't choose. In retrospect, this caused me great difficulty. Focusing on a specific product is paramount to the highest success in any business. I loved expensive things and enjoyed selling them, but that wasn't where the profits lay.

A friend of mine warned me, "If you sell to those who ride in limousines, you will ride the bus. But if you sell to those who ride the bus, you'll be the one in the limousine."

Sometimes the shows overlapped each other. In the summer season Avanti of California had a booth at the Los Angeles Gift Show, while Adriana K Collection Jewels had a booth at the New York Jewelers of America Show, the same weekend at opposite ends of the country. I engaged one of my jewelers, Sergey Z., who agreed to work at the LA show along with Margo, so that I could go to New York to sell to the trade at the Jewelers of America Show. At least twice a day, I phoned Los Angeles to see how the show at home was doing. Margo had a cell phone, but she was with a customer, so Sergey was the one who answered. This time he had something pressing to tell me: *Margo had shown a pair of earrings to a client, and when they weren't sold, she put them in her pocket.* Sergey had confronted her, and she covered by saying she was saving them because the customer was coming back later. Sergey didn't believe her and warned me to be watchful in the future.

"Why would Margo put jewelry in her pocket instead of in the back tray?" I wondered. *"Surely she wouldn't steal from me."*

I trusted Margo implicitly. My customers loved her and came to buy from her specifically. She knew everyone and their families, and was also an outstanding worker, able to take over all my duties when necessary, always cheerful and wonderful to be around. Yet on the other hand, to the best of my knowledge no employee ever took an item from the showcase and put it in her pocket. We always set aside items for a "be back later" client in a tray on the back table. I was in New York and didn't see Margo put jewelry in her pocket, but I should have taken Sergey's warning more seriously, as more and more merchandise began to disappear.

I had a fleeting thought at this point: Margo used to sell a lot of jewelry for me. She ordered from me all the time in the past. Why had she stopped buying? Later on, when I asked her, she said simply that her business had slowed down, and she wasn't working as hard.

I thought I was lucky to have her. She sold more than anyone. She never let anyone leave without buying. She was competent, cheerful, and enthusiastic. I made money with her on my staff, and without her my life in business would be so much harder.

Margo told me exactly what she'd told Sergey: "The customer said she'd be back in a little while, and I was saving the earrings for her." Ignoring the obvious signs, truly deluded, I buried my head in the sand.

At least twice a year we took a physical count of the inventory, and each time I would write off the inventory we couldn't find. The unaccounted inventory continuously bothered me. I couldn't believe that Margo would steal from me. She was paid generously and treated well.

Sometimes we'd get so busy that items were carelessly handled. Upon returning from a show in Seattle, I couldn't find an expensive diamond ring—one of my best. I looked for it frantically, only to discover that it had been shipped inadvertently on a truck with my showcases, tossed in with a bag of ring displays. I also noticed there was no record of a sale for three of the always popular twisted gold bangle bracelets. I'd seen them at the close of the show, but where were they now? I phoned Margo in exasperation. She said she could have sold them for cash at the closing hour of the show in Seattle. But our cash sales had all been accounted for, and the cash for these bracelets wasn't there.

I weighed the pros and cons in my head. Margo was a phenomenal salesperson. Even though she saw our customers just twice a year in Los Angeles, San Francisco, and Seattle, she was always genuinely excited to see them. She remembered their names and what they had purchased the last time. She would ask about their children while enthusiastically bringing new items to their attention. Surely without her we wouldn't sell nearly so much. I was fortunate to have her by my side. Yet jewelry was going missing far too often, and I was in denial about why this was happening. Tens of thousands of dollars went unaccounted for each year.

I wanted to trust Margo because I needed her, and I needed her because she could sell better than anyone, even better than I. In fact, at times she cared more about moving the merchandise than she did about helping the customer. How could I not respect a woman who was so gifted at sales? But regardless of her prowess, laudable or otherwise, Sergey was right. When he told me she put earrings in her pocket instead of in a tray on the back table, I should have done something about it. I did nothing because I didn't *want* to believe she'd steal.

You were obtuse, Adrienne. It ended up costing you plenty.

The business was growing but not without a struggle. It would be a while before Sergey introduced me to Dan, and *that* would change my life dramatically. Working together with them would make my life better at first, but later I would suffer greatly, as I ended up riding a roller coaster from high hopes to heartache, from trust to suspicion, from triumph to frustration, from glee to rage, and from glad to sad and back again.

Who was Dan? He was Sergey's twenty-one year old son, born in Odessa. Some would say he possessed admirable qualities, such as great ambition and desire for prosperity, a competitive attitude, and a winning personality. He was charming and clever for sure, but his cunning would leave me deceived and disillusioned, and in the end, his actions would complicate my life in ways I could not prophesy.

CHAPTER 13

SERGEY, DAN, AND
A SPECIAL OFFER

As a teenager growing up in Odessa, Ukraine, in the 1960s, Sergey Z. had been a good boy, honest, truthful, well mannered, and kind. His mother was a schoolteacher, his father a jeweler, the family Jewish by birth but not in practice. Stocky and strong, soft-spoken and unassuming, Sergey had a boyish face and happy disposition that earned him many friends. In school, he played and mastered the game of soccer. It was also there that he met Inez, a gorgeous buxom blonde. They fell in love right away, married very young, and had just one child, a son they named Dan. Life in Odessa, a city on the Black Sea in Ukraine, was difficult under Communist rule. Sergey followed in his father's footsteps and became a jeweler. He was adept with his hands, and because of his love for shiny well-cut stones, the profession came to him naturally. His strong, thick fingers and eye for beauty spawned perfection in his workmanship. Yet as much as he loved his work, he earned little and was barely able to provide for his family. Far from lazy, Sergey went down to the wharf to look for extra work. He met an older man who had a high paying job under the Communist regime, building boats that could transport goods. The two made a deal: They decided they would build a boat they could sell on their own, with Sergey providing all the labor and the older man providing materials he would somehow manage to obtain. Illegal under the regime, the money from the eventual sale would help them get by.

For several months thereafter, Sergey spent after-hours and weekends building the boat by himself, with his strong hands and only a few tools. He worked hard, long into the nights, taking precious time away from his wife and son. When finally finished, the boat was a fine vessel, a joy to behold. It would bring a great price and secure their future in a land where many had nothing except that which was provided by the government, more or less equally to all.

With great pride, Sergey brought his partner to see their finished product. The older man said, "Good job, kid. This beautiful boat is mine now. Sorry I have to break the bad news. Our deal's off. I've got a buyer, and I'm keeping the proceeds. There isn't a damn thing you can do about it either!"

When Sergey told me this story, I could see the emotion on his face. "What did you do?" I wanted to know.

"What could I do? I wanted to kill him. I worked so hard on that boat . . . I tried to talk to him. I needed the money. I trusted him to be a man of his word. It was so unfair. I was so mad and could do nothing." Sergey blinked and swallowed hard from the memory. "The guy didn't care. He told me to get the hell out of his sight, and if I caused trouble, he'd tell the authorities I stole the wood and all the materials, and I'd go to jail, maybe even Siberia, and never see my family again."

Sergey paused for a second before continuing. "My stomach burned inside me like a hell. I really wanted to kill the guy. At night after dark, I went down to the dock. I took a power saw and cut the boat completely in half, right down the middle. It made me sick to do it, but I wasn't giving him the boat. That boat was half mine. I had every right. I finished just before daybreak. It split in half. Finished. But then, I knew I had to get out of there or I'd be dead the next day. So I took my wife and son, and a small pouch of rubies from my workbench and whatever money we had, and we left the country immediately. We took a train and a boat to Italy, and from there I planned to go to Philadelphia, where we had family. But I had bad luck on the train. I lost the small pouch of rubies. It was very hard. Eventually our cousin in Philadelphia sent us money to get there."

Listening to this story, I was in awe. I'd heard of gangsters on the Russian trains who snuck into rail cars and injected chloroform under cabin doors so they could enter during the night and ransack the luggage while travelers were dead asleep. Indeed, this practice was widespread in those days in this country of thieves where life was so hard.

I tried to imagine what it must have been like to run from the law. Here was a man who conspired to violate the communist rules of the Russian regime, who suffered betrayal and guile and retaliated bitterly. Here was a man who became a fugitive shanghaied by robbers, a victim of circumstance or careless ignorance, a man who acted defiantly without consideration of consequences.

Philadelphia in the 1970s had a thriving Jewish population. The city was diverse, and Sergey and Inez felt free for the first time in their lives. Sergey got a job with a jewelry manufacturer downtown. He and others at the shop made rings from scratch and did repairs for stores all over the US. Inez procured part-time work as a bookkeeper and also as a masseuse. She was actually a trained cosmetologist. Their son, Dan, at the age of five, learned to speak flawless English, just like a native American. At some point, they all became United States citizens.

At work every day, Sergey was a natural expert at grading diamonds. He worked with large center stones almost exclusively, and judging them for their beauty was easy for him. In fact, in just a short time, working with stones every day, Sergey knew more about how to judge a diamond than most gemologists with diplomas on their walls. He truly enjoyed his work and became a highly valued, trusted employee. It was he who walked to the post office at 4:00 every afternoon, laden with shipments of everyone's daily work. His employer gave him a gun to carry to protect the packages more than anything else. They were valued at thousands of dollars. It was important to watch your back whenever you carried goods.

Sooner or later it was bound to happen. If you left every day at the same time from a jewelry factory, carrying packages on your way to the post office, someone would notice and follow you. One day Sergey was accosted on the street. The guy was young and skinny, no match for Sergey's strong athletic build and quick instincts. He had a knife and approached Sergey from behind, threw his arm around his neck, yelling, "Drop the packages, man, or I'll slit your throat!" Sergey stepped backwards, in an attempt to stomp on the man's toes. He dropped the packages, and, with a cosmic power that came from fear, he pushed against the arm that was hooked around his shoulder. He broke free in a flash and swung around, adrenaline coursing through his veins. With his life at stake, in blind fury he lunged at his attacker with all the strength he could muster, kicking him squarely in the groin. The man dropped his knife and grabbed his crotch, and it was then that Sergey punched him in the jaw. He would have hit him again if the man hadn't fallen to the pavement from the force of the blow. His heart racing, Sergey picked up the man's knife and the sack of packages and ran like hell all the way to the post office.

Trembling and scared, out of breath and barely able to

speak, he felt like a marked man. An immigrant from Russia, a refugee without citizenship and so little English, he feared the authorities, not to mention future retribution from gangs and gangsters who might try again. Sergey knew he had to uproot his family and leave town. No questions would ever be asked or answered.

I listened to this story, completely in awe. It takes guts to be in this business. One must anticipate. That thought never leaves you. It becomes part of your soul. When everything you've worked for is suddenly at stake and it's time to do or die, adrenaline kicks in, and you don't recognize yourself. Even Piero Milano, so distinguished and refined, once told me, "Two robbers accosted me as I was opening the door to my showroom. When it's your merchandise, you do what you have to do."

After this incident, Sergey and Inez ended up leaving Philadelphia for Los Angeles, a city with a thriving population of immigrants, including 300,000 Russians. It was a city of great opportunity. They found a place to live in West Hollywood and looked for work. They were able to get by, although there never seemed to be quite enough money. Dan grew up speaking English like a native and after high school began working at the age of eighteen as a traveling salesman for a factory that sold to jewelry stores and dealers all over the country.

Dan was a natural-born salesman and was making good money. Sergey, on the other hand, was having a tough time at his jeweler's bench all day. He began working at a small store, mainly offering diamond setting and jewelry repairs. Open to the public, but with little inventory to sell, the shop welcomed individuals who stopped by with rings to be sized, chains to be shortened, and other such work. He had a partner, but there wasn't enough work to support two families. At least once a week, Sergey would visit jewelry stores in Beverly Hills to offer his services. And that's how we met.

Sergey knocked on my door one day, asking if I had any repairs he could do. The owner of the store up the street recommended him highly. Of course I had repairs, and mountings that needed to be set, and I could see right away that Sergey's diamond setting was impeccable. Once or twice a week he'd pick up and drop off jobs, always on time, always at a fair price, creating beautiful jewels from the dozens of mountings I'd imported from Italy. It wasn't long before Sergey told me he wanted to work for me full time. He was leaving his job and starting over again.

The reason? At their store in West Hollywood, Sergey and his partner had suffered a real calamity. Whether a careless blunder or a costly screw-up, a simple case of negligence destroyed the partnership. The electric ultrasonic machine had been full of dirty jewelry cleaner, so dirty that it was impossible to see what the tank contained. It was an everyday occurrence, pouring out the liquid and replacing it with fresh jewelry cleaner. However, care had to be taken not to throw out any jewelry that might have fallen unnoticed to the bottom of the tank. Due to fatigue or carelessness or desperate times, a large diamond ring disappeared. Perhaps it was in the tank when someone poured the dirty jewelry cleaner down the toilet to change the liquid. In any case, this expensive ring with a large center stone was nowhere to be found. Neither one of them knew for certain how it happened. An argument ensued. Could a customer have come to the back room, normally not allowed, and swiped it off the jeweler's table? No matter, the missing ring had to be paid for. The situation became intolerable, and Sergey, as stubborn as always, quit.

He knew I had enough work for a full-time jeweler on premises. Within two weeks, he brought his bench and tools to my showroom, paying me rent and subleasing one of my rooms in order to set tiny stones in mountings for me. With strong hands and unrivalled patience, Sergey could make anything from start to finish. Occasionally he took jobs from other jewelers. They would marvel at his work, as Sergey could set even the most fragile, precious emeralds in any metal including brittle platinum without a hitch.

You could count on Sergey to be there every morning at 8:00 a.m. He'd make coffee, turn on the ultrasonic machine, smoke a cigarette, and begin his work at his bench. At least once a week he would visit the jewelry district downtown to pick up supplies, usually at 10:00 a.m. when traffic was light, so he could be back before noon. His work ethic could not be faulted. Occasionally when my friends came to the showroom with special requests for jewelry, he would leave his workbench and come out in front. He had a sincere way of explaining to customers how he would do the work, often creating detailed drawings to point out why a job had to be done this way instead of that. No one questioned the price. His work was exemplary, and he was good for my business.

Sergey's son Dan also loved the jewelry business, although he never learned to work at the bench. Right out of high school, he became the number one salesman at a wholesale company that was well known for an extensive line of diamond engagement rings. The owners of the company were two street-smart Russians who sold their product to dealers throughout the United States. Dan proved to be of great value. From the very first week, he revamped the computer system and organized the factory, and then went on the road to sell. He was a soft-spoken, cute kid with a pretty face. He had an endearing manner and tremendous charisma. Everyone he met thought he was special. Determined to make his way in the world, he would sit on the toilet in the men's restroom and quietly study the jeweler's bible, the thick Red Book, published annually by the Jewelers Board of Trade. The famous Red Book was full of information about most of the jewelers in the United States, wholesalers as well as retailers, an absolute "must" for anyone in the jewelry trade. Everyone of any importance in the business was mentioned there. The book provided necessary details: storeowners' names, addresses, credit worthiness, years in business, number of locations, and more. If you were a jeweler with a good credit rating, you would want to be listed in the Red Book so everyone in the business could see that you paid your bills on time.

Reading the book and wasting no time, Dan made appointments with the biggest companies, those with the greatest number of stores and the highest sales volume, and before he turned twenty-one, Dan was selling and making a commission on over $2,000,000 of sales a year. When he wasn't working, he spent his free time with a pretty Russian girl, a raven-haired beauty, whom Sergey referred to as a spoiled brat. Regina was an only child who had always had her way. Her parents owned convalescent homes and were financially secure. Dan got her pregnant, and he married her right away. It was an expensive wedding at the Sephardic Temple in Westwood, with a fabulous evening of dinner and dancing. A group of professional dancers was flown in from Las Vegas to entertain with a show. The cost of the wedding was split by both sets of parents, which Sergey could not afford, but he was too proud not to contribute his share. He had little money saved and borrowed on his credit cards to pay for it.

After the honeymoon, Dan would leave work at the end of the day and come to my showroom to visit his dad before we closed. He didn't really want to go straight home after work, a telling sign that his marriage would not last. In fact, after less than two months he was already thinking of divorce. Actually,

Dan had good reason to spend time in my showroom after hours. He had a grand plan to quit his job and start his own company with his father. Many days the three of us would talk of the future. Dan's only problem was he had no money, but that would not deter him.

"Would you like to be a partner?" Dan asked me. "We're going to need money, at least $100,000."

I didn't really want to be his partner, or maybe I just wasn't ready for that. I didn't know him well enough. Could I really trust him? Ambiguous thoughts began churning in my head as I weighed the reasons for and against being in business with him, debating with myself.

Dan could sell anything, and more importantly, if he didn't have exactly what his customers wanted to buy, he knew where to find it.

Dan could copy anything and make it for whatever price point it needed to be, with quality to match any price. He could make more expensive pieces with better diamonds, but he also knew where to find cheaper diamonds to bring the cost down.

He wasn't just a cute, likeable guy. He was a go-getter who made things happen. When he and I visited one of his customers, she didn't need to buy a thing, but she gave him a nice order anyway. It was uncanny how no one ever turned him down.

But he wanted an investment of $100,000. That was a lot of money, a big risk.

Dan can sell ice to Eskimos. And Sergey is okay. He's always been forthright and truthful to me at least.

But will they make money or lose it?

I'm tempted. I'd love to be part of their business.

What should I do? Yes? No? I'm not sure, not sure at all.

CHAPTER 14

A PENNY SAVED

The first few years in my own business at Avanti, I watched expenses like a hawk, trying to keep them as low as was feasible. The shows constituted my biggest expense by far. When flying to a show, I brought my bags as carry-on luggage instead of sending them insured with an expensive courier. I used my own showcases and sent them on a truck from city to city rather than rent showcases on site. I brought my own low voltage lights and hung them myself, rather than pay Exhibitor Services the high union wages to hang them. In Seattle, we stayed at the Holiday Inn Crown Plaza, three women in one room with me on a rollaway bed. In San Francisco, we stayed at my dear friend's house instead of paying for a hotel. Irene made breakfast and lunch for us every single day, even when I begged her not to. When we were there, she cared for us as if we were her children. The only thing I splurged on and insisted upon was a relaxing dinner in a nice restaurant each night, from drinks to dessert for everyone who had worked so hard during the day.

In those days, two carry-on bags were allowed on flights, but many times no one stopped me as I boarded with four of them. They didn't look like jewelry cases, having evolved over time as my wares grew. One was a zippered yellow vinyl bag; one was a red toolbox; and the two others were identical black fold over leather cases with the handles on top like the ones lawyers often used. These last two would have been perfect for documents, but my velvet rolls filled with jewels fit inside superbly. As I rolled my luggage cart through the airports, no one suspected the bags contained rolls of gold or boxes of rings with little diamonds and gems. On the plane they filled the space under the seat and fit in the overhead bin as if made for that exact purpose. I often traveled this way to San Francisco and Seattle, where I would meet Margo and Elsa, my two cracker-jack saleswomen who worked with me at all the out of town shows.

Eventually the TSA cracked down on sneaks like me, and I had to adapt to their strict rule about carry-on bags. The day before a show in San Francisco, a taxi took me to the airport to board an early flight so I could meet my staff at the convention center and set up the booth that afternoon. We always prepared like this. It would take us several hours to put the showcases in place, hang the lights, set up our tables and chairs, and decide the best way to display the pieces. As usual I was flying by myself, anxious to board early to be sure the overhead bins would have space for my bags. As I approached the jet way leading to the door of the plane, I heard a loud voice ask, "Is *that* your carry on luggage?"

"Yes," I replied.

"You are *not* getting on *this* plane with all those bags!" the attendant insisted.

"Oh," I said nonchalantly, "they are small and fit under the seat and in the overhead. I can't ship them as luggage, since the contents are valuable."

"That doesn't matter," said the attendant. "You can take two, but that's all. The other two must be checked and go in the baggage compartment."

"I can't check them. Please, *please* let me take them on the plane."

"Sorry. It's a full flight, and the rules are two carry on bags per person. If you check two of them, I'll let you board."

There was nothing I could do but tearfully watch through the airport's large window when the gate closed and the plane backed out of its slot. Heavy-heartedly, I went to the bank of pay phones on the wall and called another airline. Air Cal had a flight leaving in an hour from a different terminal. I quickly took the escalator to the street to find a bus to take me there. The bus driver watched as I unloaded the four bags from the luggage cart and boarded his bus, two bags at a time. He watched again when I took two trips to off-load the four bags and tie them to the cart at the sidewalk. Soon I was standing in front of the ticket agent at Air Cal at Terminal Two with my precious bags piled four feet tall on the luggage cart by my side.

"Is that your carry-on luggage?" the agent asked.

"Yes," I replied, dreading what she was about to say next.

"Well, you have to check two of them," she said.

"I can't do that," I said, turning away, shoulders slumped. Once again, I dragged my cart to the pay phones, this time to call Stan at his office.

"Honey," I asked, "instead of flying up to be with me tonight, can you drop everything and fly up with me now? They have seats on United's next flight . . . Oh, fantastic! You're the best! I'll wait for you back at United in front of the gate."

Stan came to my rescue as only he could.

I waited at curbside for the next bus to take me back to the United Terminal. When the bus pulled to a stop, there was a line of several people getting on in front ahead of me, so I decided to board in back. What I didn't realize was that the driver didn't see me. After the last person in front had boarded, only two of my bags were on the bus while I was on the sidewalk getting the other two. The driver closed the rear doors in my face and started to take off with two of my bags on board. What! My blood-curdling, ear-piercing, gut-wrenching scream, "S-t-o-p!" could have been heard around the world! Amazingly, the bus did stop. Completely drenched in sweat, I then boarded with the other two bags.

It was only after this happened, I came to my senses and began to question my sanity. What woman would travel alone with so much jewelry—four carry-on bags, a purse, and a luggage cart? And come to think of it, what *was* the dollar value in those bags, anyway?

CHAPTER 15

D & G JEWELRY
MANUFACTURING, INC.
A START-UP COMPANY

With a baby on the way, Dan was anxious to start his own company. If his father Sergey could make rings cheaply in silver, set them with cubic zirconia, and gold plate them, he could create a sample line of rings for as little as $60 a piece. It would be easy to extrapolate the cost in fine gold, ten, fourteen, or eighteen karat, with diamonds in various sizes instead of CZs. The gold-plated silver rings looked beautiful, and Dan would tell his customers, "If we can do this with silver, just imagine how much better it will look in gold." He was already taking orders, with no funds to produce the pieces. Dan really needed investors. A Russian co-worker where Dan was working gave him $15,000. Dan's father-in-law gave him the same. With a handshake and a huge desire for success, The Diamonds & Gold Jewelry Manufacturing Company was born.

Dan didn't leave his job right away. While the company where he worked was still footing the bill for travel expenses,

Dan would fly to see customers all over the United States. First he would take orders for his boss. Then he would show his own collection with CZs and sell under his D & G company name. This of course was unethical, but Dan had no scruples. Ambitious to a fault, he would do anything to get ahead, even bite the hand that fed him. But as it would happen, he got off to a bad start when his line of silver rings was left unattended and stolen from the trunk of his car. It may not have had much monetary value, since the rings were just silver with CZs, but it takes time to produce a well-made line of samples. Starting over once again, Sergey had to produce new samples in his spare time, delaying the true start-up date of their new company by several months.

When the line was stolen, both Dan's father-in-law and his co-worker started having second thoughts about their investment in the Diamonds & Gold Jewelry Manufacturing Company. They lost faith in Dan and wanted their money back. Dan, however, was determined to become successful and would never lose faith. He was consumed with desire for success, and nothing was going to stop him. He went to "Uncle" Yefim, his boss's accountant, to see if he would invest. "Uncle" Yefim was over six feet tall, a large man in his seventies. His size alone was imposing. Opinionated, over-confident, boastful, filled with self-importance, Yefim spoke with great authority as an accountant. He believed in Dan, and Dan trusted Yefim. Yefim's participation would ensure the company's success. Yefim gave Dan $50,000 cash and also guaranteed a loan for a $50,000 line of credit at his bank in exchange for a 10 percent ownership interest in the company. Yefim also insisted that the endeavor should be a "C" corporation under California law, and even though this would prove detrimental in some ways, Dan's faith in Yefim was unwavering. Dan trusted him implicitly and treated him with great respect. From now on the company would be known as D & G Manufacturing, Inc. With Yefim's money in place, Dan quit his job, rented space in an old building on Hill Street, and hired one of his cousins and her husband, as well as Sergey and another Russian jeweler, Vladimir. Then he went back on the road to sell, this time at his own expense. He loved selling, and because of his trustable boyish face and his likeable manner, people loved buying from him.

Sergey moved out of my showroom the following weekend. Watching him pack his things to move ten miles away to the jewelry district downtown, I felt a deep ache in my chest. He would no longer be there to talk to my clients or give me advice. His son would no longer visit every day after work. I was unhappy to see him go. I would miss them both. As sad as I was, Sergey was glad, full of anticipation over his promising future. He would work hard, as hard as he could, with undying dedication and purpose to grow his company, a company I wanted to be part of in a most illogical way.

Right away, they had a problem. Yefim's money didn't go very far. Dan had to buy gold, get diamonds on consignment, produce and ship the first orders, and then wait thirty days after he shipped the finished product for his customers to pay him. It was normally ninety days from the date the order was taken to the date payment was due. But already there were so many purchase orders that all the money was gone. Some suppliers would give diamonds on an open invoice, but gold was strictly cash and carry. The more Dan would sell, the more money he would need to buy goods. There was at least a two-to three-month time lag from the date he bought the gold to the due date for what he'd delivered. His customers had open accounts and thirty days to pay. With margins at 25 to 30 percent, and selling as much as he was, Dan was constantly in arrears. Without the cash to buy the gold, Dan was taking orders he couldn't fill. It was like a never ending game of catch up. The company had to pay to produce the orders well before getting a penny of it back, and the more orders there were, the worse it was. One month in business, with credit cards maxed out and no assets whatsoever, he needed another investor to fund his purchase orders right away. Nothing less than another $100,000 would do.

Again, Dan offered me a partnership.

I had a little more information now. Orders were coming in, and production was underway. All the signs of a good investment were there. I had been lucky with some but not all of my investments. I mulled it over a few weeks longer.

Russians in general, I thought, had a poor reputation. Dating from the time of the czars in the 1800s to the present day shift to free enterprise, corruption was a long-standing problem in that country. In Russia a centuries-old thieves' world existed, a secret criminal culture comprised of vicious, shadowy characters and extortionists who demanded ransoms from small businesses in exchange for "protection." The worst offenders were from Odessa, which was Sergey's hometown. I'd heard about this first hand from a close friend who was doing business there. He'd become successful for one reason only: he paid the Russian Mafia to be on his side. They collected his money for him.

But then, I thought, Dan, Sergey, and Yefim were different. Sergey's mother had been a schoolteacher with education and culture, and his father had been in the army in a highly respected position. These men were not savages or racketeers. And now they were Americans in my country. This was the land of opportunity, their chance to fly high. *Surely,* I thought naïvely, *they would obey our laws. Why wouldn't they?* Dan was just twenty-one years old, trying to start his own legitimate business. These were good people, not criminals. I wanted to help them, partner with them, and be in business with them.

Pivotal to my decision was a visit from Sara Roth, George's wife in Mexico. George was having difficulty moving his *Avanti Internacional* silver, just as I had. Sara came to Los Angeles to buy gold and diamond jewelry to sell back home. After she met Dan, she was very excited. "He's going to go places. You should invest in his company for sure," she said without hesitation.

Yefim knew I was interested. He called to arrange a meeting with Stan. "This is a good opportunity for you," he said in his heavy Russian accent. "You will see when the company will grow up." He didn't reveal that they were desperate for another infusion of capital, that no one would give them gold for their orders, that Dan's father-in-law wanted nothing more to do with him, only that this was a good chance for me to take. "They are good, hard-working people," Yefim said. "You will not lose."

I had a little nest egg to invest and could borrow the rest of the money. We had a meeting at our house on a Sunday morning, with Stan, Dan, Sergey, and Yefim. Yefim was not a wealthy man, but he believed wholeheartedly that Dan could create a viable business. The two men knew each other well, since they had worked together for the same company for more than two years. I thought if the business were truly good enough for Yefim, it probably would be good for me, too. My husband believed these were decent, hard-working people and didn't say no. This was a window of opportunity. I could invest in a business on the ground floor and own stock in a company that might some day be worth a great deal. Dan was ambitious. There was a chance he'd hit pay dirt and make a lot of money for us all.

Just as Yefim had done earlier, I wrote a check for $50,000, and I took out a line of credit for another $50,000 to give them, in exchange for 10 percent stock in Diamonds &

Gold Jewelry Manufacturing Company, Inc. Just the fact that this was a California corporation gave me a feeling of comfort because corporations had to follow certain rules. The following Sunday we had our first stockholders' meeting at the tiny one-room factory on Hill Street. Stan came to the meeting with me. "Uncle" Yefim, the accountant, decided that Dan should have 40 percent of the stock, Sergey and Inez should have 40 percent, Yefim would have 10 percent, and I would have 10 percent. Dan would be president, Sergey would be vice-president, and Yefim would be both secretary and treasurer. So, what would my role be?

I really wanted to be on the board of directors and was wracking my brain about how I could participate, since I was so involved with my own business at Avanti with little time to spare. While I was wondering what my position in the company might be, Stan, who is ever so wise, surprised us all by saying right away without asking me first, "Adrienne doesn't want to be on the board of directors." I was ready to object but kept my mouth shut. We'd been married a long time, and intuitively I knew Stan had his reasons. If my husband, a smart lawyer, didn't think I should be on the board, he was undoubtedly right. So I kept quiet. I would ask him later. Stan is brilliant at assessing potential problems. I agreed to be just a passive investor, and although I suffered greatly later on due to the directors' covert activities and secrets, which were often discussed at their meetings without me, taking Stan's advice would prove to be the wisest business move I ever made.

Stan didn't want me involved in the event these men might partake in illegal conduct, not the least of which would be to line their own pockets while cheating the IRS and others. And he was right. Why didn't I see this?

I wasn't thinking logically. I just wanted to belong, to belong to this family, to belong to a bigger world of businessmen.

At that first meeting, where our roles were decided, I felt the pain of not belonging to the board of directors. Stan was right; there's no question about that. But I still longed to be at their board meetings, to be part of their conversations, to know all the details of Dan's business dealings, and get his phone calls after a successful business trip the way his parents did.

When I was much younger, my father had taught me to be wary of men, but he never suspected I'd end up in business with nefarious characters. Dad's old-fashioned ideas were all about sex. I was his only daughter, and he was very strict. Throughout my teenage years, I endured his constant admonishing, "Don't let a guy get into your pants. Almost any guy will sleep with you, but that doesn't mean any of them will marry you." Unfortunately, Dad wasn't around to proffer a warning now. He would have been skeptical, staunchly advising, "Don't let these guys get into your bank account. Do not get in bed with them. You're not one of the family. Who are you kidding? What makes you think you are?"

Dan was still young, his future perfidy not yet perfected. Ambition drove his psyche, and affluence was all that mattered. This charismatic kid, full of confidence, dangerously disarming, charming and manipulative, would succeed beyond everyone's dreams. Selling the product satisfied his soul, but since he was constantly hungry for more, if he sold a hundred pieces today, he needed to sell two hundred tomorrow. It was a game at which he excelled. Cool, calm, and emotionally detached, he cared more about numbers than family, more about achievement and influence than ethics and honor. With Yefim as his teacher, he would master the art of questionable accounting practices. In the beginning, we all accepted a touch of white-collar crime. He was making money for us, and that made everything all right.

When Dan and Sergey paid themselves a "bonus," I found

out the board of directors had made that decision. No one asked me. I thought there should have been a legal distribution to all stockholders, but that didn't happen. Impossible. Dividends are not deductible in a C corporation. Yefim wanted his piece of the profit, and he found a deductible way to get it. For accounting purposes, he and I became consultants so we could receive consulting fees instead of taxable dividends. I had a feeling this wasn't right, but the decision was not mine. We'd be paid, rightfully or wrongfully. However, either way, the two of us weren't actually paid enough. We received too little for our 10 percent stock ownership.

For their 40 percent interest, Sergey and Dan each took $10,000, while Yefim and I received only $1,000 apiece. I calculated that the company should have distributed $25,000 instead of $22,000, so that their 40 percent interest would mean $10,000 each for Sergey and Dan, and our 10 percent interest would mean $2,500 each for Yefim and me. I disagreed with what they did, but I had no standing, and even if I had been on the board, I would have been outvoted. To tell the truth, I was glad to get a check for any amount, and I had to let it go, because father and son were working day and night for very low salaries, just $36,000 each that first year. They truly needed the extra money more than Yefim or I did. I didn't know it then, but this was an early indication of how Dan and Sergey would always treat their two small shareholders.

It's a slippery slope, the ways of questionable ethics. I knew they made me a consultant so they could play with the books, but I had no idea what was to follow in the years to come. No one did.

CHAPTER 16

FLASHBACK

"Now I lay me down to sleep. I pray the Lord my soul to keep. If I should die before I wake, I pray the Lord my soul to take."

I'm four years old. It was the night after my mother's funeral. Tucking me in, Aunt Estelle taught me to pray. She assured me my mother, Martha, was up in heaven watching over me, and even though she was no longer on earth to take care of me, no matter what, I would be fine. Each night at bedtime my aunt taught me to pray. Together, we asked for God's blessing on all the good people we knew in the world.

My brothers were babies. Alan was two; David, an infant. A year would go by before Dad would remarry. On a business trip back east, he would meet Pearl and be smitten. Pearl was young—twenty-three years old and seventeen years his junior—beautiful, street smart, and witty. Dad promised her the sun, moon, and stars if she would move from New York to California to become the mother of his three little children.

A bossy little kid, I was ruling the roost until Mother Pearl came along. She put me in my place in no uncertain terms.

My younger brothers looked up to me, as did their friends later on. Surrounded by boys in my youth, I was comfortable around them, and when we all grew up, I was comfortable around men. It was a man's world, especially back then, and I wanted to be part of it. But boy! As much as I tried, I certainly didn't know how.

Barely out of college, Pearl had no friends in Los Angeles, and to make matters worse, she was often lonely at night because Dad worked long hours. We had a nanny and a cook. Pearl kept busy by studying interior design. She tried and tried to have feelings for us, but that didn't come easily. After three years of marriage to my father, she got pregnant with my brother Neil, and we moved to a beautiful large house in the flats of Beverly Hills. After that, Pearl begged Dad to retire. They had enough money, she told him. So he did as she asked, and then he lost more than half his money in a bad investment. Suddenly we were middle class, living frugally when compared to many of our neighbors.

I wish I'd been closer to my stepmom. She took great care of us throughout the eighteen years she and Dad were married. She made sure we had the best doctors, clothes, and after school activities. She was beautiful and wise, but we weren't really close, and as I grew up we disagreed on many things. Appearances meant a lot to her, but not to me. I cared much more about books than whether my shoes were polished or my torn hem was properly sewn or held by a safety pin. She loved jewelry and gave me a gold charm bracelet on my sixteenth birthday. I seldom put it on. Shortly after I married Stan, she was diagnosed with breast cancer. Dad told us that it had metastasized in her bones and she was given six months to live.

I suppose I'll always rue the day I didn't let her buy us the furniture she wanted to give Stan and me for our first apartment. Even though her doctor didn't tell her she had terminal cancer, Pearl instinctively knew she was facing imminent death no matter how much we tried to convince her otherwise. She wanted so badly to decorate our apartment. Looking in a catalog at pictures of chairs she loved and wanted to buy for our first anniversary gift, I demurred. It caused her great pain. I didn't like the chairs and couldn't let her waste her money. *Thoughtless child . . .* I should have let her do it. She was, after all, a self-proclaimed interior designer. It was a selfish mistake to deprive her of the pleasure of giving us that gift, and then adding insult to injury by choosing Stan's Aunt Elsa to be our decorator. I deserved the anguish I felt the night the family came over for dinner and Pearl exclaimed, hiding her aching heart with surprise in her voice, "Oh, I see you got new chairs!" If she could only hear me, I would beg her forgiveness.

Mom, I'm so sorry. I never wanted to hurt your feelings. I'm sorry you're not well. If only I had the power to help you . . . I see your expression change in the middle of a sentence and can't imagine your silent suffering. The doctor told you it's just arthritis, but that's not what he told Dad. We're all liars now. We know you are dying. Are you afraid? Why can't we talk about this? Where are the words? Why aren't they said? I don't want you to die.

Indeed, where was my courage then, stuck in my head? The two of us were sitting in the den. Pearl was trying. Just forty-two years old, she knew what was going on.

"I'm sitting on a keg of dynamite," she said. But that's all she could say.

Stone cold reality. I couldn't deny it, but like a coward afraid to confront the truth, I couldn't acknowledge it either. We all tried to tell her it was nothing serious, and that she would be okay. Alone in her bedroom, she would cry. It's horrible to know your death is imminent, but even worse to have to face it alone.

She suffered horribly, and Dad suffered with her. A year or so later, Dr. Weinberg, Dad, and I walked the hallway of the hospital. "Perhaps we can remove her pituitary," the doctor offered. But it was too late for such a drastic measure. As I watched her, rolling her eyes and writhing in pain in her hospital bed, I begged God to help her. She looked like hell. Every now and then when the pangs would strike, she'd stare so hard at the heavens, her pupils would disappear. Stan's older brother, a pediatrician, advised a morphine drip. She wanted to be buried near Al Jolson at Hillside Memorial Park, at the top of the hill in the grass. She passed away on Mother's Day, 1965. Heavy hearted and grieving, we could not avoid the reality of the warmth of the sun on that bright spring day or the cheerful sounds of the chirping birds so utterly incompatible with our loss. Stan and I hadn't been married two years. Mother Pearl never got to see our children.

She hadn't given birth to me, but I became her legacy. It would be up to me, the designated matriarch, to keep the family together. I'd follow her footsteps. She would be my guide.

From adversity comes strength. I would be self-sufficient. I had to be.

I'd lost two mothers now. With a history like mine, one develops the ability to move through all sorts of obstacles, problems, and negative events, such as those I would encounter later in life. After the funeral, I started shopping at Mrs. Lindberg's Nutrition Center, where they sold organically grown fruits and vegetables, and in desperation, I read every book I could find on how to stay well. Stan's father and grandmother had had cancer, and later his mother would suffer from it as well. I worried, "Our children might not have good genes." I studied nutrition and began to proselytize, "Butter is good. It's margarine that's bad. Trans fat deprives your cells of oxygen." Ahead of my time, I tried to convince everyone, "Sodium nitrite is a deadly carcinogen." I canceled the monthly pesticide service. Friends referred to me as a health nut, yet decades would pass before what I was preaching in 1965 became accepted as common knowledge.

Not long after Pearl died, Dad started dating. He was a young man at fifty-nine, still attractive and financially comfortable. Women loved him, but he was picky, and he remained a widower for several years. It was Sally Crandall, a gorgeous strawberry blonde, who finally won his heart. He had her phone number a long time before he called. Apparently she had been expecting him to call her months prior. It was a short conversation that went something like this:

Bob: "Hello, Sally, this is Bob Schlossberg."

Sally: "Bob? You son of a bitch, you're calling now? What took you so long?"

Bob, laughing: "Give me your address. I'll be there in five minutes."

Sally was smart and funny, down to earth, easy-going, warm, and wise. She and Dad adored each other, and we adored her. They were married twenty-seven love-filled, fabulous years.

CHAPTER 17

EVERY MAN FOR HIMSELF, AND EVERY WOMAN

Even though I wasn't privy to the official board meetings at D & G, I visited the factory often. Sergey, Dan, and Yefim spoke English most of the time when I was there, but not always. They would lapse into Russian now and then, since it was easier for them, but whenever they spoke Russian in my presence, I was miserable. I was truly an outsider. They could have been talking about the weather, but if they were discussing business, I wanted to know. It was bad enough being the only woman in the group. I didn't feel secure when I didn't know what they were saying. No secrets, please, gentlemen. I was good at languages. Perhaps I should learn a little Russian? UCLA offered Russian classes an hour a day at 9:00 a.m., Monday to Friday. The campus was walking distance from my house. Anyone could attend for a fee. I would learn to read and write in Cyrillic. It would be fun. Unbeknownst to my Russian colleagues, I signed up and took classes. Russian isn't easy. It was four years of classes before I could understand enough to know the difference between when Sergey, Dan, and Yefim were talking about the weather and when more important things were on their minds. Truth be told, I never actually learned it well enough to speak it fluently.

Things at the company rolled speedily onward. By the end of the first year in business, D & G had four traveling salesmen, each with a full sample line of rings. Sales totaled over $1,200,000. Even I became a customer. I ordered many items for my clients and visited the factory at least once a week. Dan was rarely there, constantly on an airplane, selling and developing relationships with the largest jewelry companies in the country. The first two years, business jumped in quantum leaps. Married a very short time to bratty beautiful Regina but long enough to have two children, Dan knew he'd made a mistake. This was confirmed the day he came home early from a business trip. Approaching the house in a taxicab, he caught his wife making out with another guy in a car parked at the curb.

After their divorce, Dan rarely saw his children. His business took precedence. Traveling all week long, he was too tired on the weekend to deal with little kids. At the age of twenty-three, he was probably too young to want to be a father. He was far more interested in making money. By the end of the second year in business, 1993, D & G had fifty employees—casters, diamond setters, and polishers.

The company moved to larger quarters downtown, up the street from where it started. The profits appeared to be high, but the funds flowed out as fast as they came in. Because the sales constantly grew, there was never enough money to buy gold and diamonds to work with to manufacture the incoming orders. The company borrowed more and more money when the credit line was extended and extended again, as both payables and receivables grew constantly higher.

Sergey and Dan took bigger salaries, justified by the eleven-to-twelve-hour workdays. Yefim had convinced Dan and Sergey that all three of them should take more money, based upon gross sales, even though there was no money in the till. The saving grace was a new customer, Galaxy Diamonds, Inc., a major wholesale jewelry distributor located on the East Coast that sold to retailers across the country. Galaxy had salesmen traveling on the road from north to south and as far west as Chicago.

The owners of Galaxy Diamonds desperately needed a manufacturer and even agreed to provide the gold and the diamonds in advance so that D & G could produce the orders with contract labor only and without a large outlay of cash. The orders were so huge that D & G once again needed to rent additional space to accommodate more employees. The company leased not only all of the ninth floor they occupied, but also part of the tenth floor in the same building. More jewelers were hired, and the computerized system was upgraded.

At the end of the second year, D & G Mfg. again paid its shareholders, and again the accountant categorized it as consulting to avoid the adverse tax consequences had they declared a dividend.

That year I received a $15,300 "salary" for consulting, with a W2. Even though this didn't seem to be enough, and even though I had not given any useful consulting advice, I was still a very grateful shareholder. My investment was paying off.

At the end of 1993, when D & G expanded the space on the tenth floor, Yefim came to me to complain. He'd discovered through his bookkeeping that another company was using D & G's newly expanded premises without paying rent. The company was called A Galaxy of Bracelets. Yefim didn't know what they were doing on our premises, making jewelry for our customers and not paying us any rent. When he found out, he told me immediately. A Galaxy of Bracelets was a separate company owned solely by Dan and Sergey. Yefim and I were excluded. D & G lawyers created the company for the sole purpose of making bracelets for Galaxy Diamonds. When our biggest and most important customer, Galaxy Diamonds, was sending orders for bracelets, instead of producing the bracelets, Dan and Sergey gave the orders to their new company, A Galaxy of Bracelets, which they owned, just the two of them. When Yefim realized he and I were cut out of the deal, he came to me to ask what we should do about it. He was hopping mad.

How dare Dan and Sergey take company business away from the two of us? How dare they establish this separate company just for themselves? How dare they convert a customer of ours to an exclusive customer of their own?

Yefim was standing near my desk. I picked up the phone, dialed the factory, and asked for Sergey.

"Explain this to me, Sergey. Did you and Dan open another jewelry company without Yefim and me as your partners? Because you can't do that. That would be taking business away from us."

"We didn't do anything wrong," Sergey replied.

"You didn't do anything wrong? Yefim is here. He thinks you did. He says there's a new company making bracelets, thousands of them, and neither of us can benefit because it's a separate company where we're not part owners. Don't you know you can't do that? You can't just create another jewelry company for yourself and do business there. Jewelry is *our* business, and we have to be included. You can open up all the separate companies you want, as long as they aren't making jewelry. You can sell shoes for all I care. But you can't take jewelry business away from the two of us. That's just plain wrong! Yefim says your new company isn't even paying rent. You expanded your space, and D & G pays for it all. You can't own a separate company on our premises and make our company give you free rent. We won't tolerate it! We'll shut you down."

It was outrageous to siphon off profits from our company and even worse to have our company pay for the space they were occupying.

Sergey replied, "We're working so hard. It's not fair to share everything with you."

"It's not fair? I'll tell you what's fair! When the banks wouldn't lend you a single dollar and we gave you the money so you could buy gold, what was fair then? What was the risk two years ago, when D & G Jewelry was just an idea, with nothing more than a handful of purchase orders and no way to produce them? It was Yefim and I who provided the funds for your first orders. We took a chance with our money. We gave you money when no one else would. We didn't get any collateral. It wasn't a loan. It was an investment, an investment in the two of you. All we got is a piece of paper that gave us each 10 percent of the shares. You lived in a rented apartment and didn't even own your own refrigerator! We didn't know if we'd ever get our money back. And now that you're making money, you think you can cut us out of your profits? That's what's not fair! You think you can make us go away? Well, you can't."

Sergey's resentment was palpable. "How is it possible you each own 10 percent of everything we do? You own 10 percent of every table, every chair, every piece of inventory. We have to buy you out!"

"Buy us out then," I challenged, "if you can. But you can't create your own separate jewelry company and take away our business!"

I hung up and turned toward Yefim. "We are making money, aren't we? I don't want them to buy us out, do you?"

"We are making money," he said. "That's not a problem. We have a lot of profit, but we are growing up so fast there is no money in the bank. Maybe some day we can sell them back our shares, but not now. Now all I can do is make sure they pay us at the end of each year. We are in this together. I can check up and look over."

Yefim had my back even if his English wasn't perfect.

It was about this time that Dan and I had our first full-blown argument, at a trade show in Las Vegas, an argument that caused irreparable damage to my relationship with him. The confrontation arose over an invisibly set six-carat diamond ring.

Invisible setting, a technique developed in France in the eighteenth century, was difficult to do and beautiful to behold, requiring that diamonds sit side by side, with no space in between them and no visible metal holding them in place. At the time, only a jeweler trained in France would understand how to do this successfully, with specially cut square diamonds that could slip into a metal framework from below, so that only the solid diamond surface could be seen. It was a new look, it was labor intensive, and it was difficult to achieve. When I saw the first pictures of invisibly set wedding bands, I ordered them right away. The wedding band made of three rows was the one that sold the best, but my favorite was the wide wedding band made of five rows. It held six carats, it was expensive, and it was so new that I couldn't wait to have it in my collection. The price for six carats of diamonds would be high, but not too high for my clientele. I'd sell a few of them for sure. Dan's customers, on the other hand, ordered less expensive rings that were more for the masses. I had doubts he would sell the six-carat ring at all.

Dan had promised to make this ring for me to present to my customers at the JCK (Jewelers Circular Keystone) trade show in Las Vegas. I had the foresight to know the ring would be unusual and quite enticing. But when Dan saw the finished product, only then did he decide he wanted it for his own collection. The day before I left for the show, Dan told me the ring wasn't ready, but he would bring it to my booth on the morning the show opened. I knew the factory would stay open late that night to finish it. It was a prototype and needed to be perfect. The next morning, when the show opened, Dan came to my booth.

"I can't wait to see the ring," I said with great anticipation.

Dan replied, "It's not finished. They couldn't do it in time."

"Oh, come on, that's not possible. I don't believe you. They were finishing it yesterday. Give it to me. I know you have it!"

Dan shrugged his shoulders, a habit he had when he didn't want to answer.

"You know how important this is to me," I said. "Most of my customers are coming to this show, and this is my once-a-year chance to show it to them."

I paused. Dan remained silent.

"Give me the ring, Dan," I insisted. "I ordered it, and you promised it, so take it out of your pocket and give it to me."

Dan just stood there in my booth, and finally said unconvincingly, "I don't have it."

"You most certainly do have it. I've been patiently waiting for weeks to get it. I know they were working late last night, and you wouldn't come to Vegas without it, so give it to me."

Finally, completely exasperated, like a mother talking to her child, I demanded, "Empty your pockets!"

I must have said this three or four times before Dan emptied his pockets and gave me the ring. I was practically yelling at him in frustration. It was awful. In retrospect, I should not have forced his hand. Embarrassed and caught in a lie, he finally fetched the ring from his pocket with the snide comment, "I could sell more of these than you can." Even if he could have, that wasn't the point. I had ordered the ring to show to my customers, and if he had thought ahead of time, he would have made another one for his own line as well. The result of this confrontation was that we became silent adversaries. I had exposed him for the liar that he was. Sergey had no comment, none whatsoever. His allegiance lay with his son. Our friendship became ever more tenuous, which saddened me deeply.

Sergey didn't care. He was on the road to making money. Detached from all else, he turned his back on me, leaving me forlorn and alone without his support. They had convinced me to invest with them, but now they didn't need me anymore. My mere presence was a reminder that I was on easy street, taking a consulting fee but doing no work, while they put their heart and soul into building the business.

I must admit, though, as far as Dan was concerned, there was no one better at selling than he was. With his winsome way, he was a charmer. If you were subject to his patience and fortitude, his uncanny, intuitive ability to know what you wanted, and his desire to please you, you had to buy. He made you feel that it was always in your best interest to do so. If you wanted diamond tennis bracelets with a full carat of diamonds at a cost of $49.00 apiece—an impossible, incredible price—Dan would make them for you when no one else could. At retail you would then be able to double your money at $99.00 each, a price that would bring hoards of people at Christmastime. Each bracelet would have fifty small diamonds, continuously set all around the wrist. It would be 10 karat gold. No matter that the diamonds didn't shine, they were genuine diamonds. No matter that Dan didn't make money on these, he'd make money later on future business from the buyers who knew he had good deals for them. The gold was so thin and lightweight, and the diamonds so haphazardly set, surely the bracelets would break and stones would fall out after they'd been sold and worn a few times. Then when broken bracelets came back, the company would charge for all the repairs.

Galaxy Diamonds, Inc., our biggest customer, ordered 15,000 bracelets, to be delivered 5,000 at a time during the months of October, November, and December, with special ninety-day payment terms. After delivering on time each month, Dan became the go-to person for quantities large or small of whatever the customers needed at unbelievably low prices. Delivering on time with such special terms and pricing, Dan had solidified a relationship with the largest jewelry company in America that would last for many years to come. I watched and learned a lot from this young hustler, how he searched for diamond cutters from India and contrived to procure 15,000 carats of small full-cut diamonds at $19 a carat, how he negotiated and contracted with diamond setters to complete the orders at a fraction of the usual price. Since he was ordering large quantities from suppliers and promising his workers a secure job in the future, he got them all to do his bidding at the prices he needed to pay. I knew Dan was an opportunist who took advantage of others, but I never thought he was a crook. He was just a shrewd guy with an innate sense of what people wanted.

My apprehension receded as I watched this company grow in the blink of an eye. When he ran out of liquid cash, Dan asked me nicely, and I agreed to a ninety-day loan to cover the bracelet order. I was mesmerized by his prowess. Plus, I was glad he needed my help, and it was only for ninety days. I regretted our former confrontation over the six-carat ring and would have done even more for him, just to be treated well in return.

Ninety days came and went. More and more orders came in, and Dan needed the loan a little longer. He paid the interest, but it was years (years!) before I saw the principal, and only then because I placed orders with him and reduced what he owed me by not paying for what I purchased. By then he was borrowing elsewhere and far too busy to notice.

I did what I could to regain our former friendship. After our big fight, it was obvious that our objectives were not aligned. Even so, I wanted desperately to be a part of this Big Boy's World, which appeared to be so much more exciting than mine.

It was at my uncle's ninetieth birthday party in Wilmington, North Carolina, where I thought I might be able to do something to help Dan and the company, something he might appreciate. Stan and I flew across the country to celebrate with all the relatives. It was a lovely evening, with dinner and dancing. That night I met Bill Zimmer, my uncle's good friend and owner of a chain of jewelry stores. Bill was interested in seeing my collection at the upcoming annual trade show in Las Vegas, but he was even more interested in visiting the D & G factory and placing an order with Dan. I innocently arranged for them to meet, giving the Zimmers Dan's personal contact information. Little did I know this introduction would be the catalyst for a chain of events that would change the course of D & G forever after. If Dan could sell to the Zimmers, he wouldn't be so dependent on Galaxy.

Galaxy Diamonds had been taking orders and distributing D & G Jewelry over half the country, and Bill Zimmer had been one of Galaxy's big customers. When the Zimmers came to Los Angeles to buy from Dan directly, they were cutting out Galaxy, the middleman. Dan was tempted and decided to forge ahead, but he had to be careful, since Galaxy was by far his biggest customer. Galaxy, the company that had ordered 15,000 tennis bracelets, had its own team of salesmen traveling around the country, and even though the orders were huge, it was no longer enough for Dan, who was driven to increase sales year after year no matter what. He was dependent on

Galaxy now, because they fronted the gold and the diamonds and kept his factory busy, but what he really wanted was to have his own team of salesmen traveling around the country producing orders to fill. This would be his big chance to break away from dependency on Galaxy. Zimmer's orders would surely be substantial. So Dan's ambition got the best of him, and at the risk of "biting the hand that feeds you," he made a decision that some might consider unethical. After all, it was Galaxy that had put him "on the map" so to speak, and if word got out that D & G was indeed selling directly to Galaxy's customers, Galaxy would drop D & G for sure. Nevertheless, Dan would find a way to sell directly to Galaxy's customers surreptitiously, by using a different company name. The name was D & S Trunk Shows.

At trunk shows around the country, individual customers would bring their old rings to their favorite jewelry store to have their center stones remounted in a new D & G design. Zimmer would advertise the event, and D & S would send salesmen with new settings and center stones so clients would have a large selection. This way D & S began selling to Zimmer's stores, and Galaxy never knew D & G was involved. While it was wrong to cut out the middleman, everything else was on the "up and up," at least in the beginning. I thought a lot about my role in this. What if I hadn't given Zimmer Dan's personal information? It would simply have taken Dan a little longer to get where he wanted to go. This was just the beginning. In no time, he would have salesmen nationwide, running trunk shows and selling directly to large chain jewelry stores from coast to coast.

With so many orders to fill, cash flow was tighter than ever. There were always more dollars going out than coming in. Yefim's creative accounting was an enigma to me. At the end of every fiscal year, I would receive the company financial statement. Normally I wouldn't have trouble figuring out year-end financials, but in the case of D & G Jewelry, it was impossible to understand all the line items. The financial statements showed large sums to and from shareholders and related parties, but the names of the parties were never given. There were many activities cloaked in general terms, and getting an adequate explanation for what was actually happening was impossible. I knew Yefim was determined to avoid taxes, and I didn't like his scheming, wangling, and manipulating the books. Indeed, the books were impossible for a neophyte like me to understand. The company had sold over $2,000,000 in its second year and should have turned a profit, but it didn't. Yefim, our chief financial officer, was quite adept at avoiding taxable profits. Retained earnings swelled during the year but always disappeared by year's end. On September 30, 1995, the D & G quarterly financial statement showed retained earnings of $1,881,742, but by year's end, this amount was stated to be next to nothing.

Indeed, Yefim knew how to manipulate the books in such a way that all the profits disappeared at the end of the fiscal year, only to reappear the following year on a quarterly statement. I didn't receive quarterly statements and didn't see any of this. I knew only that the company was making money and spending it all, and that our consulting fees were part of the expenses.

To tell the truth, I believed that Yefim was using legal loopholes. I started wondering if my agreement to be a passive investor, and not take a position on the board of directors, was to my detriment. It was profoundly frustrating. I wanted to know what was really going on. Yefim was playing with the books, and I was too naïve to figure it out. To placate me, he kept assuring me the company was making money. He also made sure I received compensation. At the end of the first year, I got $1,000 toward a return on my investment. The second year, I received $15,300 as a "salary" for consulting, with a W2. Subsequently the company paid me handsomely—many times my original investment—for my advice, which they didn't need, want, or ask for. As such, these payments were deductible to the corporation. Yefim did what he could to create deductions and avoid corporate taxes. Paying for his fancy vacations and my consulting advice would justify the officers' enormous salaries and bonuses, which had become so huge they absorbed all the profits. Without profits there was no corporate tax, and there was never anything left over for a dividend.

Accounting was Yefim's specialty. Characterizing payments to shareholders incorrectly was certainly not kosher. To the extent it wasn't legal, I wasn't sure. I had no proof that what they were doing on the books was a crime. Certainly, as a shareholder, I deserved to be paid. I rationalized that by paying me in this manner, they were trying to be fair to me. I cannot say I'm without flaws or that I acted properly, but I did my best at the time. They wanted to pay me as a consultant, and I acquiesced without ever telling Stan.

CHAPTER 18

SUDDEN WEALTH

D an never got over his anger toward me, or his resentment
over the fact that I'd become a proud shareholder. He and
his father were faced with the unavoidable dilemma that, while
making their fortune, their efforts made money for me as well.
"Uncle" Yefim would visit my showroom occasionally to keep
me posted about the company's progress. It was only at the end
of each fiscal year that I was given the financial statements to
review. At the end of the fiscal year in 1993, I became quite
troubled by this entity, D & S, whose expenses were paid by
D & G, whose profits were high but somehow camouflaged
or concealed because of additional salaries and payments to
unnamed related parties, and whose activities caused inventories to soar. Dan used to tell me he hated having inventory
on hand. He used to make merchandise to fill orders, and
everything was presold. Not any more. Inventory on hand grew
and grew. It was impossible to understand. It was worse in
1994, and even worse in 1995. Apparently some stores were
permitted to return what they couldn't sell, as long as they kept
ordering new things. Each year the company safes contained

more and more returned goods. Yefim insisted the company was making money, all the while manipulating the numbers to show it wasn't. To make matters worse, inventories were never actually physically counted, no matter how many times I requested it, and no matter how often I complained. Even years later when D & G borrowed millions of dollars, and the lender demanded that physical inventories be taken, it never actually happened. Instead of a physical count, inventories were always estimated and "guess-timated."

By mid 1993, sales at D & G soared to $3,400,000, and by the end of that year, the euphoria at the factory was undeniable. This was success on a speeding train that would only go faster and faster. Greed and ambition reigned supreme, and the excitement at the factory was monumental. There was a lavish Christmas party and another party for Sergey's birthday in 1996 that spared no expense and even went to extremes. Surprised to see such incredible waste of company money, I was glad at least to be invited. By then, Dan and I were barely on speaking terms. While the music played, the exotic food, drinks, and band at Sergey's birthday party went on for hours. When the guests had their fill of meat-filled pastry appetizers and caviar, we were served six colossal shrimp in elaborate crystal bowls, each shrimp the size of a lobster tail, each a meal in itself. This was followed with delicate slices of smoked salmon, sturgeon, and white fish. Then potatoes were served with lavish portions of prime beef filet, exotic fruits, and more. Bottles of liquor on the tables were replaced when empty, along with the platters of food, which arrived one course at a time. Even a large appetite would have difficulty consuming so much in one evening. The liquor flowed like water. Then, before midnight, to show off extreme wealth, enormous trays of exotic pheasant were elaborately presented. It was beyond extravagant—ridiculous, vulgar even. After this ostentatious party, Dan's family—even the children—were seen only in designer clothing, driving around in fancy cars, attending private schools, purchasing Beverly Hills residences, hiring nannies, and more. In 1994, Dan and Sergey each took home close to a million dollars in income. They stopped paying Yefim and me for consulting. Yefim would travel around the world on the D & G Jewelry payroll, but I would receive nothing further from D & G at all.

With the officers raising their own salaries to new heights, Dan told me to my face that I had already received enough in return for my investment and that, really, I didn't need more.

Brazen faced, cocky, and insolent, he said, "It's time to build equity in the company, and next year that's what we'll do."

"Good," I replied. "If you build equity, I'll be able to sell my shares for what they're truly worth."

One day, during the company's fifth year in business, a letter arrived from the attorney who worked for Yefim and also for D & G Jewelry. The letter stated that the shares I held in the company were not valid. However, the letter also said that D & G was willing to buy my "bogus" shares for $100,000. Reading this utter nonsense, I could not believe their slimy tactics. I called Sergey, of course, and accused him and his son of an attempt to cheat me, but they both pretended to know nothing of this letter from their lawyer.

"What letter? We didn't send you a letter," they professed.

Livid, I drove to the factory to show them the letter in person. "Can you honestly, truly tell me I am not a shareholder here?" I asked. No one could. Unable to look me in the eye, they insisted they knew nothing about it. But of course, they did. Instructing his lawyer to send me that letter was simply another one of Dan's desperate attempts to remove me.

I demanded and, within days, received a second letter from the same attorney, stating that the first letter was sent in error and that my shares indeed were valid. *Nice try, Dan,* I thought. *By the way, you are still using my credit line.* Truth be told, I was glad Dan was using my credit line. I longed for a meaningful connection and thought in some way that needing the use of my credit line was proof they still needed *me.*

But in fact, they didn't need *me* at all any more. It became quite apparent that Dan wanted me out, no matter what it would require. I prevailed upon Sergey and "Uncle" Yefim to maintain a cordial communication. Sergey was not only over-worked trying to keep up with continuously expanding orders, but also overstressed by the large company debt and the continuously expanding payables. He simply couldn't fathom how much money they owed, and he worked ever harder to make more. As stressed as he was, he admired his son's ambition and let him run the show, which was to my detriment, because Dan certainly did not give up his intentions to eliminate me.

At this point, Dan found himself with a considerable amount of excess inventory, and the D & S salesmen invited their wholesale accounts to take merchandise on consignment without paying for it unless it was sold. As a result, inventory was constantly moving about the country from one customer to another, without an invoice but just a memorandum that stated the goods belonged to D & G until paid for. In spite of this, D & S was making money, and Dan did not want to share the profit. He couldn't eliminate Yefim, because Yefim was at every board meeting and wouldn't stand for it. Hell-bent on depriving me of the D & S profit, Dan, Sergey, and Yefim convinced the D & G lawyers to convert D & S Trunk Shows to a separate corporation, with Dan, Sergey, and Yefim as the only shareholders. I was not informed of this and thought all along that the D & S entity was still 10 percent mine. I certainly could not decipher anything to the contrary from the financial statements, with line items such as "to and from related parties." There was no way to know that the trunk shows were no longer a part of D & G or that D & S had become a completely separate corporation in which I had no ownership. Sadly, I instinctively knew that I was being treated unfairly and kept in the dark, and again, there was nothing I could do about it.

Or was there? Could I just walk away? If they hadn't achieved astonishing success, I certainly would have walked away. I'd invested in other businesses before, such as a restaurant that lost money, and I'd simply let it go. But successes like D & G are hard to achieve. When you take a chance, when you risk hard earned, after-tax capital, if you're lucky, you hit pay dirt once or twice in a lifetime. I deserved to be compensated commensurate with the risk I had taken at a time when they had nothing, a time when no one else would lend them a dime. It would have been foolish to walk away.

Dan decided to hire a director for his newly incorporated D & S, a salesman from New York who appeared to have great qualifications. To induce this man and his wife to move to Los Angeles, Dan promised them the sun, moon, and stars, or should I say a home, a new Jaguar, $100,000 a year in cash off the books, and an all-expense-paid American Express Card. The wife was put on the D & G payroll, even though she never worked there.

With Yefim handling the books and Dan selling on the road, D & G experienced continued success. Sales in 1994 were $24,900,000; and in 1996 alone, they reached $92,000,000. Dan and Sergey's income skyrocketed, starting in 1992 at $36,000 per year, passing $200,000 per year by 1994, and reaching over $850,000 by 1996. One might ask how a company can grow so fast without equity. Beginning in 1996, Dan factored every invoice the day he shipped the goods. So even though sales were in the millions, the company owed millions to Equity Factors, a lender that paid D & G immediately eighty percent of every invoice the day after every package was shipped.

Verily, Dan had lied to me. He never had any intention of building equity, even when annual sales approached $100,000,000. True to his word, he no longer paid me consulting fees. I waited. And I watched. And I waited some more. Three years went by, and there was no equity. Had there been equity, my shares would have had real value, and the company would have been attractive enough that outsiders would want to own it. But Dan and his family never built any equity and continued to line their own pockets instead.

It was true that with all my previous "consulting advice," I received several times my money back. But that's not the point. The point was that four years prior I had taken an enormous risk, a leap of faith, with the chance of great reward one day when the business would grow. I was, in fact, a start-up investor with 10 percent ownership of the company. Defenseless and vulnerable, I watched silently from 1995 to 1998, despondent and sick at heart, because, of course, equity never happened, I received no compensation, and as a small shareholder, I could do nothing about it.

CHAPTER 19

ABCDEFG

At the rate Dan and his family were spending company money, if they were to build equity, it would take a while. In the meantime, I continued to focus on my own business at Avanti and Adriana K.

I'd been in the business several years without ever having studied at the Gemological Institute of America, where students learned all about how to judge and grade gemstones and diamonds. I didn't think it was necessary for me. I was a wholesaler who sold diamonds as part of my business, but I wasn't a diamond dealer who sold only diamonds. Most diamond dealers were schooled and generally reliable when they described what they had to offer. However, it was always better to sell diamonds that had a grading report from the GIA. The grading report described a diamond's four major qualities: color, clarity, cut, and carat weight. It contained other details as well and included a description of the flaws and a map of the interior of the stone to indicate where the flaws were located. These factors determine the price on the Rapaport List, which is actually a four-page list, published bi-monthly, that states the prices of diamonds recently sold. Since 1978, dealers all over the world have relied on the Rapaport List as the authoritative guide for the current diamond prices based on the four C's. In fact, ever since it was created, everyone in the business buys and sells their stones at various discounts off "the Rap sheet," and it's not uncommon to hear dealers offer diamonds at 20 percent or more below the listed prices.

Whenever a customer came to me in search of a larger diamond, I jumped at the chance to help. Dealing in larger stones was definitely a field dominated by men, and it felt quite special to be in the midst of it. One day a potential customer and his fiancée walked into the showroom, looking for a four-carat diamond. They wanted a high-quality round with a grading report from the GIA. This would be a major sale.

Diamonds come in many colors, but the ones most commonly accepted for engagement rings are white. There are many shades of white diamonds, and most people cannot discern the difference between one shade of white and another. A grading report from a gem lab will state the degree of whiteness with alphabet letters from D to Z. (There is no A, B, or C designation.) Stones labeled D, E, and F are basically colorless and considered by most people to be the most beautiful, since color impedes the refraction of light and detracts from the brilliance. In fact, D, E, and F stones seem to disappear when dropped in a clear glass of water. They are also rare. Far more common would be the designation of G, which is considered to be a very fine white. The further one goes into the alphabet, the more color the stone is said to contain. Stones labeled X, Y, or Z definitely appear yellow, whereas the whiter diamonds are given a letter designation from D through I. Only with J color diamonds can one discern a tinge of yellow in the body of the stone.

The flaws inside a stone are also noted on a grading report, according to intricate criteria that affect the stone's beauty.

"Flawless" diamonds are rare and expensive, whereas "included" diamonds are plentiful and cheaper. Designations are stated on a scale from internally flawless to highly included. Very Slight inclusions (VS clarity) cannot be seen with the naked eye, and often even Slight Inclusions (SI clarity) cannot be seen with the naked eye either. Flaws located in the top center section of the stone under the flat "table" affect the refraction of light, scintillation, and brilliance to a greater degree than flaws located elsewhere.

Grading reports today describe how a stone is cut. Back in the day, we had to judge this for ourselves. The cut is extremely important. I could write an entire chapter about symmetry and how the width and depth of a diamond affect its beauty. Proper proportions and polish will give a stone its greatest fire, but proportions are definitely part of the cut.

On this particular day, I didn't have any large diamonds in stock, so when my customer asked for a four-carat round one, I called my suppliers to see what was available. Most independent jewelers would do the same, since it's certainly not practical for jewelers to keep all sizes and qualities in stock, and almost every diamond dealer will readily consign them as needed. It takes a lot of capital to own them outright and to insure them as well.

I knew Irving K., one of the biggest sellers of GIA diamonds in Los Angeles at the time. He was an older man, had been in the business for decades, was highly thought of by many, and all his stones had GIA grading reports. A likeable guy, who was also quite savvy, he gave out his diamonds right and left to all the dealers on the street with merely their signature and a handshake. Everyone dealt with him, and I did too, until he did me wrong.

The diamond Irving gave me was perfect for my customer. No one could refute its beauty.

"This stone doesn't have a GIA report," he told me. "But it's a rare beauty."

"I thought all your diamonds had a grading report, Irving."

"Not this one. I would say it's I color, VS1 clarity. It's the only four-carater I've got right now. Show it to your customer and see if they like it."

I thought Irving had just purchased the stone and hadn't had time to send it to the GIA for grading yet. He gave me the diamond on my signature. There was mutual trust. If the customer didn't like it, I'd bring it back.

I was a fairly good judge of a diamond's interior flaws, but color grading stumped me. I couldn't tell the difference between an H and an I or between an I and a J. There was such a slight difference between these white colors. Irving was the real expert. With so many years of experience, certainly his knowledge was exceptional. When a major dealer like Irving says a diamond is an I, you tend to believe him, because you don't know half as much as he does, especially if you're a newbie with diamonds, which I was. Even so, no matter what color it was, this diamond was truly beautiful.

I presented the stone to my client and his fiancée and told them what Irving had declared to me. It was I color, VS1 clarity. I knew they would love it. Checking the Rapaport List for H, I, and J stones, they knew the price was low. They bought the diamond without hesitation, and I designed a gorgeous ring. In the meantime, while the ring was being made, I sent the diamond to GIA to get the stone graded.

When the diamond came back from GIA three weeks later, it was judged to be J color, not I. I told my customer he didn't have to buy it, since I'd sold it to him as an I.

"I'll give you a refund in full," I offered.

"I don't want a refund," he said. "We love the stone. I paid in advance, and now I want a discount."

There wasn't enough profit to give him the discount he wanted.

I went to see Irving. If Irving would lower his price, since the stone wasn't what he said it was, I could close the deal. That's when I found out that Irving had lied to me. With his years of expertise, he had judged the stone to be an I. He purchased the diamond at the price of an I, sent it to GIA, and when GIA graded it harshly as a J, he couldn't go back and insist that they were wrong. They never change their decisions. Not wanting to lose money on his investment in the stone, Irving tore up the GIA report and told me it was I color without a grading report.

How stupid of me not to tell Irving I was going to send it to GIA! All his other stones have grading reports. Why wasn't I suspicious?

I'd been an easy target, a guileless woman easily misled. Many experts would have thought the stone was I color. On its face, it certainly appeared unquestionably white. But that was not how the GIA graded it. Here in California, when the GIA grades a stone to be J color, it will always be J. My client took me to small claims court. He had no case, since I'd offered him a full refund. When he lost, he filed against me again, only this time, in regular court. He wanted to keep his gorgeous ring and get me to pay him $1,700. Sadly, I had to do so. He was a lawyer representing himself. Stan was too busy to represent me, and it made no sense for me to hire a lawyer.

I was upset with myself but also blamed Irving, a liar, a scam artist, and a villain who used my lack of expertise to his advantage. It seemed I was out of my league here. I was lucky it didn't cost me a whole lot more.

Clearly, I needed an education in diamonds. I took the time to learn, and it was time well spent, to say the least. One learns a lot about diamonds by taking the time to look at them, to *really* look at them under a fluorescent light and a ten-power microscope. The more you look into the body of a diamond, the more you can discover about it. It would take a while, but I was determined to become a self-taught gemologist. In those days, you could find me at my desk for hours at a time, loupe in one hand and tweezers in the other, as I studied and compared stones under a fluorescent light. I learned to judge them fairly well. I became adept at sorting the smaller ones for my mountings. It was time-consuming, but I insisted on doing this myself in order to know the exact quality of the finished product. Throughout this process, Stan watched with quiet approval. I didn't attend classes at the GIA the way my brother Neil would do, but I would bet more than half of diamond dealers today never took the classes either. For sure, Sergey and Dan never took them.

Learning how to judge diamonds was not the only lesson I needed. One might think that because I handled repairs for my clients, I might notice when my own diamond ring needed attention. There's an old expression that the shoemaker's children have no shoes—understandable, since their father is making shoes for everyone else and has no time to make them. In my case, my personal jewelry needed repair, and I was so busy making jewelry for others that I neglected my own. The jeweler who had been doing simple repairs for my clients noticed that my engagement ring had suffered some wear and tear.

"How many years have you been wearing that ring every day?" he asked.

"Twenty-five," I answered.

"It's time to make a new setting. The platinum is brittle and can break. If it does, you could lose your center stone, or even the entire ring."

I was busy. I didn't have time to take care of my jewelry right then. Anyway, the ring seemed okay to me. At least, not having examined it myself, I hoped it was okay. I suppressed the thought, *Maybe repairs are slow now and he's looking for business?* And I went off to San Francisco to do another show. Of course, I should have listened.

We were setting up the booth, and I needed to put up the lights by attaching them to the poles around the booth. But first, the poles, which were on stanchions sticking out in the aisle, had to be moved, and I had to unplug the wiring. The wire was stretched to the max, and the plug was stuck. I had to use great force to pull it out of the outlet. My hand hit the pole with a bang, but oddly the blow didn't hurt my hand. I thought nothing of it. It didn't occur to me that it was my ring that hit the pole. We finished our work and went back to a friend's house for dinner. Stan would be flying up for the weekend to join us, along with our daughter Pam, who was currently going to school at UC Berkeley, a short distance away.

We were sitting at the dinner table when Stan looked at me quizzically. I was resting my left hand on my cheek. "What happened to your ring?" he asked. I looked at my hand. The ring looked really strange. The center diamond was gone!

How come I hadn't noticed this? Was I really that tired?

I decided to go back to the convention center immediately to look for the stone. The place was closed, but the guards let me in because I showed them my badge and told them I had left my medicine in the booth. One of the guards accompanied me to the booth, where I searched everywhere for the diamond, pretending I was looking for my prescription pills. I even searched the wastebasket in the women's restroom. I didn't find the diamond, and left utterly disappointed. I prepared signs to hang the following day on doors throughout the convention center, offering a reward of $1,000 for the return of the diamond. No one came forward. On Monday, Stan notified our private insurance company. They would send a check for $12,000, about half of the current replacement value.

Lesson learned: Reappraise your diamonds at least once every two years. And listen to your jeweler as well.

The entire week in San Francisco I felt as if I had a giant pit in my stomach. Sales were strong, but having lost my diamond, I had to pretend to be happy. Finally the show closed, and it was time to pack up and fly home. A young man our daughter was dating came in from Berkeley to help us pack up. While unplugging the lights, he saw something scintillating on the rug under the table near the pole and stanchion. He picked it up and threw it in my lap. "I guess you'll be glad to see this!" he exclaimed. I felt it land on my skirt. Unbelievably, it was my diamond! I wrote the young man a check for $1,000. Accepting it, he said, "I'd rather have your daughter."

Was it all sheer luck? Or was my mother up in heaven watching over me?

When the check arrived from the insurance company, I was truly glad to return it, asking only for them to pay for a new setting, which they did.

Not everyone collects the insurance money when they suffer a loss. Stan's Aunt Elsa had magnificent jewelry, including a ring with an 18 carat emerald cut diamond from Harry Winston. Whenever she wore it, I couldn't help thinking how lifeless it was. After she passed away, Stan and Uncle Mike were the executors of her estate. The diamond needed an appraisal, as it was to be sold.

I suggested taking the diamond to the GIA, which was then located in Santa Monica.

"Let me take the diamond ring to GIA," I said to Stan. "It should have a diamond grading report to confirm the color and clarity."

How wise is Stan. He didn't want trouble with Uncle Mike. "No," he said. "Let Uncle Mike have someone appraise it, along with the antiques and the paintings."

I felt a bit slighted, because my expertise wasn't taken seriously, and my services were free. But this was Stan's family, and if he wanted me to stay out of their business, I didn't really mind.

Uncle Mike called an appraiser to get an expert opinion before deciding what to do next. The appraiser at first thought the diamond was a D flawless, perfectly colorless and perfectly clear, which was in keeping with all the other possessions that were quite valuable. At the end of the day, just before leaving, the appraiser took out his diamond-testing device to check the stone again. Imagine! The diamond wasn't real! It was a fake! The real stone could have been switched years before when Aunt Elsa had her ring sized. I certainly dodged a bullet there. Had I taken the ring to GIA, Uncle Mike would have blamed me. We would never have been able to convince him that I wasn't the one who switched it.

CHAPTER 20

TRUST AND DECEPTION

I f Dan and Sergey were not building equity, I was building
my own at Avanti. D & G wasn't paying me any more, and
since I couldn't do anything about it, I tried to keep a positive
attitude and bide my time.

I was walking along Rodeo Drive one day and came
across the window of a tiny little jewelry shop close to Wilshire
Blvd. Quickly analyzing the window display to determine if
the owners would want to buy from me, I looked beyond to
see that the store inside was filled with customers, and all of
them appeared to be Asian. At the time there were hoards
of Japanese tourists flooding our shores. The yen was strong,
and for the Japanese our prices were cheap. Two girls stood
outside the front door speaking fluent Japanese and enticing
potential buyers to come inside. When the buyers entered, the
salesgirls, who were also Japanese, showed the buyers beautiful
baubles at what appeared to be, for them, extremely low prices.
Curious to see all the action, I went inside the store as well. I
met the owners and told them if they needed 18 karat jewelry
on a short term consignment, they should come to my office,

a stone's throw away. I would give them jewelry to sell, and if it didn't sell quickly, they could return it.

The next day this little "mom and pop" store had its windows filled with my jewelry. The pieces sold so fast that at least twice a week I replenished their stock. They paid immediately for everything they sold. Our relationship lasted for years until they finally sold their lease for close to half a million dollars to their neighbor, Bulgari, who not only wanted to expand but also wanted them out of the way. But in the meantime, for years I would walk on the street and say in jest, "I have a store on Rodeo Drive, and I don't pay any rent!"

While it was nice to have several clients in my hometown, I really loved meeting jewelers all across America. One of my customers I met at the JCK Show was Abe Katz, a nice man from Houston, Texas. Abe was a big, confident man who liked to talk about his successful business and wealthy clientele. He placed a large order, and I liked him immediately. I checked him out thoroughly in June before sending him the goods he wanted in October. Everyone said he was credit worthy. Everyone liked him as much as I did. But I stopped liking him the following January when he couldn't or wouldn't pay his bills. Then I truly disliked him in February and March when he refused my phone calls.

To be fair, Abe's recent problems weren't entirely his fault, although anyone in business should have a sure-fire way to pay back bank loans. Abe was heavily borrowed and dependent on his bank, and his bank was even more dependent on the price of Texas real estate, having lent large sums to the commercial sector. In the late 1980s in Houston, office vacancies soared, bank deposits decreased, and the result led to a banking crisis. Abe's loan was callable. When his bank called his loan, he had no available cash. Not only couldn't he pay his suppliers, but soon he might not be able to pay his rent.

In this business we do a lot of networking with other manufacturers and wholesalers. When I couldn't reach Abe by phone, I contacted his references again and found out he was dragging his feet everywhere, not paying anyone as promised. Finally I heard his bank had called his loan. He could be out of business any day. Hearing this news, without waiting another moment or discussing my plans with anyone, I booked an early flight to Houston the very next morning to catch Abe by surprise in his store. A face-to-face meeting would take only an hour or two. I'd fly there and back and be home in time for dinner. If he didn't have the cash, at least I might get my goods back.

A short flight and taxi ride, and I was there. A young woman greeted me.

"Is Abe here?" I asked.

The woman called upstairs. Thinking I was a customer, Abe came down right away. Needless to say, he was surprised to see me.

"Abe," I said, "you won't pay your bills, and you won't take my calls, and if you can't pay me, I want my goods back."

Abe replied, "I'm not sure I have much left. Almost everything sold."

These words were familiar to me, as it had happened more than once with customers in trouble, who sold my jewelry and paid their bills with the proceeds instead of paying me.

"If you have anything left, I'll take it back," I said, "and then give me other merchandise you have, at your cost to make up the difference. I just can't afford to lose the $128,000 you owe me."

Fortunately, Abe didn't put up a fight and was most amenable. He gave me the keys to his showcases and told me to take whatever I thought I could sell. Two hours later I left, goods in hand, hopped on the next plane, and came home. In time, I sold all his pieces.

My son Randall told his friends, "My mom is so nice to her customers. Too bad her suppliers aren't as nice to her." In later years, he would say, "My mother is not one who takes no for an answer, and somehow she proves her doubters wrong, again and again."

Around this time, my office manager told me she wanted to retire. Without an assistant in the showroom, I asked Margo to come to Los Angeles for a few weeks until I could find someone to take over permanently. Margo had helped me just recently at a trade show for Adriana K in Atlanta. I felt confident she could run both businesses without my constant surveillance. She agreed to fly in from Northern California and stay with us as a houseguest for a few weeks.

With Margo in charge of the showroom, I felt free to run errands during the day. In retrospect, this was a mistake, but Stan and I were remodeling our kitchen at home, and it was time to choose the granite slabs, tile, and fixtures. One day I had to leave the showroom for several hours, and when I returned, Margo was distraught.

"Adrienne, I don't know how to tell you this," she said sheepishly. "A woman rang the bell and I let her in. She looked at several things and really liked a necklace, the 18 karat one from Italy with the diamonds in front."

"Your favorite necklace? The one you love so much?"

"Yes," she said. "The lady also wanted to get a large diamond, so I went in the back to get the Rapaport price list. When I came back out to the front, she said she was going to buy the necklace for sure and just needed to go to the bank to get cash. After I pushed the buzzer to let her out, I went to get the necklace to put it back in the showcase and saw that it was missing from the back shelf, where I had set it down. While I was in the back, I guess she walked around the showcase and took it off the shelf, and then she left for the bank but didn't come back."

I asked Margo for a description of this woman. Her description was vague—a large woman, with worn out shoes, wearing a scarf on her head. I wanted to know why the closed circuit camera hadn't been turned on. I didn't really believe Margo's story, especially because she had let it be known that the stolen item was her favorite piece of all. The necklace at cost was worth $3,000, less than my insurance deductible, but one of the prettiest and among the more expensive pieces in the collection. I wondered if Margo had taken the necklace and shipped it to herself surreptitiously. She couldn't afford to pay for it. I didn't have the nerve to tell her that her story was suspicious, and I did not search her belongings.

If shoplifting is part of the cost of doing business, you can't afford such losses. Why are you so blind? Why can't you let Margo go?

I thought I couldn't do without her.

On paper, the Adriana K wholesale business was beginning to make a little money, finally, after its second year. However, all the profits were in the receivables, and I couldn't find a way to get my hands on the cash. There were no fewer than seven accounts in Miami, Boca Raton, and Palm Beach that were not paying in a timely fashion. In fact, most were overdue more than ninety days, and one of the bigger accounts was a full year past due. I was becoming increasingly uncomfortable about these receivables, especially when I had to fly to Florida, rent a car, and tempt the owners with more merchandise just to get checks for what was past due. My banker had offered a large credit line to grow the business, but as time went on, I became more and more reluctant to use it. It seemed as though I was funding everyone else's business with money I was borrowing, and then I'd have to beg for payment like a pauper. My buyers were using me and taking advantage of my good nature. How much longer would I put up with this? Was this the type of business one would want for one's children? Why was I having so much trouble with my receivables, while Dan seemed to have no problem with his?

I certainly enjoyed going to the jewelry shows in Switzerland and Italy to search for new designers, and I actually did fill a particular "niche" that my clients always needed. My eye for upcoming trends never failed me. Yet, increasingly, the jewelers wanted me to send them merchandise on a consignment basis, so that they weren't committed to buying what didn't sell. Or when buying new merchandise, they always had a few pieces of unsold, year-old stock they wanted to return for credit against new items. In the past, when buyers got stuck with old merchandise, they simply put it on sale. Those days were gone. This business was much harder now. The future appeared grim. In the meantime, my trade shows on the west coast in Los Angeles, San Francisco, and Seattle, were fairly successful with relatively low margins and very few receivables. As difficult as it was to stay in business, I wasn't quite ready to give it all up.

And yet, I was tired all the time. When I'd ask Stan, "How would you feel if I stopped working?" he would never answer this question. He knew this was a decision I had to make on my own.

It was Sergey who told me about Vera. Her husband was a jeweler from Kiev in Ukraine, and they knew each other well. Vera came for her interview and seemed like a lovely person, but her English was spotty. In Ukraine, she had been an electrical engineer. Although she had few qualifications, she was willing to work hard. She had a quick mind. She was good with numbers, had an exceptional work ethic, and was completely trustworthy. I loved her open, candid demeanor and hired her immediately. Each morning she would take two buses from home, traveling well over an hour to arrive early. She would spend most of the morning studying the computer, learning its ins and outs. I watched her brilliant mind absorb the language like a sponge and was amazed how she tackled each task and anticipated every need. In short, she was a unique and rare find.

Vera hadn't been with me more than two months, when the first of two challenges arose. The first one occurred at the San Francisco Show, where another expensive piece of jewelry mysteriously disappeared. It was a ring Sergey had given me to sell.

Sergey had made a large onyx and diamond ring for a client who didn't accept it. He thought perhaps we could find a customer to buy it. It was beautifully made, but it was massive, heavy, and frankly, quite difficult to wear. Sergey gave it to us before the show, and when Vera and I first saw it, we almost burst out laughing. We debated whether or not to take it with us. Who would buy it? It didn't belong with the collection. It was borderline ugly, and also expensive. Our collection was huge, almost unmanageable, and we didn't need another ring like that at the time. However, just before leaving for San Francisco, we decided to bring it. We would see many customers, and one never knew. There was always that slim chance it would sell. Margo and Elsa and Vera would all be there to work. It was, after all, a busy show.

On the first day, we couldn't find an appropriate place for Sergey's unusual ring in our showcases, so we put it in the duplicate box on the back table. Margo tried it on and fell in love with it. "This is a great ring," she said, looking at her hand and admiring her finger.

On the third day of the show, I thought I'd show the ring to a client with large fingers. I looked in the box of rings, but it wasn't there. In fact, the ring was nowhere to be found. We searched everywhere, but it was gone.

I was livid.

You can take an inventory count every day, if the collection is manageable. We took a physical count twice a year, and it was a lengthy process that took two people an entire day to complete. Yet lately after each physical count, I'd be missing thousands of dollars of inventory. In fact, the most recent loss was over $18,000. I simply could not account for it. Yes, we had some cash sales, but those items were accounted for. This was so disheartening, especially because I'd put my heart and soul into the business. Surely there must be something wrong. There was only one show where nothing went missing, a small show in Atlanta where Margo and I had worked together. But right now, at this San Francisco Show, no one had even shown Sergey's ring to anyone. It had been in the box of duplicates, on the back table, or so we thought. Every night at closing, that box had gone to security lock-up along with everything else. This disappearance, of a ring we thought nobody wanted and nobody wanted to show, was the last straw.

I took Margo aside and without hiding my feelings told her in no uncertain terms I was sick of dealing with missing merchandise after every show.

She immediately piped up, "You're not missing inventory every show. You weren't missing anything after the show we did together in Atlanta."

Actually, I thought to myself, she was right about that. But now I yelled at her, "And who told you that? I certainly didn't!"

Furious now, the time had come to do something about it. I took each one of my staff aside, alone. I explained that they were not suspected of theft but that I was going to file a police report and there would be an investigation of all three employees. Elsa understood quite well how much I trusted her.

Vera hadn't worked for me long enough to understand. She remained quiet, not saying a single word. Margo objected. The three women were interrogated one by one, and strip-searched. The police found nothing. That evening the four of us had dinner in a nice restaurant as usual, but the feeling wasn't the same. We barely spoke to one another, our eyes downcast and faces blank. I knew I had been betrayed.

I didn't have to fire Margo. She left of her own accord, feeling too uncomfortable to continue after almost having been formally accused of theft. Margo called the following week after the show to say her husband refused to let her work for me anymore. It was a bitter and disappointing end of a very long friendship. I have to admit, though, that after Margo left, I never missed merchandise like that again.

The second challenge Vera encountered shortly after accepting the job was a sales tax audit from the California State Board of Equalization. Stan and I had been audited by the IRS and passed with flying colors, but this sales tax audit would be quite a different experience. Whenever we sold to dealers, it wasn't necessary to collect the tax if the dealer's signed resale card was in our files. Whenever we shipped the goods out of state, we didn't charge tax either. Most of our sales were legitimately tax-exempt. Perhaps we were being audited because fewer than five percent of our total sales were not exempt. On those, we collected the tax, or so I presumed.

It's a great temptation to avoid paying sales tax on an expensive item. Buyers who bought jewelry for their personal use often insisted they would pay the tax themselves when filing their own sales tax returns. Whether they did so or not was not my concern. However, it *was* my responsibility to document why I had not collected the tax at the time of the sale; and if I couldn't do so, I would have to pay the tax myself.

I myself had collected sales tax on every invoice I wrote

when the items were not for resale or shipped out of state. During the audit we discovered that my employees had been extremely careless about this. Time and time again people in my employ—both regular employees and friends who helped sell at the shows—had neglected to collect the tax when tax was due. Buyers who owned retail businesses would promise to send us their resale card exempting their purchases from tax, and many of them did. However, several did not. There was no follow through, and if we didn't have the resale card on file, the tax was owed. In some cases, we did ship packages out of state, exempting the purchases from tax. However, again and again, we couldn't find records of the shipment, without which the tax was owed. There were hundreds of invoices like this. It was a nightmare. Vera worked diligently for months to sort through the mess. We contacted everyone to get all the resale cards on file or obtain a personal statement that the purchase had been shipped out of the state of California. Some buyers had moved or were otherwise not able to be reached. Together, we worked with the auditor daily for over half a year. The original missing tax of $44,000 was reduced to slightly more than $9,000. I had to pay it. Vera took this lesson to heart. Since that day, every single invoice had the tax collected; or if tax exempt, the invoice had either a photocopy of the resale card or proof of the out of state shipment attached to it. Vera took care of the details. A few years later when we were audited again, every record was perfect, every exemption accounted for, and instead of six months, the audit took less than two days.

No sooner was this problem resolved that another problem came across my desk that frightened me even more. Certain famous Italian designers from the 1980s had their designs patent protected. Some pieces with ancient Roman coins, and some of the popular yellow gold and diamond rings and bracelets that wrap around the finger or wrist in snake-like fashion, as well as the famous "parenthesis" collection, were well known and frequently advertised in the finest fashion magazines. Copies of such pieces were in violation of the patent and could not be legally sold. Apparently a large jewelry store on the corner of 5th Avenue and 47th street in Manhattan had copies of these pieces in their window. Early one morning when the store opened, the owners were surprised to see authorities from the US Patent and Trademark Office at their door, questioning the items in the window. The owners claimed they had purchased the patented pieces from me.

I was not happy to be involved in this, and in fact quite concerned over the growing file on my desk sent by Italian lawyers, who wanted to know if I was manufacturing these items, and if not, where I was able to find them. I nervously assumed I satisfied their requests by revealing all my sources, since eventually the letters stopped coming, and the threat of legal actions disappeared. At least they disappeared for me. In Valenza, where my jewelers had the skills to copy anything they wanted, one of my manufacturers soon went out of business. I lost touch with them for close to two years, and when I found them again, they had changed their company name and telephone numbers.

CHAPTER 21

WHAT'S IT ALL ABOUT, ALFIE?

Why would anyone want to do the trade shows? As costly as they were, they did make money, but more importantly, they helped to turn over merchandise and bring in cash flow for new purchases. The year I did eleven trade shows was exhausting. I traveled all across the US and was away from my family those eleven weekends. Stan could have encouraged me to stay home more, but he understood that a career of my own was giving me a new sense of self. I knew all along that making money the way I was going about it wasn't easy, but it was worse after Timothy left when I had to travel everywhere myself. I didn't have other salespeople on the road. I was the one flying on planes and showing my collection to buyers. I was out of town often, not only to generate sales, but also to buy from designers abroad.

Vera was now the one who accompanied me to the Jewelry Trade Show in Basel in April. We found fabulous vendors from Italy, Bangkok, and Lebanon—gorgeous jewels that were unlike anything you could find stateside. Obtaining a new fashion-forward collection at the right price was the key to our success, but then, the new collection had to be sold before the following April, when we'd go to Basel again. Every year I felt the pressure. It was imperative that the entire collection sell through. Customers were often bored with last year's designs.

I hadn't sold coast-to-coast before Timothy was there, and now without him I was flying to stores across the country to visit the accounts he had opened. That meant living in hotels, renting cars or hiring taxis, eating alone, never leaving the jewels unattended, and watching my back for thieves every moment of every day. I constantly questioned my decision to keep my business going. As I got older, it never got easier.

Had I not put my family first, my drive for success could have made me a formidable competitor in the industry. But what good would that be if it cost me a precious lifetime next to my nearest and dearest? I understood the formula and followed it carefully: Buy stones at the right price; find quality labor at low cost; track down or create new, beautiful designs every year; and find the neediest buyers who are constantly searching for product. Calculate the risks before you take them, and take the good ones as often as possible.

On the other hand, I loved being with my family for dinner at night, helping with homework, going out with friends on the weekends, and not having to chase after another dollar. Some dealers exhibited at forty shows a year and paid a huge price in their personal lives for their success. I was not willing to do that, and to this day I'm not sorry.

I worried often about my customers. Many had trouble paying their bills on time. High-end jewelry was increasingly hard to sell. The larger stores didn't buy into the trends, merely taking merchandise on consignment. Other wholesalers had the best idea, to sell lower quality in higher quantities. I couldn't do that, though. I just couldn't sell poor quality; it embarrassed me and went against my nature. I stood behind my product 100 percent and felt ashamed to sell anything that was cheaply made. A proper polish, a proper clasp, natural gemstones of a certain standard—these were important to me. I didn't mess with diamonds or other gems that were created in a man-made laboratory. Even if the labs could simulate Mother Nature exactly, the only stones I chose to sell were created in the bowels of the earth.

My best customers were jewelers in New York and Florida, but the stores in Florida never paid their bills on time. Most of the stores in Florida didn't pay me for months. Eventually I stopped selling to them. It was beyond frustrating to call them again and again and beg for payment. It was hard enough to sell, but even harder getting my money.

Finally, I had to resort to a collection agency. When a jeweler in Boca Raton refused to pay his bill after a year, I told him to send back the unsold merchandise. He didn't do so. Days later when my youngest brother Neil happened to be in Florida, he tried to collect my money, and when he couldn't, he demanded and retrieved the year-old merchandise.

Old merchandise or new, I had to take it back. After all, it was gold and diamonds with high intrinsic value. *Sold and returned, a pointless effort. Never mind. Just put your head down and keep going . . .*

When Neil returned to California, he stayed with Dad and Sally and noticed something was terribly wrong. Dad wasn't the same. His mental acuity was off. He had dementia, he was forgetful, and he was not just losing his memory but he had also become irrational. According to Neil, Dad would get up in the middle of the night and wander around the apartment, talking to people who simply were not there. I didn't want to believe this. I just couldn't accept that our brilliant business-minded father, a self-made multi-millionaire, was losing his mind.

Dad had always enjoyed coming to my showroom to help out. One day he was leaving for the bank to make a deposit for me, and I gave him customer monthly statements to drop in the mailbox on his way to the bank. He accidentally put the checks and the deposit slip in the mailbox along with the customers' statements. Recognizing his error, he stood at the mailbox until the mailman came to collect its contents in order to retrieve the bank deposit. I thought nothing of it, as that could have been a senior moment that happens to anyone. But a week later he cashed a check at the bank for $1,800, tipped the parking attendant $300 instead of $3, and came home with $1,500. Instead of paying the maid $150 for her day's work, he gave her $1,500. When she tried to set him straight, he said to me, "Adrienne, can you deal with this? I'm confused." None of us realized then that he already had symptoms of Alzheimer's Disease, or that he would decline and suffer for the next ten years. We had no idea how terrible that would be.

Then one day, Dad said, "Adrienne, I'm in trouble. I'm going to need your help."

My heartbreak was overwhelming when the doctor gave us the news. For the first time, I knew despair. In bright daylight all I could see was blackness, a deep hole with no escape. Scream, beg, plead, pray—when Alzheimer's attacks, it is relentless. The two of us cried buckets the day he was formally diagnosed. There was no cure.

It's easy to take good health for granted. Almost everyone has it as a child, a gift so unappreciated until it's gone. And when it goes, or starts to go, the truth hurts. And so I began to question. What have I done with this gift of my life? Is the world a better place because I was here?

Dad came over to discuss his estate plans. I would become executor and have power of attorney. He could no longer work alongside me at Avanti, shipping packages from the showroom, because too many details were involved. He couldn't read the numbers. One day I took him downtown to visit suppliers, and he couldn't find his way from one to the other, even though he'd done so many times in the past. My brother David and his wife Linda did everything they could to help. When doctors said there was no cure, I took matters into my own hands, researched on the Internet, and ordered esoteric brain supplements and Serrapeptase, an enzyme to clean his arteries, from a pharmacy in Milan. I bought a child's toy with geometric shapes that fit in a puzzle. That was pointless, as Dad couldn't distinguish one shape from another and furthermore wasn't even interested in trying. Over the following decade, he would gradually lose his vocabulary, his complete sense of self, the memory of his successful life, the ability to remember our names, and everything that makes a person human. He rarely had anything to say that made sense at all, nor could he answer when we asked him questions. It is hard to lose a loved one this way, to be with someone day after day and year after year, unable to communicate. Even though we were together and he continued to live and breathe with a strong heart and healthy body, the man I loved and respected my entire life disappeared before my eyes. He'd become inaccessible to me in every meaningful way. I loved him dearly, cared for him deeply, kissed and hugged him unceasingly, but he wasn't really there. Was it so unkind of me, selfish in a way, without his approval, to prolong his life with extraordinary measures, while he battled pneumonia, bedsores, gangrene, and more?

CHAPTER 22

A FRIEND GETS IN TROUBLE

Nubar, my supplier of gold charms at Avanti, called me to ask for a favor. His casting factory in downtown LA had become very successful, but he had grown complacent and was rarely there. His work with a fellow Frenchman at Oro-America, a public company on the New York Stock Exchange, had taken all his attention, and apparently he had trusted his foreman at the charm factory a bit too much. Little by little, the foreman had been pilfering gold, and by the time Nubar noticed, so much gold had gone missing that he couldn't fill the OroAmerica orders. Forced to close the charm factory, Nubar had to start all over. His savings were slim, but he still had enough money for a down payment on a building in Glendale to house a new factory.

Nubar took his best sellers and went to QVC, where the orders were so substantial that he needed a loan to buy gold. He came to me with a signed purchase order, asking for $120,000 to buy the gold to start production. He would pay me back at a high rate of interest as soon as he was paid in ninety days. As security for the loan, he offered me a second trust deed on the

Glendale building. I went to see the property, and I compared the appraisal with the first trust deed from the bank. There was a clean soil report, and a gold reclamation system in place. Having done my homework, I knew that lending money on the property was a safe bet. There was plenty of equity, so I made the loan.

Why is it so difficult to succeed in the jewelry business? Why do so many fail or barely make ends meet? Is it the low margins at wholesale? Is it because of the constant vigilance required to prevent theft or the stiff competition? Is it due to a lack of focus? Perhaps it is because the nature of the business requires constant intensive capital with the problem of aging and dead inventory. Why are some jewelers respected as savvy businessmen and others looked down upon in disparagement as blue-collar laborers or mere peddlers? I had been in the business for more than twenty years and still couldn't answer these questions, only that, in my book, jewelers deserved respect. They were not mere peddlers. They were creative individuals, designers who influenced trends, took financial risks, and made decisions about how much to charge and to whom they should extend credit.

The truth is that it's not only jewelers who have difficulties. Any business venture can fail. With so many decisions, miscalculations are normally costly. It takes tenacity to succeed, and the main reason companies achieve success is because they take risks and keep trying. But you must believe in what you wish to accomplish and get fully behind it, heart and soul. Try and try again.

For some people, the world of academia I'd left years before held far more respect than the world of business. As a businesswoman, I learned to disagree and never stopped to question my own self-image. A woman like me was an anomaly, outside the norm. Others didn't know what to make of me, and I didn't either. But I knew it took fortitude and gumption to make it in this business. As for Nubar, even though he had failed, he was not a quitter and would begin again.

For close to a year, Nubar came to our house once a month to pay interest on the loan but never any principal. He was so successful at QVC that he could barely buy enough gold to make the new orders, let alone pay me back. His margins weren't high enough. It was a shock when one day a letter came from his bank that the building he owned was in pre-foreclosure. Nubar was ashamed, embarrassed, and worst of all, psychologically paralyzed. The building had a two-year-old appraisal of $850,000. Nubar could have asked a real estate broker for help. He could have tried to sell the property. He did neither. To this day, I don't understand that. There was equity. He should have sold the building. He never thought he would lose his entire investment. But he did.

Nubar owed $550,000, and the bank wanted its money. Foreclosure was imminent. There would be a public auction. As the holder of the second mortgage, I had to attend the auction with a cashier's check ready to pay the bank the full amount and more. If not, the building would be sold to the highest bidder, and I could lose the money I had loaned, all or a good part of the $120,000.

Stan and I had plans for a month-long vacation in the British Isles, and we were going to be abroad on the date of the auction. We enlisted a dear friend, Ray, who was quite savvy when it came to real estate. He would attend the foreclosure sale on our behalf, with cashier's checks to cover our potential purchase. Naturally I had to buy the building, even though I didn't want it. If not, I'd lose the $120,000. Ray attended the auction hoping to purchase the property on our behalf for $600,000. If he succeeded, we should be happy, although I had no desire to own it, to find a tenant, or to become a landlord looking for one.

On the day of the auction, a gentleman was there who wanted the building but didn't have the cashier's checks. He couldn't bid. Ray bought the building with no competition. Right away the man approached Ray and asked him a question. Ray said he represented the buyer and would let him know the answer after speaking to us. We were in Ireland in our hotel room when the phone rang. It was Ray.

"You got the building for $600,000. How would you like to sell it for a quick $50,000 profit?" And so it was that what could have be a disaster worked out in my favor with very little effort.

CHAPTER 23

SHENANIGANS

While I was waiting for Dan and Sergey to build equity in D & G, Yefim was exploring opportunities and investments for the company abroad. Sergey came to me one day to tell me about a chance to invest in something special. He wanted me to lend him money and become his silent partner, but I had to do so without knowing what the investment was.

"I cannot tell you a single thing about this," he said, "but I promise to give you your money back if it doesn't pay off. You asked me to let you know about opportunities, and this is it. For sure I will give you your money back. You have my word. If we make money, you do too. If not, what do you have to lose?"

At the time, because the company directors were enjoying affluent life styles, it appeared that D & G was making a lot of money and could do no wrong. I calculated my risks and decided to trust Sergey, who had always been a hard-working man. Even so, having learned from prior mistakes, it was not like me to invest in a project without studying the downside. But here there was no downside. Sergey never made a promise he didn't keep. Besides, he was not a poor man anymore. And maybe I was motivated because I wanted to be included again. Yefim had contacts in Russia and Czechoslovakia, or perhaps they were considering a diamond mine in Africa. Sergey would not tell me anything about the new venture. He said it was better if I didn't know. After some thought, I gave him the money, $100,000, and never did find out what it was for. (Stan didn't know about this.) Two years later, Sergey said the investment had come to nothing. The money was gone, but he did pay me back a little at a time, and all of it eventually. The deal had been made with a handshake. Whether he had a lot or a little, Sergey remained a man of his word, always.

As affluence found its way to Sergey and Inez, they began to have problems. When they were young and had nothing and were struggling together to make ends meet, it was obvious how much in love they were. From the early days in Odessa, they had survived life-changing events with strength and resilience. Now they were part of the newly rich Russian crowd in Los Angeles, far from their humble beginnings. Sergey remained his modest, unpretentious self, while Inez wanted to show off their prosperity. Instead of fighting because of money they didn't have, they fought because of the money they *did* have. Inez had an easy time spending. Sergey was concerned about the company debt. He wore the Versace jeans she bought him, but this trendy, expensive designer brand wasn't important to him. Money had changed Inez, but it hadn't changed Sergey. They began to disagree about everything.

With more respect for her son's business acumen than her husband's creative talent at the jeweler's bench, Inez started complaining. She put her husband down constantly with disparaging, bitter words. It wasn't long before Sergey ended up sleeping on a couch in the living room, and because he was stubborn and angry, he remained there for several months. He detested his wife's new snobbish, highbrow attitude. She had become someone different from the young woman he married, now wanting to spend time with richer friends than the people he wanted to be with. Sleeping alone, it wasn't long before Sergey would look elsewhere for comfort, while Inez watched the family fall apart. Their long history of love and affection, trial and tribulation, could no longer save this marriage. When Inez filed for divorce, Sergey did nothing to stop her.

In the meantime, Yefim was still having a hard time maintaining his grasp on the accounting. While the money was rolling in and out so quickly, with merchandise being exchanged between companies, Yefim couldn't keep the books straight at all. At one point he came to me and said, "There's been a huge embezzlement. A young Russian girl in the accounting room somehow made off with more than half a million dollars." I couldn't believe my ears. It had to be a trumped-up story. The girl's salary was paid in cash. How could she steal so much money?

Yefim said he'd discovered the discrepancy and called a board meeting with Sergey and Dan. It was then that Dan explained what happened to the missing money. According to Dan, the embezzler, who had worked at D & G just a short time, had access to Sergey's check signing stamp, and she had issued duplicate checks to vendors in exchange for a large kickback. Yefim didn't really believe this story. He came to see me and said he would get the real facts. If anyone could get to the bottom of it, he could. He would talk to her and shake her down. Just one week later, Yefim came back to tell me what he had learned.

Yefim had no reason to keep secrets from me. He confronted the girl in private, intimidating her with his formidable, menacing posture and his bombastic way of speaking. To get the truth, he threatened her with a police investigation and convinced her that she, an immigrant, would end up going to prison for embezzling funds. She had a family, a husband and two children. Face to face with Yefim's gruff Mafioso bravado, his 6'4" height looming over her, she broke down. It was a sordid but plausible story: Sergey had gotten her pregnant, she had borne him a son, and the company paid her off several hundred thousand dollars as a settlement. According to Yefim, there was no embezzlement. The girl was paid to keep her mouth shut, and she would never be heard from again.

I was so surprised with this explanation that it didn't even occur to me that the embezzlement would be a direct expense against company profit. The company would pay from its profits for Sergey's unscrupulous little affair. To make it appear real, Dan hired a private investigator to look into the situation to find out how so much money could have gone missing. But Yefim told me the investigation was a hoax, ordered to appease the stockholders (Yefim and me) and the D & G accountants and lawyers. Dan and Sergey knew all along the funds were never embezzled. They had simply paid the girl off and let her go, swearing her to secrecy. If she talked, she risked prosecution.

Sergey obviously loved women, and women loved him back. He suffered the consequence of his behavior again and again throughout his life, but this time his fellow shareholders had to pay.

According to Yefim, things were getting messy. There were too many inter-company transactions, and too much cash changing hands unaccounted for. He was losing control. He wanted to sell his shares and advised me to do the same. He told me that without him at D & G to watch my back, I would never get anywhere or anything from the company ever again. In other words, once he was gone, I could use my shares for wallpaper.

Yefim can't be right. I'll get paid again some day. He has inside knowledge and has to get out, but I don't have to sell right now. I *don't trust him somehow. He thinks $1,000,000 is a fair price. I'm not so sure. It's probably far too little.*

You think you'll ever get their respect? You'll have to sell sooner or later.

Later, okay, but not now, and not for this price.

Yefim was chief financial officer, with access to all the transactions involving the money. I was just a small shareholder who was given an obscure financial statement once a year. I had no control, no power, no inside knowledge. Yefim was on the board of directors, and as such, he was a director of the corporation. He, not I, was responsible for company improprieties. He, not I, could be accused of cheating the IRS and worse. It was he, not I, who stood at the crossroads. If he had knowledge of shenanigans, he had to leave the company or be complicit in financial lies and income tax issues. As for me, since I was not an officer or director and merely a passive investor, unable to attend their meetings and not privy to their actions, I would have no liability for their wrongdoing. Moreover, I wouldn't even know about it if Yefim didn't tell me.

Yefim finally did sell his shares back to the corporation in 1998 for about $1,000,000. Since D & G had so little cash on hand, Yefim accepted $150,000 along with the agreement to be paid the remainder in consulting fees and expenses over the next ten years. However, according to the accountant and others as well, Yefim was never consulted for advice. Even Sergey said no one wanted Yefim's opinion on anything. The consulting fees were just another ruse—par for the course, it seemed to me—so that D & G accountants could deduct his payout from earnings, and as a precedent to establish the price in case I wanted to sell my shares. Yefim still came to Dan from time to time later on, hat in hand to ask for even more money for travel expenses, and Dan always obliged, never forgetting that Yefim was the one who believed in him from the start.

Dan felt indebted to his "Uncle" Yefim. Because he received more than his contract called for, I believed he sold his shares too cheaply.

After he sold his shares, I owned 11 percent of D & G. However, Yefim would no longer be my fellow shareholder watching over the books on my behalf. He had been my tether. I'd invested in the company because he had. Now I was on my own, the lonely outsider and the only one with shares besides the family. He was the one who made sure I was paid every year those first four years for "consulting advice." Without him there, I didn't stand a chance of getting any more money, no matter how much the company prospered. They had never shown a profit or paid a dividend to shareholders in the past, so why should they ever do so in the future?

Lonely outsider, indeed . . .

If I were so unwelcome, unwanted, and unpopular, why should I want to stick around to be the butt of their disdain, so evident when they avoided my gaze and rejected my friendship? Was it just my silly pride at owning even a small part of such a successful company? Was it vanity? I knew what others did not, that without me this company would have had a tough start. But who was I kidding? I wasn't important any more, and I felt absolutely wretched. They had stopped paying me, and they never would again.

Even if I had agreed to sell my shares, I had little confidence that I'd ever be paid, without Yefim there, insisting that they do so. They wanted to make me a so-called "consultant" for the next ten years? I shuddered at the thought.

Silent anger eroded my soul. My longing to be in their world and be part of their lives would never be requited.

Sergey remarried, he in his forties, she a much younger Armenian girl. They had three children and bought a nice house in Glendale, not far from the D & G factory. So it would be that Dan's half brothers were younger than his own children. Inez, still beautiful and full-figured, had no trouble finding a new significant other.

In 1996, D & G Jewelry had about three hundred employees. Quarters were cramped. Rents were high. Dan and Sergey, acting together on their own, had made the decision that D & G should find larger space. The ninth and tenth floors on Hill St. were not big enough. I certainly wasn't aware of their desire to move. Unbeknownst to me, they had found a property for sale outside the jewelry district of Los Angeles, but convenient nevertheless. The property consisted of a building that was just a shell and two parking lots, but it was more than large enough to house the D & G factory. The building was purchased, and Dan and Sergey hired architects to design and build out the 10,000 square foot interior space to suit future factory needs.

One day when I was visiting the factory in its cramped quarters on Hill Street, as I did at least twice a week at that point, I was quite surprised to see Inez and several others standing around a table and looking at blueprints for a new, modern factory. As I entered the manager's office, no one acknowledged me. I was ignored. Invisible. I approached the table to see what everyone was talking about. The plans depicted a new factory, complete with offices for Dan and Sergey, and two offices for the accountants. There were workstations for several jewelers, polishing rooms, lockers and changing rooms, a well-designed security system, and an impressive entry. The address, near Chavez Ravine, was just minutes by car from the downtown jewelry district. The building was two stories, with a lunchroom upstairs, and several extra rooms that could become available for future use. The new factory would be a fabulous place to work, but no one ever asked me my opinion about such an endeavor. Could D & G afford to buy the property and build it to suit company needs? I wouldn't mind owning 11 percent of that. It would take two years for this vision to become a reality, two stressful years during which many changes were taking place. The company was moving onward and upward, obviously making money, even though the financial statements reflected otherwise, and even though I received no additional compensation.

But then, why wasn't I receiving anything? Why hadn't anyone told me about the company plans for the future? As I gazed at the blueprints for the new factory, I realized with a jolt that not only had I become an outsider, I was irrelevant to the future of D & G. Distress, gloom, and resentment filled my core.

With Yefim gone, I tried ever harder to understand the financial statement I received at the end of every fiscal year. But it was the annual report at the end of 1998 that I found most disturbing. A new entity had been created called DSRI, and D & G had paid this new entity hundreds of thousands of dollars for "rent."

"What is DSRI?" I wanted to know. It has to be a company owned by Dan and Sergey, I surmised.

Why would the company be paying rent to Dan and Sergey?

The stated facts, if true, made me angrier than ever. After all of the shenanigans at the company that could fill a television soap opera, and a financial statement that depicted a depleted corporation, I decided I had been silent far too long. What was really going on between the lines of these complicated financial arrangements, full of disguised self-indulgence and clandestine corporate opportunity?

I enlisted Stan and asked him to study the 1998 financials. I needed someone to tell me what to do.

CHAPTER 24

THE LAST STRAW

S tan was sitting on the sofa in the family room watching a Sunday morning football game.

I burst into the room. "Stan, there's something odd here," I said, as frustrated as ever. "According to this financial statement, D & G is paying an enormous amount of rent to a company called DSRI. It doesn't make any sense at all. We *own* this building. We shouldn't have to pay rent."

Stan took the statement from my thrust-out arm and began to study it, while the game was still playing on the television behind me.

Did D & G really buy a 10,000 square foot building, with a down payment and a hefty mortgage? The company had written a nice check for the down payment and paid all the accounting and legal expenses associated with the purchase, but elsewhere on the financial statement it seemed that all those payments were just loans to related parties. Did Dan and Sergey borrow the down payment from D & G? Was the loan interest-free? What is this new company called DSRI, the initials for Dan & Sergey Rental Income? And why are all these expenses being footed by D & G?

Who paid the architects? D & G did. Who paid to renovate the building? D & G. Who paid the mortgage on the building? D & G did, with payments categorized as "rent" from the first day escrow closed, even though D & G was renting elsewhere. The fact that the company could not occupy the new building during the design phase, because it wasn't occupant-ready, meant that the company was paying rent in both locations.

I looked at Stan in disbelief as he explained that what I surmised was true: My company, D & G, was paying rent to D & S Rental Income.

It was there in black and white. D & S Rental Income received over $100,000 from D & G in rent during the first year alone, when the company wasn't even operating out of the new building *and* was paying rent on the ninth and tenth floors on Hill Street as well, where they remained until the build-out was finished.

The architects and the builder charged over $750,000 to create the building's interior space, and D & G paid all the bills. D & G did not receive consideration by way of a rent reduction for providing all the tenant improvements, but on the contrary, paid a higher rent when the property was later reappraised at a higher value upon completion. The building was worth much more than the original purchase price because of the infusion of D & G funds. All this time I'd been glad that my company's money had been wisely spent, resulting in a property that had significantly increased in value.

Oh, but as Stan and I read between the lines of the year-end financial statement, it became apparent that my company did *not* own the building. The building wasn't *ours*. The title belonged to Dan and Sergey, who purchased the building for themselves with D & G funds. In that case, instead of being glad, I should be mad as hell.

The truth is I had been mad as hell for more than four years, holding inside myself feelings of exasperation, fury, impatience, and indignation. Maybe Dan and Sergey were mad too because they were stuck with me, a shareholder they couldn't eliminate. Dan had said, "You got enough. You should be happy." He was thinking, "Look what I did for her already." Had he considered when he started his company that shareholders have rights that can never be taken away, he would never have given me stock or any type of ownership position. But he had nothing then, and did what he had to do to get an investor. In his eyes I'd become a parasite, clinging to my shares of stock, hoping to benefit from the hard work and talent of others. He vowed to get rid of me. If he couldn't kill me, he'd find other means to eliminate me. If I got in his way, he would act as if I didn't exist at all.

Dan and Sergey shunned me, as best they could. They barely spoke to me when I came to visit the factory. I, who had helped them in friendship and longed to be a real part of the business and a family friend, wasn't privy to a single thing they were doing. I could merely watch them living high off the hog, which I wouldn't have minded and in fact was glad of, but for the fact that they weren't paying me anything anymore and treating me as if I didn't belong. So what if I'd been well compensated and didn't actually need more money? What does "need" have to do with it? I was an 11 percent shareholder, entitled to participate in profits. Yet four years had gone by, during which I'd received no compensation. It was even worse now, when they wouldn't even say hello or acknowledge my presence. Yes, I was exasperated beyond words, but I hadn't known the extremes they'd pursue to be rid of me and get me, the only outside shareholder, out of their hair. Damn right, I was mad as hell.

By purchasing the building solely as their own, they'd taken a corporate opportunity, one that should have been available to me as part owner of the company. My heart was filled with hurt and a gnawing grief that wouldn't go away. Yefim had known it would be like this for me.

When Stan finished reading the financial statement, he was angry. In fact, in all the years we'd been married, I'd never seen him so outraged. At long last, Dan and Sergey had gone too far. Their greed and obvious betrayal were loud and clear. Finally we had proof of their deceitful treachery. Finally I could fight back. I could be hopeful. Four years of helplessness might come to an end. From this day forth I would no longer suffer as a powerless, fragile victim, but would unleash a quiet vengeance they'd regret for a long time.

I had serious questions. "Why doesn't D & G own the new building? Why does the property belong to Dan and Sergey? Why did the company pay so much to their benefit? Why wasn't I asked to join in the purchase so that I could benefit too?" If D & G weren't a tenant footing the bills, I reasoned, the building would not have been purchased at all.

"This is clearly a breach of fiduciary duty, when officers of a corporation ignore their obligations to their shareholders." My husband, who is so even keeled and rarely loses his temper, became angry beyond description.

"You were not offered an 11 percent ownership in the property," he said. "What they did is called self-dealing, taking a personal advantage against the other shareholders, and using a corporate opportunity to enhance their personal wealth. They can't do that to shareholders and get away with it. It's against California law."

The TV was still on, and the Rams scored a touchdown. We watched the replay together.

I started pleading. "Please, Stan, let me do something. I have had it with them. They've taken every advantage, they haven't paid me anything in more than four years, and they don't even talk to me when I'm there. Can't you see how it's eating me up inside?"

Stan advised me to wait, to ask questions first and get answers. That Sunday morning, a day I'll never forget, the two of us created a long list of accounting questions and sent them off to D & G, requesting a response within thirty days. It was time to get down to business.

The answers we received thirty days later from the accountant at D & G were pure garbage. She gave us no information at all. We asked again for clarification but got nowhere. Finally, in March of 1999, just days before my statute of limitations would have expired, we filed a lawsuit: Adrienne Rubin, an individual, as plaintiff against D & G Jewelry Mfg., Inc., a California Corporation, and against Sergey, Dan, and their spouses, as individuals. Had I waited much longer, I would not have been able to file the lawsuit.

Stan specialized in trusts and estate planning, so he suggested a litigator in his law firm, Alan Wilken, to be my attorney. I accused Dan, Sergey, and their spouses of self-dealing, usurping corporate opportunity to the detriment of shareholders, of taking excessive salaries and other compensation, of breach of fiduciary duty, plundering company assets, and more.

I later learned that after building out their new factory, Dan and Sergey refinanced the property and paid D & G back for the down payment. But they did not pay to build out the space. When they refinanced, father and son took home close to $2,000,000 cash in personal profit. Then Dan signed both sides of a one paragraph pocket-to-pocket lease agreement between landlord and tenant (He held both positions.) that required D & G Jewelry to pay higher rent because the property was worth more as a new state-of-the-art factory. The rent D & G was required to pay was increased at first to $25,000 a month and later to $40,000 a month. Not only would the

D & G rent cover Dan and Sergey's mortgage obligation, but it would also cover all future repairs, maintenance, property taxes, and plenty of profit for them both as well. I was excluded because they had purchased the property for themselves. Had D & G owned the building, the company would not have had to pay any rent at all, and I would have owned 11 percent of the building, since Yefim was no longer there.

To say that Dan had become a thorn in my side is an understatement, but it's also a metaphor for what was actually happening to me health wise. Any attempts to restore my place as part of the "D & G team" had been disregarded, and my anger, smoldering inside for years, had finally taken its toll. During all this time I watched them benefit from profits while giving me nothing more. Coupled with the stress of my dad's Alzheimer's, and combined with my crazy zero carb dieting with no fruits or vegetables for four months, I lost a lot of weight at the expense of my health. Dan, the so-called "thorn in my side," was actually a real-life cyst on my left flank. At first the cyst was the size of a pea, but within months it grew to the size of a raspberry. A biopsy showed it was malignant and had to be excised with margins as soon as possible. I should have known not to give up fruits and vegetables. Without them, I had no protection against a malignant tumor.

It's at times like this when you take stock of your life and analyze who you are and how you would live differently if you had the chance. Surprisingly, I didn't feel sorry for myself. We all know we must die some day, but if it seems that day is coming sooner rather than later, there are certain things we would change. I began to think about my existence and whether or not I had fulfilled a purpose here on earth. Would I be remembered for the choices I'd made? I was a trailblazer during decades of rampant sexism, a naïve young woman with a maverick streak, a nonconformist, and a risk taker. Did any of that matter? I'd been on the merry-go-round so busy reaching for the brass ring that I forgot how important it was to enjoy the ride. The music could stop any minute. I decided then and there that I had to retire from Avanti and Adriana K and enjoy my life. It was time to look for someone to take over my two small jewelry companies.

I was very lucky. The surgeon got the margins he wanted. My oncologist looked at the medical report and asked me, "So why are you here?" I left his office with a new perspective on life, free of malignancy. Furthermore, I knew that with a lawsuit on file against Dan and Sergey, everything would be fine. I was no longer helpless. I'd been given the power to fight, and I would be well. Dan and Sergey were no longer a thorn in my side. Instead, I would become a thorn in theirs.

CHAPTER 25

MY DAD SLIPS AWAY

My malignant tumor was successfully excised, but my father's Alzheimer's was getting worse. His nights and days were confused. Often at night he would have hallucinations and envision imaginary people walking around his apartment. To him they were real people and quite frightening. We told him over and over again not to pay attention to these human-like figures. They weren't real, just figments of his imagination. Night after night, he fought with his demons. One was standing over him as he was lying in bed. He took his pillow to hit the man, but the pillow swung right through the thin air. He still couldn't believe it. He became fearful that the people in his bedroom were there to steal his money, so he hid his money clip where they would not find it. Then the following morning, forgetting where he had hidden it, he accused his housekeeper of stealing it, or worse, he insisted that was proof that the intruders were real. He became paranoid and wouldn't listen to reason.

One night he was sure he heard someone in his apartment. He went into the kitchen and picked up a carving knife. With the knife in his right hand, he stalked the apartment. He came into his bedroom, groped in the dark where Sally was asleep in bed. He grabbed her arm and started yelling, "Who are you? I got you now!" Sally sat up and turned on the light. When she saw her husband with the butcher knife in his hand, she was terror-stricken. The next day, still terrified, she had an auto accident. She may have stepped on the gas instead of the brake, because she ran into a post, hard. Her right ankle was shattered beyond repair, and she was bed-ridden for quite some time after that. But she was too afraid to stay in the apartment she shared with my father. She moved out, into her daughter's condo a mile away. She could not handle my dad's stressful situation any longer. We understood completely.

I became my dad's primary caretaker, but mainly to the extent that I hired his caregivers and paid his bills. Sally went to a lawyer for advice, and soon Dad was served with papers asking for separate maintenance. When Dad refused to hire a lawyer himself, I asked him for full authority to deal with a lawyer on his behalf, but he said no. He insisted he was still competent in certain things. According to the court papers, he was supposed to appear the following week. I knew if I took him to the courthouse, it would not turn out well. I also knew that if I did not take him there, it could turn out even worse. If he were proven to be incompetent, we would have a big mess on our hands. I tried hiring a friend who specializes in family law, but my dad refused to sign the engagement letter, so we ended in no man's land without a lawyer.

Sally's lawyer was Steve Kolodny. He had the reputation as the toughest divorce lawyer in town. I called him on the phone. The conversation went like this:

"Steve, this is Adrienne Rubin. My dad received the papers you filed, and he has to go to court on Monday."

Steve didn't want to talk to me. "Tell your lawyer to call me. I can't talk to you. You are not a party to the case."

"You have to talk to me," I told him. "We don't have a lawyer. My dad has refused to hire one, and he is truly unreasonable. If you ask him a question, half the time he doesn't make sense. He may not know what day it is, but he still knows who is president of the United States. Look, if I don't drive him to court, he won't go. If I do, he will be asked questions he won't be able to answer. It will lead nowhere, except eventually to determine his incompetence, and that would be horrible for the entire family."

I continued, "I love Sally. We all do. We are not going to put her on the street as a homeless person at the age of eighty, especially after their twenty-five year marriage. I have financial power of attorney and want to give her whatever she needs to find a separate apartment and pay her expenses. Dad created a trust for her that provides an income after he dies, but he has always been absolute about one thing, and that is that the trust must remain revocable. I know Sally wants it to be irrevocable, but I can't get him to change that. Anyway, he's not going to revoke it. Even if he tried, his competence could always be questioned. We don't want to go to court. We don't want to revoke the trust. We want Sally to be happy. I've been putting money in her checking account and hope to continue to do so. But if you force us and make us go to court or insist on making changes our father told us he doesn't want, we will rely on the anti-nuptial agreement they had."

Steve was quiet, and I could imagine that he was taking notes as I spoke.

"If you fight this in court," I continued, "Sally will end up with far less. We'll show how much my dad gave her while they were married, and how he dramatically changed her personal finances with monetary gifts and guaranteed investments. Plus, Dad told me that whoever dies first, the other gets the condo free and clear, and we'll honor that. It's obvious Dad will die first and Sally will get the condo, so eventually it will go to her children, not to me or my brothers. But if you fight us and take us to court, we won't honor that wish, and we'll demand half the value of the condo when he dies."

Steve cleared his throat. He asked me if my brothers and I and all our spouses would agree to create a trust for Sally with the same terms, should the current trust ever be revoked. I said, "Of course we would." So that's what happened. Before the court date, Steve sent an agreement to my brother Alan in Idaho, my brother Neil in New Zealand, and to David and me locally. All four of Dad's children and their spouses signed it, and everyone was satisfied. Amazingly, Sally found a condo for rent in Dad's building, on the exact same floor as his, right across the hall. Their front doors were ten feet apart. Sally had her caregiver, and Dad had his. They saw each other as much as ever. The arrangement could not have been more perfect.

I tried to talk to Dad. I tried to tell him I was suing the D & G Company, but I couldn't get through to him anymore. It was perhaps the most difficult time in my life. I longed to talk to him. His mind had been gone for a long time, and in some ways, it was as if he had already died. Eventually, when his body did let go, I still wasn't ready to say good-bye.

CHAPTER 26

"You Can't Possibly Be That Smart"

Almost immediately after I filed the lawsuit against D & G, Dan's lawyers took my deposition. I had made certain claims against the corporation and its shareholders as individuals, and by deposing me they could ask for proof of on what basis I had made my accusations. I had accused them all for breach of fiduciary duties to shareholders. I accused them of self-dealing and taking corporate opportunity by using the company for their personal advantage, to the detriment of the shareholders. I accused them of looting and plundering the company, of taking excessive compensation, and more. Did I have any proof? I did not. During my deposition I had no concrete answers or evidence. The lawyers got nothing from me, mainly because my discovery had not yet begun. They thought, even after a thorough examination of the books, I would come back with nothing. In fact, they told Dan that he had very little to worry about. Grossly underestimating me, they did not know me, this person they were dealing with.

We all went to court to fight over my request to examine the books and records, and as expected, I was given authorization to examine everything. My accountant and I paid our first visit to company headquarters, where there was an unlocked document room on the second floor, perhaps fifteen by thirty feet, filled with hundreds of storage boxes containing files and folders. My accountant was interested in the ledgers, but I was far more interested in the payables. "Where did all the profits go?" I wanted to know. My lawyer had said this room would be mine for as long as I needed it. A photocopy machine would be at my disposal. Every page I wanted copied would be stamped and numbered, with duplicates for the D & G lawyers.

The room was a mess, with boxes of files lettered from A to Z for each year the company had been in business. The boxes were piled up in rows, helter-skelter, everywhere, labeled only alphabetically "Payables" or "Receivables" with the year. The first thing I did was separate these and stack them on opposing sides of the room according to year in chronological and alphabetical order. I decided to concentrate only on payables, each and every one of them. Understanding that the original documents were never to leave the room for any reason, I removed the folders one at a time from their file boxes, sat at a table, and examined them for evidence of wrongdoing. Rather than make copies myself, I put designated papers on a side table, clearly marking them with paper clips and post it notes. A copying service would come on a regular basis to make three copies of every page I wanted and stamp them in numerical order, so that my accountant, my lawyer, and the lawyers of the defendants would see each piece of evidence I was gathering. Stamping each page officially with a Bates stamp number would allow everyone involved the ability to refer to the exact same page at any given time. I was determined to find proof of my accusations to develop my case no matter how many pages it would take. Two years later I had copied 29,000 pages, as evidence to show the officers had personally appropriated millions of dollars of the profits of D & G Jewelry Manufacturing, Inc.

After I put the boxes in chronological order by date and then from A to Z, I opened the first box that contained the payables in 1991 for companies or people beginning with "A." Right away I started reading about "A Galaxy of Bracelets," the company Yefim and I said we wanted shut down that year. All the incriminating documents were there, proof that A Galaxy of Bracelets was a company owned by Dan, Sergey, and one other person, operating rent-free out of the D & G premises, filling orders that belonged to D & G and keeping the profit that should have gone to D & G Jewelry Manufacturing, Inc.

When my lawyers inquired about this, Dan lied about it:

"Neither I nor any of the other named individual defendants own or have ever done business through an entity by the name of 'A Galaxy of Bracelets'. . . Although there are some documents purportedly reflecting the lease of space by 'A Galaxy of Bracelets,' no such entity was ever formed, nor has any such entity ever done business or manufactured jewelry. D & G occupied all of the space reflected in the invoices attached . . . As D & G was the sole occupant of that space, it was D & G's lease obligation to make those lease payments."

Such an out and out lie. I couldn't believe Dan signed the above statement and submitted it as an affidavit for the court. I photocopied the lease Dan had signed between D & G and this newly formed company he and his father owned. A Galaxy of Bracelets had indeed existed on premises. But they never paid rent, and what is even worse, D & G paid Dan and Sergey's bracelet company the exact price they sold the bracelets for, transferring the profit away from Yefim and me so that Yefim and I couldn't make a dime on the 15,000 bracelets our company sold.

I continued to search the payable files. There was an interesting folder from Al's Smoke Shop. Al's Smoke Shop was a kiosk on the ground floor next to the elevator. Apparently many people in the factory bought their cigarettes there, as well as drinks, snacks, and cigars, and they charged their purchases to the company, close to $10,000 a month. The file was very thick, with a running tab that included cigars Dan passed out when his children were born. I showed this to Alan, my attorney. I didn't know that during the course of doing business it is common for many companies to have such perks for their employees. I was upset.

"How dare they? Can't Dan and Sergey even pay for their morning coffee or afternoon Coke?" I asked my lawyer.

Alan looked at the evidence and silently surmised that $10,000 a month was not all that impressive. Not wishing to discourage my efforts, he said, "That's good, Adrienne. Don't be upset. Be glad. This is good work, and the more you find, the better our case will be."

So I changed my attitude, and instead of getting agitated, I was happy each time I came across personal expenses charged to the company. There were thousands of these. And each time I found squandering of company funds for personal purchases, I photocopied the details, had them Bates stamped as evidence, and labeled them "plundering company assets." I felt like an athlete chalking up points for my team.

I next opened the American Express file. *Naïve girl, why be surprised?* My company, D & G Jewelry, paid for everything, including a tuxedo for Dan, his designer clothes from Hugo Boss and every other designer in town, all his lunches and dinners in restaurants seven days a week, grocery bills and Blockbuster Video rentals from stores near his house, books, casual shoes, pharmacy items, deodorant and soap. D & G paid for an AV camcorder at World of Electronics in Florida, airplane tickets to Florida for his children and ex in-laws (who obviously were not employees of the company), theme park tickets for his children at Disneyworld, and toys from Toys R Us. Dan's wife charged spa treatments. There were charges from clothing stores for the entire family, from stores like Le Chateau, Kids Kastle, Bardelli's, and Max Studio. Dan got sporting goods and general merchandise from the golf clubs at Pelican Hill and Newport Beach and charged his dry cleaning and flowers for his wife. There were lavish vacations, expensive designer watches and other personal jewelry from Tiffany and other jewelers, and so much more, all charged to the company American Express card. The monthly bills described every purchase. Legitimate or not, good or bad, every time the card was used by any cardholder, it was recorded in detail, along with real travel expenses for all the salesmen. I had photocopies of it all.

I couldn't believe Dan charged the company for $5.00 video rentals. He never paid for anything at all. I was appalled. These small things were merely an indication of his arrogance and abuse of power, far less significant than his perfidious underhanded dealings I really wanted to find. Even so, these small things bothered me just as much. Dan's sense of entitlement was out of control.

I felt just like Columbo, the famous TV investigator.

As part of my discovery, I was very interested in interviewing the workers at D & G, so I copied the payroll list. At first, I noticed Yefim's wife was listed, even though she was at least sixty years old and not an employee. Dan's wife, and Sergey's as well, were listed as salaried employees. Sergey's wife was listed as an independent jewelry contractor but couldn't make a piece of jewelry if her life depended on it. None of these women worked at the factory, yet all received weekly checks. For most of the others, I noticed how low the stated salaries were. I knew many employees were paid a portion of their salaries in cash to avoid payroll taxes. Most of them were said to be independent contractors, even though they were truly full-time employees. There is a difference. Independent contractors don't work exclusively for one company. They pay rent, utilities, insurance, and security, and they come and go as they please. They supply their own tools and often their own goods. Employees, on the other hand, occupy a workspace rent-free and do the work they are told to do with materials and goods supplied by the employer. By designating their employees as independent contractors, D & G avoided the payroll taxes they should have paid, such as withholding social security and FUTA, the Federal Unemployment Tax.

Years before, when Sergey and I were friends, Sergey told me that some customers paid for goods in cash off the books. He never put the cash in his pocket. Instead he used it for furniture for the factory and employees' salaries. He used to tell me that by paying diamond setters part cash/part check, everyone's taxes were lower, and the cost of the jewelry was lower. Since the merchandise cost D & G a little less, they could sell more and make more profit. He also explained it away by talking about the competition, as if that were an acceptable explanation for doing this. I imagined that D & G could be receiving a fair amount of under the table cash for merchandise they sold, but I trusted Sergey when he told me the incoming cash was all accounted for and all being spent to pay bills. He said he even got a deal on the chairs and tables for the factory because he paid in cash. There was a cashbook that showed funds in and out, and Igor, a trusted employee, was in charge of keeping track. But Igor resigned and began working at another company nearby. I knew where he was working now and planned to talk to him and even have him deposed legally when the time came.

At the end of February 2001, after I'd been looking at documents for quite some time, I asked Sergey if he was going to admit that cash had been received and paid out, as he had told me years before. (I had asked my lawyer earlier if it would be okay to have this conversation, and he approved.)

"Sergey, if you simply admit that you sell off the books for cash and spend all the cash on the business, I won't have to photocopy so many pages."

"We never sold off the books for cash. And we never pay any of our employees in cash, either." He lied to me face to face full of bravado without hesitation.

"If you say that, Sergey, you'll be in big trouble. Too many people know what you did. And if you lie in court, that's perjury."

"I'm telling you the truth now. We have never sold for cash. And if I told you that we did a long time ago, I was lying back then."

Sergey wasn't deluded. He was stubborn. We both knew the truth.

Actually, I did talk to a few sympathetic employees as part of my discovery. One of them agreed to talk to me and my lawyers because he was no longer working at D & G. He said he happened to be at the factory after-hours one evening and heard voices in a nearby room. He opened the door and saw two men inside and stacks of cash in hundred dollar bills piled high like bricks on the table. Struck with fear that someone would know what he had seen, he closed the door quickly and ran out of the factory with his heart pounding, praying no one noticed him. I made a note to depose him in the future.

Legally, I was entitled to talk to anyone I wished, ask all the questions I wanted, and do whatever I deemed necessary to uncover the facts. After all, Dan had hidden so many deceitful activities from me over the years and continuously used his power and position as president of the company to take away whatever might have benefited me in the smallest degree. My opponents didn't realize that I had only just begun my discovery, just tiptoeing about and testing the waters. Soon I would don my combat boots, and they wouldn't know what hit them.

CHAPTER 27

DIVERTING AND PLUNDERING
THE PROFITS

As I was given free rein to examine all documents, I did so meticulously. Apparently my opponents didn't realize that I would find several files full of privileged information from the company lawyers. The legal firm of Hercules, Fisherman, Graystone, and Smythe described their hourly charges for advice in great detail on every invoice, including discussions regarding the incorporation of personal and side businesses. D & G paid all the legal bills, including charges relating to D & S Rental Income or "other businesses of Sergey and Inez Z." Apparently, the lead lawyer for D & G, Jim Hercules, didn't pay attention, or else he didn't mind that D & G was paying for the family's personal bills. Even though Hercules had correctly addressed his bills to the family, it was the D & G Company that paid him for everything, regardless of what he worked on. That was just one obvious error. Hercules usually warned his clients about inappropriate payments but neglected to do so here. I'm absolutely certain he had no idea that I had access to his billings. It was privileged information I was not supposed to have.

Lucky for me that Dan and Sergey think I'm just a dumb chick. But it is pretty stupid to have left the confidential legal file here for me to see. I guess they'll realize their mistake later when they see the Bates stamped photocopies.

The real kicker for me, in the first legal file I found, was reading about the decision to create two new jewelry companies I had never heard of. One was S & B Enterprises, a partnership of Sergey and Boris. The other was IDC, a partnership between Sergey and Robert D. Once again, these companies were side businesses Dan created to divert income from D & G. They were separate jewelry businesses, also on the tenth floor of the D & G leased premises, and while D & G could not benefit from their transactions, D & G did pay their rent as well as the bill Hercules charged to incorporate them. The payments were classified on the books as "miscellaneous expense," another way to conceal their activities. The existence of these companies had never been disclosed to me, yet both had received large checks from D & G, some for tens of thousands of dollars to cover their payroll, their diamond and gold purchases, their freight, and their overhead. D & G also paid invoices for their workbenches, tools, furniture, telephone installation, and more. It is possible that Yefim, as the accountant at the time, was not aware of these side businesses, where he and I were excluded from the profits, or perhaps he didn't consider them important enough to complain about. If my accountant looked at the expense report, he probably wouldn't have spotted anything wrong. It was only by looking at the actual invoices that one could see exactly what was going on.

A pattern was beginning to emerge. I would now be on the lookout for side businesses and would find multiple corporations set up surreptitiously to divert income from my company to Dan and Sergey alone. D & G would give these companies (all of them owned solely by Dan and his family) merchandise at cost, and D & G would pay their expenses as well. On the financial ledgers, all would be disguised. D & G paid the travel, advertising, freight, commissions, and incentives for all the companies, without compensation in return. These companies, owned solely by Dan and his family, never paid rent, either. It was plundering. Pure and simple.

Sometimes the companies would change names, by acquiring a DBA, a name under which they would "Do Business As." But it wouldn't matter how many companies Dan's lawyers created to take profits from D & G shareholders. Over the course of two years of watching me as I examined files in the document room, they should have known that I would unearth them all.

CHAPTER 28

GREEDY SELFISH SCOUNDRELS

The next two years our lives continued as usual, except I was much happier. With each discovery of wrongdoing, I had more ammunition. Vera managed the Avanti business while I spent several hours a day in the D & G document room, where discovery for my lawsuit was always intriguing. I began to examine D & S Trunk Shows, as this entity should have been a nice source of profit for D & G. The entity was definitely profitable, as I learned from reading about the meetings between Dan and the company's lawyers. However, in 1996, Dan found a way to take this business away from me and eliminate my share of these profits permanently. He and his lawyers decided to make D & S Trunk Shows a separate corporation, no longer part of D & G. Instead of the profits from D & S going to my company, they would go to D & S, Inc. There was no way I could have known this was happening. Had I known, I would have stopped it. It was outrageous to do this to me. Physically nothing changed. Business continued much the same. The only difference was that I didn't own any part of D & S, Inc. Dan, Sergey, and Yefim cut me out of the deal. In retrospect, it amazes me that Jim Hercules, Dan's chief attorney, didn't know that what he had done by incorporating this entity was illegal and unfair to me according to California law.

How is it possible that we were all owners of D & S Trunk Shows, and suddenly it's D & S Inc., and I'm out, and everyone else is in? They didn't kick Yefim out. He knew about it and let it happen. He wasn't really protecting me, after all. He thought I'd never find out. He wasn't really a friend. It was every man for himself.

But this was a low blow.

D & S Trunk Shows had always sold a lot of diamond rings, and plenty of large diamonds as well. The D & G salesmen visited stores all over the country, and customers would come to the trunk shows to upgrade their old engagement rings and wedding bands. Previously, D & G would procure large diamonds on consignment from various diamond suppliers and offer them to D & S at a higher price. But after D & S was incorporated as a separate company in which I held no ownership, D & S ordered the diamonds directly. D & S, Inc. was making money, but my company D & G could not benefit at all, even though it still paid all the expenses. So Dan was obviously no longer interested in making money for D & G. On the contrary, he burdened the company with expenses while stripping it of profits. Shady dealings can only be questioned if you know about them, and I was discovering them years later, well after the fact.

There was no way I could have suspected this level of greed. D & G, was borrowing from the Factor at a hefty interest rate to buy goods to manufacture and consign them to D & S, Inc. with no guarantee of sale, taking all the risks, paying the insurance and security guards, the salesmen's travel expenses, and more, and apparently not making a profit, while D & S,

Inc., which I had no stake in, took it all. When D & S had been a division of D & G, this profitable business was ten percent mine. But once D & S was incorporated as a separate business, I had no ownership in it any more. Separate shares of D & S stock were created and distributed to Dan (45 percent), Sergey (45 percent), and Yefim (10 percent). Since it was all done behind closed doors, there was no way to have known about this. Even when I studied the financial statements, I couldn't tell that this was done.

How could Dan, Sergey, and Yefim have seized a profitable arm of the company and taken it away from me? Didn't Hercules, their lawyer, know any better?

The audacity of these men who ignored me, easy for them because I was just a woman they could shunt aside . . . I'd never find out, and anyway, if I did, chances were I wouldn't pursue them.

Obviously, they didn't know me.

I didn't know myself how much I longed to be part of the team.

All three of them did whatever they wanted and didn't care. D & G—the company I owned stock in—gave up its ability to profit from D & S Trunk Shows and received nothing in return. Then, to take even more from my company and give more to D & S, Inc., Dan used his corporate advantage and his power as president of both corporations, in bold, unabashed, shameless style, by creating a marketing agreement between my company and his, requiring my company to pay his company *$50,000 a month* for the "privilege" of handling marketing and sales.

I had to stop and reread this page again. The marketing agreement that benefitted Dan, Sergey, and Yefim two times over clearly stated that D & G was to pay D & S, Inc. *$50,000 a month for the privilege of handling marketing and sales.* Considering that D & G fronted the newly incorporated D & S all its merchandise, paid all its suppliers, its overhead, its employees and its salesmen's expenses, and directed its customers to pay *his* company instead of the company I owned stock in, it seemed to me that the only lawful thing to do would have been for *Dan's newly incorporated company to pay the D & G company,* instead of the other way around.

But then, I wasn't dealing with law-abiding people. I was dealing with conniving sharks.

Nevertheless, letters went out to all the stores where trunk shows had been held, instructing the stores to pay D & S, Inc. directly for the jewelry they'd ordered from D & G, instead of paying D & G as they had in the past. If customers forgot or ignored the letter and paid D & G instead of D & S, Inc., Dan simply transferred the funds from D & G to D & S, Inc. without explanation.

When questioned, Dan lied again under oath. He vowed in an affidavit that D & S, Inc. never received preferential prices on items D & G manufactured, and that all its merchandise was purchased at arm's length. However, I found numerous records of D & G sales to D & S, Inc. at prices that did not include any profit for D & G whatsoever. For example, I found documents in the file room from I. B. Goodstein, for diamonds sold to D & G in 1997. The invoices identified the number of pieces, their style numbers and their prices to D & G. And then D & G sold the *same* goods with the *same* style numbers to D & S, Inc. *at the identical price.* This meant no profit for me, while everyone else benefitted.

Dan lied again on another affidavit I found. He stated that D & S Inc. never made a profit, but his personal tax return, which I found buried in loan documents he gave to his bank, revealed otherwise.

Isn't it amazing what you can find when you look at an application for a bank loan?

While D & S, Inc. enjoyed doing business rent-free on D & G premises, D & G continued to supply the merchandise. D & S, Inc. never had to "buy" the goods. Instead, D & G "loaned" the merchandise, so that D & S, Inc. had preferential access to an inventory of jewelry manufactured by D & G at no invested cost. Some of this inventory was physically returned to D & G, but not all. D & G was paying the now incorporated D & S overhead, including the hefty management package offered to Robert B., as well as accounting and legal fees and considerably high travel expenses, while Dan, Sergey, and Yefim received all the income, and D & G, my company, was encumbered with all the expense.

I got the evidence for this photocopied and Bates stamped, all of it—the 1997 IRS 1040 individual income tax declarations for Dan, Sergey, and Yefim, and the K-1's for each of them, showing the profit they had declared—the profit stolen from D & G. Dan, Sergey, and Yefim's stated personal income from D & S, Inc. was ironclad proof that they had cheated me. The sole reason they had incorporated D & S was to move the profits out of my grasp.

California law states: A director or officer of a corporation may not enter into a competing business which cripples or injures the business of the corporation of which he is an officer or director.

Even if there had been *no* profit, the clandestine conversion of D & S Trunk Shows from a division of D & G to a corporation of the same name was just another insidious way to exclude me.

So, Dan, you want me out of your life. You pretend I don't exist, but I'm a shareholder, and I'm still here.

To quote William Congreve, although the context is quite different in my case, "Heaven has no rage, like love to hatred turned, Nor hell a fury, like a woman scorned."

CHAPTER 29

DAN'S ACHILLES HEEL

I was sitting patiently upstairs in the document room, waiting for the accountant to print out some ledger pages I requested, when Dan invited me into his office on the first floor. He wasn't happy that the court allowed me full freedom to examine company documents and thought he might offer me something to make me go away. He had a Magic 8 Ball on his desk, which he used to predict the future. To break the ice, he showed it to me. He picked it up, shook it, and asked, "Will my sales be higher than last year?" The answer this toy produced was "maybe." I imagined he consulted his "oracle" several times a day. It seemed as if his only goal in life was to sell more every year than the year before; nothing else seemed to hold any meaning for him. After I sat opposite him at his desk, he asked about my findings in the document room. He let me know in no uncertain terms that my daily presence was annoying. I asked him just one question.

"Dan, how do you have the audacity to charge all your personal expenses on the D & G American Express card? You live off the card and just take and take."

He shrugged his shoulders, as he always did when he wanted to say, "So what? It's no big deal."

"How much can you find?" he asked. "Perhaps you will find a million dollars worth of stuff you can blame me for. What does it matter? Stop looking, and I'll give you $100,000."

"To make me go away?" I paused, realizing I'd touched a nerve. "Four years ago, you said you weren't going to pay me any more because you wanted to build equity. There's no equity. I waited, but nothing changed."

I paused again. "Take care of your shareholder, Dan, or you will have a big problem."

I stood up and turned toward the door, refusing to give him a drop of information.

As I was leaving, Dan held out his hand to shake mine. I took it. It was cold and clammy. I scowled at him, my lips sealed. He was visibly sweating.

That night at the dinner table at home with my family I announced, "I'm going to get millions from them, not $100,000."

Our daughter Pam was worried. "Mom, what if these guys are Mafia, and they kill you?"

I was fearless. "If they do, make sure they end up in prison, and then get the money I have coming to me."

Each day as I entered the factory premises, I enjoyed light banter with the company security guards while playing my cards close to the vest. Neither Dan nor his lawyers knew the extent of my findings. In fact, they didn't seem to understand the magnitude of my complaint, nor did they imagine I'd uncovered so many areas of self-dealing. The documents I photocopied were delivered to them on a regular basis, but no one took the time to look at them. When my lawyers questioned the incorporation of related businesses, clearly against the law, they sent back letters of denial, which we intended to use to discredit them and secure sanctions against them. I certainly didn't tell the opposition I had access to the confidential files that described in detail the private, privileged discussions Dan, Sergey, and Yefim had with their lawyers, since they had every right to keep these hidden from me.

Had they not been so lazy or so busy with their affairs, they could have examined all the photocopies and found out exactly what I was privy to. But as cocky as they were, they assumed I was just a stupid girl having a look around and I'd never find anything damning.

Dan became curious though. One day he sent his full-time in-house accountant, Herman, upstairs to the document room, where I sat each day reading and marking pages with Post-its and paper clips to be photocopied. Entering the room with papers to file, feigning nonchalance, Herman turned to me casually.

"Tell me, Adrienne, have you found anything illegal in these boxes of documents?" he asked.

Trying to match his tone, I said in an off-hand way, "Oh, I suppose I've found thousands of things."

Did he really think I would tell him anything important? He actually looked at me in earnest, expecting an answer.

Recalling that Mrs. Leona Helmsley, the hotel queen, had gone to prison for fraudulently using hotel funds to decorate her own home and claiming it was a business expense, I asked him, "Do you see any parquet floors here in the factory? Can you tell me where they are? And what about the swimming pool? Where is that?"

The bills D & G paid were for these luxuries installed at Dan's residence, along with other properties the family owned. There was a $25,000 dermatological treatment for Dan's wife, and payments for insurance on all his cars, even his Ferrari which he seldom drove, and for his child support, as well as checks to a private school for his children and a separate check for their after-school ballet classes. D & G even paid to install telephone service in the Z family home in Beverly Hills. During one of Dan's vacations, D & G wired $70,000 to a Caribbean hotel to pay his gambling expenses. It's not unheard of for executives to borrow funds from their companies temporarily, but I searched and could not find reimbursement from Dan or any member of the Z family for anything. It was another stunning display of Dan's narcissistic and cunning ways.

Dan's misconduct didn't stop there. My lawsuit had not deterred him from his self-dealing, and in fact, once I instigated proceedings against him, he became even more determined to amass personal wealth at the expense of the company. As far as he was concerned, D & G no longer suited his purpose. After his parents' divorce, father and son were estranged. As part of the divorce settlement, Sergey gave half his stock to his ex-wife Inez. Dan maintained his 40 percent, while his mother had 20 percent, his father 20 percent, and Yefim (before he left) and I had 10 percent each. Together, Inez and her son held the majority, and neither of them had any use for the rest of us. D & G, a C corporation saddled with taxable dividends, became an unattractive vehicle for Dan's future ambitions, and Dan was hell-bent on creating other companies and making his money there.

CHAPTER 30

RESILIENCE

Meanwhile, Avanti of California was doing fairly well. The showroom next to the elevator in the Bedford Wilshire medical building was in a decent location, and I was paying a very low rent on it. I'd been there close to fifteen years, when one day I received a phone call from the landlord. Actually, the call came from the new landlord, Sam's son, Richard. His father had passed away, and a new regime was taking over. Richard wanted to know if I would be willing to sign a new lease, since for more than four years my status had been month to month with no obligation to continue. I told him I really didn't want a lease because the current arrangement seemed perfect. I was hoping to stay at least two more years, and what could possibly be wrong with the way things were? I didn't tell him that after my tumor had been excised, I'd made up my mind to get out of the business as soon as I could sell off my inventory, nor did he tell me that the tenant next door to me wanted my space and would pay much more than I was paying.

Without warning, Richard sent me a letter, telling me I had lost the right to stay month to month. He had leased my space to the other tenant, and the small space she had been leasing, he leased to someone else. I called Hilda, Sam's wife and Richard's stepmother, to see if she could influence her son to allow me to stay. After all, we were old family friends. But it was too late. Leases had been signed, and there was nothing she could do for me. As angry as I was about being evicted, I was concerned about how I would be able leave in just ninety days with over $1,000,000 of merchandise on hand.

What would a woman with resilience do? Not retire, surely? Would I find a new showroom? I was going to have to sign a lease after all, and at a much higher rent, only this time, I thought, I could be on the street by the sidewalk where retail customers could find me, not in the back of the lobby of an elevator building. These were the Bill Clinton years, when businesses were flourishing. I'd still have fun, if not as a wholesaler, then as a retailer. But in my heart, I knew I wanted to get out.

For several months, I had been hinting to Vera that one day in the near future she would take over my business. Vera didn't want to though. Finally, feeling the pressure of a new five-year lease, I gave her half ownership in all future business. Without investing in my inventory, she would share fifty-fifty in the profits. At this point, I truly needed her. She was good at retail, much better than I. She didn't want to pursue wholesale customers and preferred individual customers instead. Together we started a new company, Avanti Fine Jewelry, on Brighton Way, less than half a block from our prior showroom, in the middle of one of the busiest streets in Beverly Hills. We each invested $50,000 to build out the space, using my showcases and safes instead of ordering new ones. Vera hired a competent employee who used to work at D & G, an honest woman who was willing to learn our business. I agreed to work Mondays. Vera would work Tuesday through Saturday, and Sundays we would be closed. I would have four full days a week to visit the D & G factory and continue to go through files in their document room.

Adrienne's Dad

Mother Pearl

Stan and Adrienne

Stan and Adrienne

Pamela, Adrienne, Randall, and Stan

Adrienne, on a bike ride for the Arthritis Foundation

Seattle Show, January 25-29, 1997

Left to right: Adrienne, Vera, Elsa

Adrienne at the Jewelers of America show in New York City

The retail store on Brighton Way in Beverly Hills

Vera, wearing 18-karat
Italian jewelry

Three-row invisibly set princess
cut diamond band with three
carats of diamonds

Piero Milano with important emerald and diamond jewelry

The Piero Milano factory

Seven portraits of Dora Marr by Pablo Picasso

This Picasso image depicts a smart girl with a decision to make, eyes wide open to the future.

This is Picasso's observation of a very unhappy woman. For me, this was the realization that I no longer mattered to the D & G Company or anyone involved in it. If I hadn't cared so much about them, it would not have been so painful.

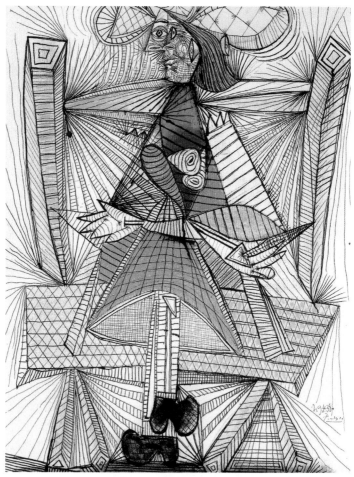

This is a painting of Dora Marr in a wicker chair. The wicker consumes her. She is tied up in it, unable to move, the tool in her hand completely useless. This is what it felt like to be a minority shareholder in a large corporation.

This Picasso painting is anything but pretty. It depicts my total exasperation. In fact, in 1937, the image is Picasso's personal statement of his feelings of anger over the Spanish Civil War. It shows anguish, rage, indignation, and resentment personified—a woman with a dangling breast who is no longer beautiful, a woman with no control.

My reaction to Picasso's painting of a weeping woman, with its purple background and her green nose, turned-down mouth, sad eyes, and tense, rigid chin, was a feeling not only of despair but also of heartache and regret—a grief that was doubly poignant, over the loss of my father to Alzheimer's disease and the loss of acceptance from my business partners.

When I first saw this painting, I was reminded of how it felt to be self-confident and smart. The art historian Judi Freeman described this as a woman who stares intently, confronting the viewer. "The red nails against the dark black hair bespeak a strong, assertive woman. Hers is a powerful force."

Back in the driver's seat! This is how it felt to wrest control.

CHAPTER 31

COLORED GEMS, INC.

Prior to August 2000, before my lawsuit had picked up steam, D & G had a substantial business in colored gemstones. Now with the lawsuit underway, Dan was even more determined to strip D & G of its assets, and one of the first assets Dan claimed for himself was the D & G colored stone business.

In February of 2000, the D & G colored stone inventory had been $85,206. After that it gradually diminished in value until July 2000, when it was reported at $17,293. Then, in the following months, the colored stone inventory simply disappeared.

What happened to the colored stones? Dan and his lawyers formed a new company, Colored Gems, Inc. Dan took the gems off of the D & G inventory list and gave them to the new entity. He took a partner, Ivan, a former D & G colored stone salesman, as CEO in charge of sales, and then he installed the new company, rent-free, on the second floor of the D & G factory with the D & G colored stones in the new company's safe. The inventory was transferred gradually so that Equity Factors, the company's big lender, wouldn't notice the disappearance of the colored gems from the D & G inventory over time.

As it was, D & G kept very sloppy inventories. I had heard from one of the employees that when Dan's cousin was working in the diamond department, he left a bag of diamonds under the table during a physical count of inventory. When the employee pointed out that they forgot to include the bag of diamonds in the total, he said, "Oh, don't worry. We don't have to count that."

In fact, the journal entries on the financial statements always showed large inventory adjustments, often over $1,500,000 a month. Incredibly, two months into the fiscal year, inventory suddenly increased by $2,250,000. It was easy to see that the accountants wrote off inventory and added it back at will. With credit memos to customers, returns and allowances close to $3,000,000 in one month alone, it was a mammoth effort to keep track of all the transactions.

Dan authorized substantial sums to be given from D & G as loans to Colored Gems, Inc., transferring up to $385,000 in funds in one month alone. These loans were always interest-free. Using the D & G relationship with Equity Factors, Dan also provided Colored Gems, Inc. with a personal guarantee to obtain all the financing it would need. In short, the D & G suppliers, the D & G customers, the D & G leasehold, the D & G inventory, the D & G employees, and the D & G goodwill were all transferred to or used by Colored Gems, Inc. without any compensation to D & G, while D & G paid all of the Colored Gems, Inc. expenses.

My lawyers insisted that the Colored Gems, Inc. business truly belonged to D & G. Nothing about the business had changed except the ownership on paper. D & G paid for Ivan's travel expenses before and after Colored Gems, Inc. was formed, including a trip to Italy where Ivan was introduced to the D & G mountings supplier, Italgold. When Italgold shipped mountings to D & G before and after Colored Gems existed, D & G paid the bill. Even the employees and salesmen for Colored Gems were actually employees of D & G, as D & G continued to pay for their travel expenses.

My lawyers confronted Dan with this complaint, and his response was that he wanted to focus on the D & G diamond business, not on the colored gemstone business. Ivan told me he himself had invested $900,000 into Colored Gems, Inc. and Dan had invested $60,000. But Dan's investment had come out of the D & G checkbook. We looked to see if any of these invested sums were ever paid back to D & G, but they were not. D & G received no compensation from either Dan or Ivan for giving away its colored stone business. It was obvious to all that this business still belonged to D & G, and at this point, with Yefim gone, 11 percent of it belonged to me.

Had Yefim still been a shareholder, Dan would not have been able to get away with this. But he wasn't there. It was easy for Dan, carefree and unbothered, to do whatever suited him.

I couldn't say I hadn't been warned.

In any case, to justify his wrongdoing, Dan offered me 11 percent of his alleged 6 percent interest in Colored Gems, Inc. (the equivalent of .0067 ownership in this company), but only on condition that I pay hard money to Colored Gems, Inc. and also become jointly and severally liable for a $2,000,000 credit line. This was ridiculous. Why would I pay for Colored Gems, Inc., when D & G had received nothing for giving it away? I had no obligation to pay for .0067 of this portion of D & G's business when I already owned 11 percent of it through D & G. The offer was a sham.

While it's self-evident that no one would pay for a .0067 interest in a new company and become jointly and severally liable for its entire $2,000,000 line of credit, nevertheless, to ensure that I would not accept the offer, Dan told me that if I did buy into Colored Gems, Inc., he would leave, and without him the company would die.

CHAPTER 32

SELLING DIAMONDS
CAN BE TRICKY

M y partner Vera was keeping the business together in Avanti's new location, where I worked every Monday. I had just shipped a special order engagement ring to New York City with a 2.69 carat round brilliant diamond as the center stone—truly beautiful—so I wasn't surprised when the groom-to-be gave my number to his best friend, Dean. Dean loved his friend's ring and the price as well. He called to say he wanted something just as beautiful, but it had to be different. He wanted an asscher cut diamond instead of a round one. Asscher cuts are square, and the prettiest of them are perfectly square, all sides matched to zero hundredths of a millimeter. Because they are square, they weigh more for their size. A three-carat asscher cut doesn't look like three carats. Its length and width are similar to the diameter of a two and a half carat round.

"Dean," I said, "If you want an asscher cut, you'll need to get a bigger diamond, at least a three-carat asscher, or it will look smaller than your friend's diamond. And the price per carat will jump at that size."

Dean really wanted the lower price of a two-carat diamond, as the price jump is significant for a three carater, but accepting my advice, he asked me to show him some three-carat stones in spite of the additional cost. He could just imagine the two girlfriends holding their rings side by side to compare them.

"Can you wait a week?" I asked Dean. "I'll be in New York then and will have several stones you can look at."

Fortuitously, there was a trade show coming up, and I had to be in New York for that. I could bring Dean whatever he wanted to see. I quickly researched online through my suppliers' diamond inventories to see what was available in fine quality asscher cuts between two and a half and three carats. One of my dealers was in New York City, actually just walking distance to Dean's office. I made arrangements to pick up several asscher cut diamonds from him the following week.

The diamond Dean selected was the only perfectly square three-carat asscher cut available in the United States. This was almost certain, since it was the only one that size in the online inventories of diamond dealers coast to coast. It was graded by the GIA to be G color, VS1 clarity, excellent cut, polish and symmetry, with perfectly equal measurements on all sides. It was also more than Dean planned to spend. I showed him asschers that were *almost* square, but he was a perfectionist and wanted just the impeccable one. I left him a copy of the GIA report, then walked back to the diamond district on 47th Street to return all the diamonds except the one Dean was considering. He was going to let me know his decision the next day.

The following day I called Dean. "What did you decide?"

He said he had found the exact same diamond online for $500 less. It was the same perfectly square asscher cut with exactly the same measurements, color, and clarity, and exactly the same GIA grading report. If he paid by credit card, he could have the stone in two days from his online source.

"There is only one diamond like this," I replied. "No two diamonds are exactly alike. I have the stone here with me, and your online source doesn't have it and never will. How can he say he'll send it to you in two days when he doesn't have it? Who is he, anyway?"

Dean gave me the name. I hung up and called this online seller immediately. His phone number had a Los Angeles area code, but he said he was in Beverly Hills, off Coldwater, in a residential area. I told him I was calling because I had seen the aascher-cut diamond online and had a customer for it.

I wasn't serious, but I did want to see his reaction.

"Can you bring the stone to my Beverly Hills store, just ten minutes away?"

"Not today," he replied. "I'll bring it tomorrow afternoon."

He didn't tell me he didn't have the stone or that it had to be shipped to him overnight from New York. Nor did I reveal that I already had the diamond in my pocket.

After that phone call, I went back to see my dealer on 47th St. "Saul," I queried, "How can a guy in Beverly Hills go online and sell your diamond $500 less than I can?"

Saul was perturbed. This had apparently happened to him a couple of times before. He asked his receptionist/assistant if they had received any requests that day for a three carat aascher cut. She said someone did call, but she told him that the stone he requested was out with a customer.

Saul shook his head. "That guy takes my online list of available stones and claims they are his. He makes his own list with my online inventory and offers my stones to the public. One of the biggest stores in Chicago dropped me when they lost a sale because of him. I should have stopped sending him stones back then, a long time ago. I can't let him do this any more. He'll never get another thing from me now; that's for sure. This can't happen again."

Then Saul lowered my cost by $1,000 so I could make the sale.

It used to be that stones changed ownership on a handshake from one dealer to the next. Dealer A gave it to Dealer B who gave it to Dealer C. It was hard to know who really owned the stone. With the advent of the Internet, the diamond business radically changed. Today, with very little research, the primary sources are instantly available to all.

I called Dean back and gave him $1,000 discount on the already very low price. I also made him a gorgeous ring. I tell this story as an example of why it is so difficult to make money in the jewelry business today.

CHAPTER 33

HEEDLESS GALL

As I was leaving the D & G factory at the end of the day, Inez ran after me. I was heading for my car when she called after me. I turned around to face her. "Do you have any idea how much our bill is for photocopying your documents?" she asked. "Will this never end?"

Wow, she sounds upset. She wants it over with.

"Whatever your bill is," I said, "it's a pittance compared to what you've taken from me. If you don't like paying for photocopies, then pay me what you owe me."

Actually, by 2001, I had gathered almost all the evidence I needed. I had more than enough to build a strong case and was now examining recent transactions. The latest chicanery was when Dan decided it was time to get rid of D & S, Inc., where his father and Yefim were still shareholders. Once he knew I was complaining that he'd created D & S, Inc. for everyone else but me, Dan instructed Zales *not* to pay that company, but to make their payments to Creations Jewelry Manufacturing, instead.

Will he ever stop fabricating new entities? Does he think I won't find out about them?

To prove Dan's devious ways, I photocopied an invoice from D & S, Inc. to Zales, the nationwide chain of jewelry stores, where the payee, D & S, Inc. had been crossed out by hand and replaced instead with the hand-written payee, Creations Jewelry Manufacturing. Creations Jewelry did not exist at the time D & S, Inc. shipped the goods. The new company began a month later with the publication of a Fictitious Name Statement in the newspapers. I made a photocopy of that as well. Dan had successfully cheated me, and now he would cheat Yefim and Sergey, the other shareholders of D & S. He no longer wanted anything to do with them either. His parents had divorced, and Dan blamed his father. He had no use for Yefim any more. Since he did not wish to share D & S profits with anyone, Dan established Creations Jewelry Manufacturing and would funnel D & S profits to himself and himself alone.

My lawyers' questions about this were answered with a signed declaration from Dan that D & S, Inc. had ceased operations years ago. I could see him shrugging his shoulders as he perjured himself without compunction. Committing perjury on the Defendant's Declaration was no big deal for him. In April of 2001, D & S, Inc. was still in business, shipping goods and invoicing customers, even though Dan declared otherwise.

When I was the victim, a shareholder on the outs, neither Sergey nor Yefim stood up for me or cared. When Sergey and Yefim became victims, there was no one left to stand up or care for them.

There were other companies Dan established for himself even before Creations Jewelry. The more I looked into the books and files, the more wrongdoing I found. Moving from the payables to the receivables, I saw the name Manufacturers

Jewelry Outlet, a business owned and operated by Dan and Joan, Dan's second wife.

After seven years in business, D & G had millions of dollars of surplus inventory and unsold samples, most of which consisted of merchandise returns. A few customers, including Zales, were given very special perks, such as inventory balancing, which allowed them to return a small percentage of unsold merchandise with no questions asked, as long as the store continued to place purchase orders. The returned merchandise was considered "unsalable," so Dan and his wife decided to open an outlet store with merchandise taken on consignment at a deeply discounted closeout price, far less than the cost to manufacture. D & G would lose money on every piece given to Dan and Joan, allowing Dan and Joan to keep all the profits themselves.

As usual, D & G paid all the store's expenses. D & G paid the lawyers to incorporate the company, and also paid for the rent, the safe, the showcases, and more. According to Joan's one employee, who was actually on the D & G payroll, Dan and Joan's outlet store sold quite a bit of merchandise for cash off the books. When the merchandise simply "disappeared," D & G didn't get paid at all.

Chasing after business was not the only way Dan sought to enrich his family. When he decided to move from Hill Street and purchase a building to house the D & G factory, using D & G funds for the down payment and acquisition costs, Sergey and Dan took the mortgage in their names so that title belonged to them. Then when they refinanced the property after the build-out, they obtained a new loan from Universal Bank.

My lawyers asked me to look for the loan documents. I couldn't find them in the document room. They just weren't there. Looking at the loan documents would reveal crucial information my lawyer needed, but Dan's lawyers considered them to contain privileged information, so they kept them in their offices, not in the document room. To gain access to the file, I had to petition the court. The request racked up more than $15,000 in my legal fees, but it was worth it. The documents proved to be damning in more ways than one.

It is interesting to note that once we had access to the file, instead of going through it himself, my lawyer had the documents delivered to my home. He trusted that I would read the file carefully and let him know what I had learned. I set the box filled with thousands of pages next to my bed and began reading, while Stan lay next to me watching television.

I opened the box with anticipation. Surely there was something here they didn't want me to find. I was determined to read every page.

The first interesting document was a letter from Universal Bank with an inquiry. The bank wanted to know why Dan's income, as stated on his W-2, was so vastly different from his income as stated on his 1040 IRS declaration. I wanted to know the answer too, possibly more than the bank did. I couldn't wait to read on.

"The answer must be here someplace," I told Stan.

It took some doing to uncover the facts. The W-2 income statement for the IRS Dan gave to the bank in order to get a bank loan showed a much higher income than what he actually received. It was false. He had correctly reported a lower salary to the IRS that year. The false W-2 that the bank received was corrected later on, after the loan had been made. The accountants had it all figured out. When Dan needed the loan, they produced a W-2 that told the bank he had earned more. It was so simple to present a false document to the bank and reverse it later, after reporting his true income to the IRS.

I get it now. They defrauded the banks.

As I dug further into the box of documents they had fought so hard to keep from me, I couldn't believe my eyes. *"Voilà!"* I told Stan. "This is BINGO! Here's what they didn't want me to see."

It was a signed balance sheet for D & G, dated December 12, 1997, stating Retained Earnings of almost $11,000,000, and a full market value for the company at $25,093,020. "This is great," I mused, proud to own 11 percent. Then I found the signed IRS form 1040, dated the same day, signed by the same accountant, where the Retained Earnings were close to zero! So which document was true, the higher one for the bank loan or the lower one for the IRS? There was an $11,000,000 difference!

Wait. This is outright fraud! And yet, they have no compunction.

It seemed to me that the financial improprieties were endless, and the misstatement of corporate financial records was an everyday occurrence. The more I looked, the more I found. For example, Dan's cousin, his very first employee at D & G, had been working faithfully every day since the very beginning, when the company was a struggling start-up Her salary was $500 a month and remained there for years until I instigated my lawsuit. How could she survive close to a decade on just $6,000 a year? The answer became obvious when employee salaries were no longer supplemented with cash, because then her stated income went from $6,000 to $70,000, which is what she'd actually been getting all along, I assumed.

The ledgers themselves were full of lies. My accountant called it smoke and mirrors. Inventories changed drastically from month to month and were always high except during the last month of the fiscal year, when they mysteriously diminished to a fraction of their previous month's value. Low inventory would reduce the profit and avoid taxes. However, two months into the next fiscal year, inventories would increase dramatically to satisfy the lender, Equity Factors.

Having read through all the payable files, I began looking at the receivables. File after file contained dozens of unpaid invoices for merchandise shipped to D & G customers with no proof of actual payment. Some invoices showed payment, but for the wrong amount with no credit given. The records were indeed sloppy.

As far as the financial statements were concerned, even if you were astute and savvy, you couldn't know the truth. At the end of each fiscal year and the beginning of the next, after the facts were stated and written in stone, there were multiple reversals and adjustments of general journal entries. As it was, I tried to understand some of the financial statements, but there were many inter-company transactions that were impossible to follow because they were listed as "interco" without mentioning any of Dan's companies by name. Not only that, the accountants did their best to hide the loans to and from officers, who also weren't identified. A line item in the ledgers labeled "suspense," often held unallocated sums of over $1,000,000.

I asked my accountant to explain the term, "suspense," and he said it's a term for funds coming in or going out with no explanation, not attributed to anything in particular. I supposed this would be normal for a nominal sum of money, but a million dollars? How can you not reconcile such a large amount?

Easy, if you sell a hundred million, that's just one percent.

I knew for a fact that with over three hundred employees at D & G, the vending machines in the second-floor lunchroom brought in a tidy sum every month, but this money never made it into the bank. Yet, every month, D & G wrote a check to Advantage Vending as a rental fee. The vending machines in the lunchroom were simply another source of income never mentioned on the books. Why bother? That was merely chump change no one cared about, even though it added up to a tidy sum.

One of the requirements of a California corporation is the keeping of proper financial records. Because of what I thought was deceit or sloppiness of those in charge, I hoped to prove that D & G defrauded both the IRS and its shareholders, in spite of Henry Finsterman's admonitions. As the CPA (certified public accountant) for D & G, Finsterman felt there were irregularities and tried to protect himself by writing letters describing the tax laws. As early as 1996, Finsterman wrote to Dan and Sergey about the company's irregular bonus accruals in an attempt to explain illegalities. The company gave them huge bonuses on the books, $500,000 each, money that it didn't actually have available to give. How did it give them the money when it wasn't there? They said they got it even though they didn't. And then they "lent" it back to the company at 6 percent interest. It seemed to me that if they got the bonuses, they should have paid tax on the money, but I had no idea whether or not they paid attention to Finsterman's warnings or ever paid taxes on their bonuses.

If you really didn't get the half-million-dollar bonus, could you afford to pay tax on it?

Dan was a gambler, not just in business but also at the gaming tables. During the Las Vegas trade shows, I used to run into him night after night at the casinos. He loved black jack and roulette and would risk losing tens of thousands of dollars in tall stacks of chips just for the thrill of it. I watched him do so and couldn't believe it.

One day while looking at the D & G ledgers, I noticed that D & G had transferred $40,000 to a bank in the Bahamas. I presumed this was to pay gambling debts when Dan was on vacation there. Henry, the accountant, explained it as a "loan to an officer," but of course, when Dan borrowed from the company, he had no intention of ever paying it back, and he certainly didn't pay interest on it, either. In retrospect, I think he might have been a gambling addict.

My accountant examined all the ledgers. "Is this company making money?" he asked hypothetically. "It's hard to tell."

This was one of the pivotal questions for my case against Dan and Sergey. Indeed, D & G seemed to be surviving only on cash flow.

CHAPTER 34

SEARCHING FOR ANSWERS

In the early years, D & G had trouble paying its suppliers on time because the company was growing too fast and in constant need of gold and diamonds to manufacture its orders. In fact, creditors were owed so much that Dan was told not to drive his Ferrari around town because his creditors would get angry.

"Look at this guy," they would say. "He runs around in a fancy car as if he's a king, but he doesn't pay his vendors."

In 1996, D & G found a lender who would lend 80 percent of every invoice on orders that were filled and shipped. Factoring invoices this way gave the company funds to work with. Even with this help, D & G was in dire need of suppliers who had deep pockets and didn't mind waiting for payment. Dan looked to India and China to find new vendors. He always found a way. He hooked up with Indians from Mumbai and Chinese from Hong Kong, well-heeled suppliers able to manufacture cheaply as much as Dan could sell. D & G began importing goods at a million dollars a year at first, but this quickly grew to a total debt of $15,000,000.

It took quite some time for me to put the pieces together. I noticed someone named Dixit Shen was flying in from Hong Kong, but I didn't know who he was. D & G paid all his expenses, leased an apartment for him downtown, and paid for his office in Hong Kong, but I didn't know why. Then later a man by the name of Adil Kumar came from Mumbai, and he ran up enormous expenses that D & G paid. Kumar was flying in from India, staying in Los Angeles for months at a time, and charging everything to the company. He stayed at the Residence Inn in Beverly Hills. He flew first class on Singapore Airlines and even charged expensive clothing when he'd been in London. I wanted very much for my lawyers to subpoena him for questioning. Who was this guy, really? Shen's expenses were high, but Kumar's were even higher.

I called The Residence Inn and asked to speak to Mr. Kumar. I wasn't even sure he was in town at the time. The hotel operator connected me to his room, but there was no answer. At least I knew he was in town. My lawyers drew a subpoena, and a court messenger took it to the D & G factory, where Adil Kumar presumably spent his days checking the receivables. But each time the messenger went to serve the subpoena, he was told Mr. Kumar was not there.

So, Dan, you think you can keep Adil Kumar hidden from me forever? I'll find a way to subpoena him.

Since we didn't know what Kumar looked like, how were we going to serve him his papers? The messenger couldn't get past the security guards, let alone the factory entrance. I wanted Dan to know that I had every right to question Mr. Kumar, and I would find a way to do so. I told my lawyers to hire an investigator to catch Kumar at his hotel and serve him there.

I'm going to get to this guy, and you can't stop me.

The investigator telephoned me. "What does Mr. Kumar look like? How old is he? How tall?"

I had never met Kumar. I had no idea. I certainly couldn't ask anyone at D & G. All I knew was the name Adil Kumar appeared over and over again in the payable file and on the ledgers. He ran up huge bills, and D & G paid every one of them. That's all I knew. But investigators are very smart and have their ways of getting information. The next day a beautiful gift basket arrived at the front desk of the Residence Inn, with a note from Singapore Airlines that said, "Thank you, Mr. Kumar, for your business." My investigator waited around in the lobby for Kumar to pick up his gift. He took his picture, and the next morning in the parking lot, Kumar was served with the subpoena.

That triumph felt amazing. I do believe it was the catalyst that would cause Dan to cave. *I* was merely an annoyance in the document room, but *Kumar* was too important, and Dan didn't want my lawyers to mess with *him*.

Just watch me, Dan. I'm much more than a thorn in your side now.

As it turns out, I didn't have to take Kumar's deposition. A week after he was served his papers, while I was examining documents, Dan introduced him to me, and we had a nice conversation. I found out he was an important accountant hired by Indian suppliers in Mumbai who had given millions in diamonds to both Colored Gems, Inc. and D & G. Kumar thought I was a rich investor. He wanted me to help him get his suppliers paid in India.

"Do you have money to lend here?" Kumar asked me again and again, as if obsessed with need. His native accent was typical. "Where can we get money? We need money here." For a very long time he had seen money flow out as fast as it came in.

I shook my head from side to side without an answer. He didn't have a clue about my investigation into the very man who couldn't pay this debt. *Poor Adil,* I thought, knowing he and his Indian friends were owed close to $15,000,000. I didn't tell him what I presumed—that they would never be paid.

Days later, knowing everyone at the factory was sick and tired of my constant presence, I saw Dan's cousin in the parking lot. She wanted to talk to me to find out how much longer my investigation would take.

"I told Dan to pay you," she said. "You are right to fight him. I don't know why he doesn't pay you. He really should. You come here every day. We are getting tired of it. We all want this to be over with."

Her words were comforting. Even so, I knew where her loyalties lay. Obviously, my daily visits were beyond exasperating for all of them. They complained to their lawyers to do something.

CHAPTER 35

ENOUGH IS ENOUGH

Dan was tired of me. He called his lawyers. "We don't want her hanging out here any longer. It's annoying, and if she talks to Kumar, that could hurt us."

We got a list of sixty-four questions to answer. What had I learned over the past two years? They wanted to know. My lawyer said I didn't have to answer, but I was proud of what my sleuthing revealed and wanted them to realize they were in trouble. A judge or jury would likely put them in jail for what they'd done. At the same time, I wasn't about to give away my case. They had the thirty-six boxes of photocopied documents pointing to illegal improprieties, but they hadn't opened a single one of them.

My lawyer was a great litigator who did not want to make things easy for them. "We're not going to hand them our case on a silver platter. If you really want to answer their questions," he said, "direct them to the Bates-stamped photocopies. Answer with page numbers, not with words."

Alan had our set of all thirty-six boxes of documents delivered to my house so I could reread every page and create an orderly spreadsheet to prove each of my accusations against them. Organizing the documents took me most of the summer, more than two months for sure, but it solidified my case for my lawyers and saved me tens of thousands of dollars in legal fees. My legal bills were small when compared to the size of my complaint. By summer's end, we sent my answers off to Dan's legal team—no words, just lists of Bates-stamped page numbers as an answer to each question. I was gloating. My opponents were about to find out I wasn't the patsy they thought I was.

You want answers? You want to know if you did anything wrong? Go to the boxes. Read the 29,000 pages I photocopied for you.

Finally, they opened the boxes and started reading. Self-dealing can be found again and again. Look on this list of page numbers. Excessive compensation can be found over here, on this list. Depriving shareholders of corporate opportunity while usurping it for yourself can be found elsewhere, on this list. And so forth . . .

The evidence was all there, but we were not going to spoonfeed them. We were going to make them discover it themselves.

It wasn't long before Stan got a phone call. One of Dan's lawyers wanted to meet for lunch to discuss a settlement, lawyer to lawyer. I told Stan to feel them out. He shouldn't go unless the offer was at least a certain amount. They did *not* want a trial. They wanted to pay me.

After the lunch, when it was evident they had a high number in mind, we scheduled a meeting in the Loeb & Loeb conference room on the 19th floor of 10100 Santa Monica in Century City. Jim Hercules, Dan, Sergey, and Alice V. (the accountant), sat on one side of the table; my lawyer, Alan, and I sat on the other. Jim Hercules began the meeting with a statement saying they recognized they had done "a few things" wrong. I wanted to laugh out loud at his phrasing, but I kept my composure. Even so, they wanted to answer any questions we had.

Of course, we had questions.

Be calm. Be confident. Just sit tight and see what they do.

Alan began with his first question, which was really several questions in one. "Let's talk about excessive compensation. Aside from your excessive salaries, perhaps you can begin by explaining this long list of your personal expenses the company paid." He handed the list to Dan, across the table.

All eyes turned to Dan. He barely glanced at the page, winced slightly, and shrugged his shoulders. His father, who was sitting next to him and wasn't happy to be there, said, "That is not an answer! Say something!"

I can't believe Sergey is attacking his son. All that admiration he had for him, where'd it go? I've never seen him get so angry.

Alan waited. When no answer was forthcoming, he continued. "As officers of the corporation you voted yourselves large yearly bonuses that the company couldn't afford to pay. You didn't actually receive the money because it wasn't there, but the ledgers show you claimed it and lent it back to the corporation at 6 percent interest. Then at other times, you borrowed large sums from the company as a completely separate transaction—interest-free, so you didn't *pay* any interest—and more importantly, you didn't repay the loans either."

I was pretty sure we had proof of this, but in any case, the question was out there, and no one uttered a reply.

If they weren't concerned at this point, they were all about to be very worried.

Next, Alan presented them with two conflicting documents, both dated December 31, 1997, signed by the company accountant, "Alice V., CPA". The first was an application to the bank for a loan. The second was a statement of company income for the IRS.

"Which document is correct," Alan asked, looking directly at Alice, "the one with the higher number you gave to the bank for your loan, or the one with the lower number you gave to the IRS to avoid taxes?"

There was an $11,000,000 discrepancy in company assets on the same day.

At this point the opposition all huddled together around the table to study the evidence. They were understandably troubled. One way or the other, it was clear they were guilty of either bank fraud or tax fraud.

Now, at least, they know we mean business.

Later, Alan presented an analysis of diamonds the company had sold, some that had been invoiced and some that hadn't. It was a nineteen-page report of sold diamonds, and it was a real "Gotcha!", proof of consummate crime. More than one hundred large diamonds were listed, from one to five carats each. The spreadsheets, written in ink by hand, documented all the details of diamond sales, from the date the diamonds were acquired to the date they were sold. The data included the name of the diamond supplier, the cost of each stone, the customer who purchased it, the salesman who sold it, the selling price, the date of sale and the invoice number. At least one-third of the stones on the list had no invoice number, even though all of them were tallied in the profit column. Our question: "Why were so many large diamonds sold without an invoice?" The unasked question, of course, was, "Did you pocket the cash and cheat not only your shareholders but also the IRS?" It was the elephant in the conference room. When they had no answer, I knew they were dead, then and there.

We got a hefty settlement offer the next day. It was a good offer; but hoping to do better, I called a dear friend who had been a judge on the bench. I wanted his opinion. Bob had been a no-nonsense adjudicator, and we truly respected him. He had read our brief, with our list of accusations and general statements of proof, and was ready to give us his advice.

He came over one evening to talk.

"These people are out-and-out crooks! I'm surprised they didn't kill you." Bob went on with a tirade for several minutes about all their wrongdoings, all the things you cannot do to a shareholder: breach of fiduciary duty, deceptive financial practices, misappropriation of funds, self-dealing, excessive compensation to officers, usurping corporate opportunity to the detriment of shareholders, unreported cash transactions, tax evasion, and so forth. Then he offered his opinion, telling us he thought their offer was high enough, and I should probably take it. In fact, he said, "I'm not supposed to think like this, but the thought did cross my mind. Where can you invest $50,000 and get such a huge offer like this one?"

Nevertheless, we didn't accept the settlement offer right away. The court ordered us to hire a mediator to convince both sides to agree on a price instead of going to trial. We each had to select a person acceptable to the other, someone whom everyone deemed objective and impartial. We all decided on Eli.

The Z family had had enough of me. They were anxious to buy my shares. Their offer was actually fair, but I was hoping to up the price. I wanted punitive damages, yet without a trial, that didn't seem possible.

Eli went back and forth. Alan, Stan, and I were in one room at Loeb & Loeb; Hercules, Dan, and Sergey were in another. Eli went to their room and told them if they didn't pay me what I wanted, there would be a trial, and they would most certainly go to jail. Then he came to my room and told us if I didn't settle for their already generous offer, there would be a trial, they would go to jail, and the IRS would take the bulk of the money, so I might get nothing more than the satisfaction of punishing them. In addition, it would be costly. Then later on when they would get out of jail, they would go back to what they had always done as if nothing had ever happened.

Eli negotiated both sides. They agreed to give me a little more, but the company had a lot of debt and would have to pay me over time. They didn't want to pay interest on the unpaid balance, but I said that if the company could pay Sergey and Dan 6 percent interest on officers' loans, it could pay me 6 percent as well.

In the end, Eli commented, "The only person I know in this town who can negotiate like Adrienne is the divorce lawyer, Steve Kolodny."

I smiled and said, "I had to deal with Steve a few years ago. He was my step-mom's lawyer when my dad was very sick, and I found him quite reasonable."

In this world, if you win, you're respected. And I had won a hard-fought battle along with a substantial sum.

It took four years for Sergey and Dan to pay me with a nice check every month. Everything the family owned, including their homes, cars, jewels, and thirty-one of their most valuable personal possessions, was attached as security until the last payment was made. I had been through a riveting two years of research and undercover work that ultimately led to this agreement, one that might never have happened had I not prevailed and stood on principle for what I believed. My family was proud of me, but more important, I felt respected by many different people. In fact, the day before meeting with Sergey and Dan and their lawyers, I was in the conference room at Loeb & Loeb. Stepping away from the table, I had trouble squeezing my body between my chair and the sideboard next to the wall. Laughing about my recent weight gain, I said, "I guess I'm not as small as I think I am." Alan's reply was a pleasant surprise. "There's nothing small about you, Adrienne."

Eventually, D & G went out of business. Although I had no further contact with Dan, I heard he joined a diamond firm and then left to become president of a trading company, probably working for the investors in India to whom he owed a fortune. He never lost his extraordinary gift for sales. He and Joan divorced, and in fact, Joan called me one day to try to dig up dirt about him. As of this writing, he remains unmarried. I'll always believe that selling is Dan's true love. Sergey divorced his second wife and went back to working on the bench on his own, a victim of his son's anger and greed, just like me. Older, living alone, Sergey had come full circle, from rags to riches, to an ordinary life like any other, his main happiness coming from spending time with his children on the weekends. Dan remained close to his mother, who I believe is still single. Later on, when Sergey's health began to fail, Dan felt compassion for him and gave him space in his office rent-free.

This is the lesson. Each of us must live the life we create, according to our actions. Every day we are faced with choices. What we choose and how we react will determine our future. As for me, the money did not change my life. Stan wasn't ready to retire, and I still had the store on Brighton Way.

CHAPTER 36

ASSESSING THE FUTURE

A nd so, it was done. D & G was no longer part of my life
or daily consciousness. I felt a moment of awe, a sudden
freedom, as well as a sense of accomplishment. It was time to
acknowledge the past and look to the future, a new day, and a
time without demanding pressures. Where was I at this point
in my life, and where was I going?

I started playing bridge again, once a week, while Vera
continued to take care of business at Avanti. Philanthropic
causes beckoned, and I joined the Board of Governors at
Cedars-Sinai Medical Center. With our children out of college and living on their own, Stan and I decided to remodel
our home. As beautiful as it was, the closets were tiny, the
plumbing was old, and the bathrooms needed updating. It was
a fifteen-month project, adding square footage and a new roof,
moving walls around, installing copper pipes throughout, and
rewiring the entire house. Soon I'd be planning a wedding for
our son Randall and Galit, his beautiful bride-to-be. Life was
busy, and I was blessed.

After our son Randall married Galit, I enlisted my daughter-in-law's help. Residential real estate was on the rise, and I wanted to invest. Together Galit and I would buy a house, remodel it, and sell it for profit. The housing market was booming, and we could do no wrong. It seemed like an easy business, if you were smart about it, much easier than selling jewelry. With just six months from the purchase to the sale, we did very well. Our daughter Pam wanted to do a house with me after that. However, by the time this second venture was purchased, remodeled, and ready to sell, the bubble had burst. When we couldn't sell this house for profit, we rented it out instead. It was a beautiful colonial-style house in a sought-after area near UCLA, so why not hold onto it until its value went up again?

Home prices had suddenly plunged, while oil prices surged. A huge number of mortgage delinquencies, a weaker job market, and the nose-diving value of the dollar meant higher prices for foreign goods and less consumption overall. A financial crisis was looming.

Life at Avanti was not so busy any more. Mondays, when Vera was off and I managed the store, I rarely saw any customers. President Clinton was out, Bush was in, and business was definitely at a standstill. Our first years on Brighton Way had been good ones, and we renewed our lease, but conditions had changed. The economy all over the country seemed to be failing, and by 2008 we were in the middle of the Great Recession.

Vera and I tried not to invest any more money in inventory. We had more than $250,000 in stock that was more than a year old, and another $250,000 that was almost five years old. In an effort to sell more, we dropped prices, which weren't high to begin with. We gave up exhibiting at the Los Angeles gift shows and the San Francisco shows as well, because the tradeshow expenses had become so high we couldn't make a profit, and the money we did glean from the shows didn't warrant closing the store to be there. We bought new displays to spiff up the showcases and relied on vendors who allowed returns. Instead of buying, we took merchandise on consignment to show the new trends. Profits disintegrated, so I stopped taking a salary.

In 2009, despite the consistent success of my thirty-five years in the business, Avanti Fine Jewelry lost money. For five years in a row, sales had steadily declined, without even a hint of an uptick during the downward spiral. Our lease would expire in 2010, and the new rent was going to be too much to swallow. Vera had grown weary and began to have health problems. She was exhausted and emotionally out of steam. I wanted to retire. She needed a long rest. When our landlord wouldn't budge or negotiate a new lease or even allow us to stay on a month-to-month basis at the old price, we began making preparations to close for good.

With $1,250,000 of inventory, you don't just close your doors. We needed a marketing plan to unload our stock quickly, complete with promotion and advertising. I researched. What is the best way to have a going-out-of-business sale?

I'd heard about cars that roamed the streets with advertising. The cars had large "Liquidation Sale" signs on top. It was a great idea. A caravan of cars like these would bring in customers who never knew we existed before, customers who would be thrilled at the bargains we offered.

We all got on the phones and called everyone we knew. When our loyal clients realized we were actually going out of business, they came in droves to buy at closeout prices. In the six hectic months that preceded the end of our lease, we sold 90 percent of everything in our inventory. Our vendors were sad that we would not be buying any more, and they supplemented what was left by allowing us to choose from their inventories on a consignment basis so we could continue to have product until we closed our doors. To this day, when we have jewelry parties or private showings, these same vendors continue to sponsor us with consignments. It's a warm, fuzzy feeling to be trusted.

Vera paid off her house. We sold the showcases and safes and put the leftover stock in a bank vault. When I officially retired, Vera started her own company, Avanti Designs.

Fully retired from the jewelry business, except for a jewelry party now and then, I bought a road bike and became a cyclist. I'd heard about the California Coast Classic, a 525-mile bike ride from San Francisco to Los Angeles that takes place each September to raise funds for the Arthritis Foundation. I'd never owned a road bike before, but, as with everything else in my life, I was determined to learn how to ride it. I took lessons, and even though I fell down many times, failure was not an option. Eventually I would master the sport. The California Coast Classic was just another challenge that turned out to be the opportunity of a lifetime. Striving to conquer the hills on a bike, I truly believed that if others could do it, I could do it also. This bike ride for charity, eight days along one of the most beautiful coastlines in the world—through fields of strawberries, artichokes, avocados, and more, on back roads with few cars and the sound of the ocean waves crashing and the smell of the sea—became a Zen experience of wonder, surprise, joy, apprehension, exhaustion, amazement, humility, and pride. More important, though, was that I raised awareness and a great deal of money for the Arthritis Foundation. I also inspired others to do the same and made many new friends.

Now I spend days with our grandchildren every week, while slowly improving my skills at bridge. I'm also building a huge house on spec in the Palisades of Los Angeles. It's a risk, a big one, in fact, but I'd faced bigger challenges than that over the last ten years dealing with businessmen who were out to get me.

As a rebel who tried to exceed the limits of normal boundaries, I never sought to harm or injure anyone along the way. I've rejoiced in a feast of blessings, all the miraculous gifts I'd been given at birth in our spectacular world, and I've never stopped feeling grateful. It's easy to say I would have loved to have known at the beginning what I came to realize at the end. I was young and willing to take chances. Starting a business, today more than ever before, requires youth and a daredevil attitude.

It was all worth it, though. The business world had changed me and made me the woman I'd sought to become. Looking back, I could see how I'd dedicated decades of my life in pursuit of personal growth, true self-respect, and a sense of accomplishment. A youth spent with few regrets, I'd kept many friends and my family close. Life taught me well. Fears and doubts notwithstanding, in every endeavor I'd invested myself fully, calculated the odds, endured long hours and many unpleasant incidents, overcoming challenges with courage and resilience. Whatever the task at hand, I would become adept at it. I certainly made people happier through the years, creating beautiful things and serving a purpose in the business world. Reconciling the woman I'd been with the woman I'd become, content as a person of "character" in spite of mistakes, I felt fulfilled. Most of all, the incessant yearning of my youth was at long last requited.

I could see the world had changed in many ways. No longer constrained by society's traditional roles as housewife, schoolteacher, or secretary, women were now CEOs of major corporations, and in fact, women dared to seek the highest office in the nation, president of the United States. In my thirties, the fax machine had appeared to be the most significant invention. Now cell phones, laptops, tablets, and computers were *de rigeur*, offering instant information and communication to everyone. With tremendous access to competitive pricing and overnight shipping, business itself had changed. Jewelers that survived would have to develop a topnotch website and deal with online comparison shopping and same-day Uber delivery. They would have to muster fierce dedication, focus, and discipline. To become successful in this new world would be much harder than in the past.

As for me, I shall go on to future endeavors. I shall look for new opportunities. Older and wiser, I'll find a new career. You only regret the things you don't do when the opportunities are there, and I've learned that determination can trump almost anything as long as you believe in yourself.

I'll always take calculated risks as a way of living life to the fullest, never forgetting the words I'd heard at the age of four when my mother died. They were engraved in my conscious being. Aunt Estelle was right. Life would test and reward me, but no matter what, when obstacles blocked my way, I could conquer them. The world was mine. I could be, and I would be, just fine.

Book Club
Discussion Questions

1. What makes the jewelry business so vastly different from other endeavors?

2. In Chapter 9, the author philosophizes existentially about that indescribable thing that remains forever beyond her grasp. Is she on the right track? Does it seem she will ever get there? She believes she alone is in charge of defining her personal development toward leading a meaningful life. What does this reveal about her character?

3. How does the author feel about the theft of her precious merchandise while it was under her husband's care? Why doesn't she reprimand him? How does she feel about the men in her life who take over because they think it is in her best interest? What does this say about women in general?

4. What are the character flaws of Dan, Sergei, Yefim, and the author? What are their strengths?

5. The author briefly describes her early years and life before going into business. How has her past shaped her character?

6. When the author's business partners try to buy her out, should she take the money and walk away? Would you have done so in her place? What does her refusal show about her character? Does she suffer as a result?

7. The author weighs the importance of devoting herself to her family against creating a successful career. Did she make a choice?

8. When speaking of women in the workplace, what are the major differences between the last decades of the 20th century and the first decades of the 21st century?

9. What life lessons can you take with you after reading this book?

CASE STUDY OF
THE DIAMONDS AND GOLD JEWELRY
MANUFACTURING COMPANY, INC.

PART I

Abstract:

This case is based on Adrienne Rubin's complaint that the officers of a corporation, the Diamonds and Gold Jewelry Manufacturing Co., Inc., breached their fiduciary duty and violated their obligations to shareholders by personally benefiting themselves at the expense of the minority shareholders. In addition, Adrienne also accused the officers of usurping corporate opportunity for their own personal benefit, to the detriment of the shareholders.

Background Facts:

Dan and Sergei, son and father, and their respective spouses owned a majority of shares in the Diamonds and Gold Jewelry

Manufacturing Corporation (D & G). Adrienne was a minority shareholder who invested $50,000 cash and signed a loan to the corporation for another $50,000 as seed money. The company started off well and appeared to be profitable through the years, although there was minimal equity. There was one shareholder meeting at the end of the first year that Adrienne was aware of. There may have been others through the years that she did not know about. Sales substantially and rapidly increased, and by the third year, gross sales reached over $3,400,000. Dan and Sergei's salaries substantially and rapidly increased as well, and bonuses of half a million dollars each were taken as well. When Adrienne complained to the president of the company, he told her he would build equity in the future and her shares would greatly increase in value over time. However, when equity didn't grow at all over the next few years, she became frustrated. Her frustration turned to anger when she received a letter from the company lawyer stating that her shares were improperly granted, along with an offer to purchase said shares for an unacceptable sum. Adrienne demanded and received a rescission of this letter. She was, nonetheless, ignored and dismissed, even as the officers raided the corporate treasury through excessive compensation and loans, depleting assets to such an extent that there was little profit and never any dividends. Some examples of this are the purchase of new $2,000,000 homes in expensive areas, company-leased new $100,000 S-Class Mercedes-Benzes, and expensive designer clothing charged to the company American Express card. Family vacations in Europe and the Bahamas were also charged on the American Express corporate card, and categorized as "salesmen's travel expenses." Dan once lost $40,000 gambling in the Bahamas and ordered the bank to wire the funds from the corporation to pay his debt. This was done without a loan agreement and without the knowledge of the other shareholders. The loan was interest-free and remained on the books, unpaid, when the company closed its doors years later.

Questions:

How does a minority shareholder find out about excessive compensation to officers or abuses on the company credit card?

What can be done about it?

What are the tax consequences of the $40,000 loan to Dan to pay his gambling debt?

Additional Facts:

The company soon outgrew its rented premises. The company acquired a bank loan to purchase a $2,000,000 building with a large down payment, and paid architects and contractors to design and build out the interior to suit company requirements. Adrienne was happy with this decision, as she assumed the company to be the rightful owner of the building. During construction, however, Adrienne examined the latest annual financial statement and discovered that the company was paying rent for two locations—not only for the rented premises where it was still located but also for rent due on the new building under construction. She decided to ask who was receiving the rent, and learned that the proprietors of the building were these officers: Dan, his father, and their spouses.

Further investigation revealed that these same individuals, who together had a majority of shares, had agreed to borrow the funds from the company in order to take title to the property under a new company name owned exclusively by them, all without the knowledge or consent of the other shareholders.

Questions:

Should the loan to the officers, for the purpose of transferring ownership of the property, have borne a fair rate of interest? What if the annual report to shareholders shows no interest was ever due or paid?

Discuss the principle of corporate opportunity. Discuss rent participation, depreciation, other tax benefits, and equity appreciation. The corporate opportunity doctrine is the legal principle providing that directors, officers, and controlling shareholders of a corporation must not take for themselves any business opportunity that could benefit the corporation, because all shareholders should have the same opportunity.

Additional Facts:

Several months later, the build-out was finished, all improvements having been paid for by the D & G Company. The newly refurbished building was appraised at double the original purchase price. The officers of the corporation (who were also the owners of the building) agreed that the company should pay a much higher rent, based on the newly appraised value of the property. Dan signed both sides of the rental agreement, a lease between landlord and tenant. He held both positions.

When the property was ready for occupancy, the officers, as owners, refinanced the building with a larger loan. In this way they were able to put several hundred thousand dollars in their own pockets. The higher rent D & G paid to the officers according to the new lease allowed them more than enough money to make the payments themselves on the new loan.

Question:

Did the officers of the corporation usurp corporate opportunity for themselves to the detriment of the minority shareholders? Explain the answer.

PART II

Facts:

The D & G Jewelry Company sold 25,000 bracelets during their second year in business. These were hastily produced at such a low price that the quality was poor. Within months, several hundred bracelets were returned to the factory for repairs. While the company was quite capable of handling all the repairs, a decision was made not to do so. When the damaged bracelets came in, they were given to Sergei, the father of the president of the company, who was an experienced jeweler. Sergei received, repaired, and returned the damaged bracelets to the D & G customers, billing separately for the repair work he and others at the factory performed. As such, 100 percent of the overhead attributable to the repairs was borne by the corporation, at no cost to Sergei. He used the D & G premises, as well as the company's labor, tools, gold, and stones to do all repairs, but he sent his own invoices for all repairs to the D & G customers and deposited all payments received into his own, separate account.

Think of an automobile dealership that had a service department on its premises. The company might not make much money on the sale of cars, but that would not be of major importance if enough profit came from the service or maintenance department, as long as both the dealership and the service department shared the same ownership.

Question:

How would a shareholder be able to determine that profits from repair work that the corporation could have (should have) charged for were going elsewhere?

PART III

Facts:

By its second year in business, the D & G Company was selling mostly engagement rings, which the store buyers ordered as semi-mountings without the center stone. There are several reasons for this. The center stone in an engagement ring is often much more expensive than the ring itself. The end user could choose a ring he or she liked and use his or her own diamond for the center, or the customer could purchase the center stone separately, according to his or her budget and taste. The primary business at D & G was the manufacture and sale of rings, not center stones, and the D & G Company did not purchase these outright for its customers; through relationships with diamond dealers, the company often procured diamonds for customers on a consignment basis.

Dan and Sergei thought it would be a good idea if jewelers held an "event night" at their stores, whereby the end user would come to see the entire line of D & G rings. Customers could exchange their old rings for new ones and even upgrade their center stones, often walking out the same night with their new purchase, as usually there was a jeweler on premises to size the newly purchased rings and set the diamonds in the center. Store owners especially benefited by this, not having to buy anything that night unless it was sold.

"D & S Special Events" was known as a separate division of the D & G Jewelry Mfg. Co., so the corporation paid all expenses (including the cost of goods sold, the salesmen's travel, and all commissions). On the books, expenses were paid by D & G and profits were attributed to D & S, and this was fine because profits from the event nights for the first two years went to the corporation. However, the third year, Dan and Sergei created a new, separate corporation of their own in order to take over this arm of the corporate business. They did not pay the D & G Corporation anything for the transfer of this business, but took the profit of $50,000 for themselves on their individual tax returns.

Questions:

Is this one more example of abuse of the doctrine of corporate opportunity? Or is it simply the plundering of assets?

After D & S became a separate company from D & G, how would the actual costs associated with the events be calculated?

Without forensic accounting or a lawsuit, how would a shareholder be able to discover the transfer of this business to another?

Please visit www.adriennerubin.com for more on this topic.

Acknowledgments

So much gratitude is owed to so many. My husband Stan has been by my side encouraging my every endeavor, telling everyone all the while, "Life with Adrienne is full of surprises." I also want to thank our daughter, Pamela Cohen, and our son, Randall Rubin, for understanding my absence on those occasions when my business became a top priority. I wasn't present at every gymnastics event or baseball game, but like most working mothers today, I cared with all my heart and tried to do as much as possible for them.

I owe a debt of gratitude to my suppliers, who offered me staggering credit and 30 day terms, particularly Milano Piero, Sirom, Hagop Dakessian, the Hanasab brothers, and the many diamond dealers who placed their trust in me.

I would also like to acknowledge Wendy Werris and Elizabeth Bailey for their editorial guidance, as well as my readers Lynn Klinenberg Linkin, Peggy Ehling, Suzanne Rosentswieg, and Caron Broidy for their keen, insightful suggestions.

I've included a few portraits of Dora Marr by Pablo Picasso, taken from the book *PICASSO and the Weeping Women,*

The Years of Marie-Therese Walter & Dora Maar, published in 1994 for the Los Angeles County Museum of Art by Rizzoli, New York. When I first saw these paintings at the museum while dealing miserably with scoundrels in the business world, I thought, "Picasso has portrayed here the exact emotional turmoil I'm going through." Several of his paintings of weeping women are right on the mark. Standing in front of them, my empathy was stunning, swift, and profound. Picasso was a genius at showing us the way it feels to feel that way.

About the Author

Originally a high school French teacher, Adrienne Rubin published two cookbooks for charity before making the decision to go into business as an importer of fine jewelry, selling to the trade. She sold to stores all across the country and the Bahamas and eventually opened Avanti Fine Jewelry, her own jewelry store in Beverly Hills. Today she pursues other investments while spending time with her husband, children, and grandchildren in Los Angeles. You can find her online at adriennerubin.com.

Author photo © Alan Weissman

SELECTED TITLES FROM SHE WRITES PRESS

She Writes Press is an independent publishing company founded to serve women writers everywhere. Visit us at www.shewritespress.com.

In the Game: The Highs and Lows of a Trailblazing Trial Lawyer by Peggy Garrity. $16.95, 978-1-63152-105-8. Admitted to the California State Bar in 1975—when less than 3 percent of lawyers were women—Peggy Garrity refuses to choose between family and profession, and succeeds at both beyond anything she could have imagined.

Blue Apple Switchback: A Memoir by Carrie Highley. $16.95, 978-1-63152-037-2. At age forty, Carrie Highley finally decided to take on the biggest switchback of her life: upon her bicycle, and with the help of her mentor's wisdom, she shed everything she was taught to believe as a young lady growing up in the South—and made a choice to be true to herself and everyone else around her.

Postcards from the Sky: Adventures of an Aviatrix by Erin Seidemann. $16.95, 978-1-63152-826-2. Erin Seidemann's tales of her her struggles, adventures, and relationships as a woman making her way in a world very much dominated by men: aviation.

Army Wife: A Story of Love and Family in the Heart of the Army by Vicki Cody. $16.95, 978-1-63152-127-0. A rare glimpse into the heart of the Army, as seen through the eyes of Vicki Cody, an Army wife of thirty-three years who fell in love with a lieutenant and stayed by his side as he rose up through the ranks, all the way to four-star general and Vice Chief of Staff of the Army.

Operatic Divas and Naked Irishmen: An Innkeeper's Tale by Nancy R. Hinchliff. $16.95, 978-1-63152-194-2. At sixty four, divorced, retired, and with no prior business experience and little start-up money, Nancy Hinchliff impulsively moves to a new city where she knows only one person, buys a 125-year-old historic mansion, and turns it into a bed and breakfast.

Seasons Among the Vines: Life Lessons from the California Wine Country and Paris by Paula Moulton. $16.95, 978-1-938314-16-2. New advice on wine making, tasting, and food pairing—along with a spirited account of the author's experiences in Le Cordon Bleu's pilot wine program—make this second edition even better than the first.